FIC

ELIZABETHAN SEAMEN

H.M. QUEEN ELIZABETH OF ENGLAND

ELIZABETHAN SEAMEN

BY
DOUGLAS BELL

With Maps and Illustrations

Philadelphia
J. B. LIPPINCOTT COMPANY

PRINTED IN GREAT BRITAIN

CONTENTS

LIST OF ILLUSTRATIONS

MAPS

vii

FOREWORD

IN this book I have laid emphasis on the deeds of the Elizabethan seamen, believing that most people would rather read what the men did, what they suffered and endured, than an essay on what they may be supposed to have felt or thought or on the significance or otherwise of their actions. Many of the stories have been often told before. I make no apology for telling them again. A test of a good story is whether or no it will bear retelling, and there are many thousands to whom these tales will be new.

In quoting from contemporary records I have modernised the spelling. It is not desired to given an impression of "quaintness." Elizabethan seamen were not in the least "quaint," but virile men remarkably like the men of to-day.

I am deeply indebted to the authors and compilers of the works named in the list of books consulted, and make my grateful acknowledgements herewith. My warmest thanks are due to Mr. Ian F. D. Morrow, who has read the manuscript, and made many most valuable suggestions, and also to those persons or bodies who have given their permission for the use of the illustrations.

DOUGLAS BELL

Ashburton,
Devon.

CHAPTER I

VENTURERS ALL

"THERE is no land unhabitable, nor sea innavigable." So spake Master Robert Thorne, in the year of grace 1527, when the offshore wind was filling the sails of English ships about to voyage into unknown seas. These were bold words, when three parts of the earth's surface was unknown to him, when the oceans were uncharted, and no man knew what lay over the edge of the world. But it was the voice of Tudor England, determined, exultant, courageous, and the men of that age made good their words.

The great age of exploration, discovery, trade, and the fighting that resulted from these aspects of man's restless activity was centred in the long reign of Queen Elizabeth. But for many years before her accession to the throne Spaniards, Portuguese and Italians had been busy blazing the trail. These pioneers had been showing the way to new unguessed-of dominions and had been carving out with their swords empires of fabulous wealth in the names of their sovereigns. As has often happened in her history England, a small minor power in those days, and cut off by the sea from the main stream of life upon the Continent, was late in starting, but had her share of the glory in due time. Even from England great deeds were done, arduous journeys were undertaken, and her flag was shown in remote regions of the earth years before the spacious days

I

of great Elizabeth. England's effort began when the first Henry Tudor grasped the reins, and started on that drive of her young men over the world and round the world which was to end in the founding of as great an empire as that of Spain in the zenith of her pride and glory.

There were many forces, spiritual and material, that urged the men of the late fifteenth and of the sixteenth century over the far horizons. The desire for honour was the first. Then, when the world seemed new and young, with strange lands beyond every skyline, honour was a fine flower to be plucked by the daring navigator as well as by the knight in armour. Humphrey Gilbert, who met a gallant sailor's death at sea, summed up the nobler side of those adventurers when he said: "He is not worthy to live at all that for fear or danger of death shunneth his country's service and his own honour: seeing death is inevitable, and the fame of virtue immortal."

This desire and quest for honour was nurtured and thrived in an air of wonder, hope, and exaltation. Men's minds were uplifted by the new knowledge that was speeding across the continent of Europe from east to west, and were released and expanded by new inventions and the discovery of new lands. Another spiritual force, that of religious enthusiasm, played but a small direct part in this era of search and discovery. Much devotion was shown by many members of the religious orders, and many of the adventurers such as Columbus and Drake were deeply religious men. Nevertheless, the Christianisation of the New World by the Spaniards went hand in hand with pillage, exploitation, cruelty and extermination. Twelve years

2

after the courteous and honourable Columbus had
come and gone the Indians on the fair island of
Hispaniola[1] had been almost wiped out; and when
as a result there was no longer any slave labour
available, negroes were imported to work under the
lash. The Protestants completely failed to Christ-
ianise anybody. Hakluyt, himself a divine, admits
this, though the Protestant nations, possessing no
lands whatever in the New World, had not the
opportunities of Las Casas and the Spanish Catholic
missionaries.

The thirst for gold was perhaps the most conspicuous of the material forces. The power and
wealth of the Spanish and Portuguese empires were
based on gold, and behind all the resolve on the
part of the English to trade where they would,
behind the call of the Northern route to far Cathay,
was the lure of gold. Gold meant wealth to avari-
cious and ambitious men; gold meant power,
influence and popularity to needy governments.
Even Columbus, who was more concerned with
honour than with greed, said: "Gold constitutes
treasure, and he who possesses it has all he needs
in *this* world, *as also* the means of rescuing souls
from purgatory, and restoring them to the enjoyment of Paradise." So thought the English as
regards this world.

The treasure that poured into Spain from
America during the sixteenth century was enormous. The total from 1503 to 1660 was 447,820,932
pesos.[2] Compared with this colossal sum the captures of the English, French and Dutch were
insignificant. Where did it all go? The answer

[1] Now Haiti.
[2] Nearly £150,000,000 in Elizabethan money, worth quite ten times as
much to-day.

must be that it was poured into the sands of costly wars in Flanders, France and Italy. Moreover, the extraordinary inflation in currency that it caused sent prices soaring, and the gold and silver disappeared. Gold was the source of the wealth of Spain, and gold was the cause of her ultimate decay.

Few people realize that an everyday commodity like pepper was the foundation on which the British Empire in India was built. For the need for spices, a need, strange as it may seem, that was even more urgent than that of gold, was another material force that drove men eastwards and westwards in quest of them. The traffic in spice was a vital trade in medieval times. The rich and powerful merchant community of Venice, the greatest trading centre in the world, was concerned almost entirely with spices, and particularly with pepper. In the Middle Ages cattle and sheep could get little winter fodder. Oil cake was unknown, and it was the practice of the farmers every autumn to kill most of the beasts, and preserve the meat as best they could. Meat and fish were salted and cured after a fashion, but it was badly done, and pepper was used as a preservative, as it is to-day in sausages. With other spices it helped to disguise decomposition and enable the food to be eaten.

For long years Venice had almost a monopoly of the pepper trade. She obtained it by the overland route from the western coasts of India, and to this day pepper is shipped from the ports of Tellicherry and Alleppy on that coast. It came to England by way of Bruges and thence to Norwich. But in 1453 Constantinople fell to the Turks, and their tide of conquest surged over the old Empire of the East.

The Turks thus cut across the trade route by which pepper came to Venice. Venice could not and would not do without it, and it was a firm of Venetian bankers that took an important part in financing the voyage of the Portuguese Vasco da Gama. He was looking for a sea route to India, and found it by rounding the Cape of Good Hope. So began the trade between Portugal and India. The English in 1592 captured an immense Portuguese ship laden with all manner of tropical produce. Queen Elizabeth's share of this booty was some hundreds of tons of Indian pepper. The keenest interest in the sea route from India was aroused in England. Men began to ask why they should not have a direct share in the trade. As a consequence the East India Company was founded before the close of the reign, and in this way a commodity, relatively unimportant to-day, profoundly affected the destinies of mankind.

While the main great trade routes to India through Syria and Baghdad continued overland, Italian city-states like Venice and Genoa held the bulk of the Eastern commerce in their hands. When the overland routes were interrupted, and the sea routes took their place, it was the Portuguese who snatched away the key to the commercial supremacy. The great invention that made ocean navigation possible was that of the mariner's compass, the "Wise Iron" that, when magnetized, pointed always to the north and south. This had been in use for well over 3,000 years in China, and was discovered independently in Europe in the latter half of the twelfth century. In 1302 a great advance was made by affixing to the pivotal needle a card on which the points were drawn, and a hundred years later the compass was in general use throughout Europe. Longer and more daring voyages were also helped by the improvement made in the design of the Portuguese ships.

The life of Prince Henry of Portugal covered the great era of Portuguese exploration. He was known as the "Navigator," though he never sailed a ship himself. He took great pains to foster the arts of navigation in others, he founded a naval college, and he enlisted all the knowledge of his time. League by league his sailors crept round the west coast of Africa. In 1487-8 Bartholomew Diaz rounded the Cape of Good Hope, pushed on up the east coast, and returned the way he had come. Diaz gave the Cape its name, and indeed it was of good hope, for, inspired by this success, in 1498 Vasco da Gama followed him and reached India. His actual voyage lasted for a year and nine months, of which a great part was in the open sea. When the size of his ship, the hazards of weather and the difficulty of victualling are considered, his feat seems marvellous. He covered 24,000 nautical miles, and half his crews died on the voyage. In 1500 King Manoel assumed the title of "Lord of the conquest, navigation and commerce of India, Ethiopia, Arabia and Persia," and soon the Portuguese captains occupied Goa in India (still Portuguese) and Malaya.

After Portugal came Spain. It was a Genoese resident in Portugal, Christopher Columbus, who started Spain on her imperial career. His conviction that the gold and spices of Cathay[1] (China) and Cipangu (Japan) were to be reached across the Atlantic was too big an idea for the Portuguese

[1] The Russians still call China "Kitai."

6

authorities, and so he sent his brother to Henry VII of England with an offer to go and look for those treasures across the ocean. Henry VII at once agreed, but the brother was seized by pirates, and was so long in returning to Christopher with the news that by the time he did return Christopher had already sailed into the mysterious West under the patronage of Ferdinand and Isabella of Spain. In 1492 he discovered what he thought were the islands of the Indies, and therefore called them the "West Indies."

The following year he sailed westwards again. On his first voyage he had touched at Cuba and Hispaniola, and this time he coasted along the islands and discovered Jamaica. He was still under the impression that Cuba was part of the mainland of Asia, and his two subsequent voyages did not undeceive him; he died in that belief. Columbus has given his name to many places in the Americas, but for the name of the two continents the world is indebted to a Florentine, Amerigo Vespucci, who made at least two voyages to the New World. He discovered Brazil when in the service of the King of Portugal.

Portugal and Spain had the New World to themselves, and much of the Old World as well. It seemed to Pope Alexander VI, himself a Spaniard, that their rivalry in exploration and exploitation would very likely lead to a breach of the peace. Therefore in 1493 he issued his famous Bull, dividing the world from pole to pole in the middle of the Atlantic Ocean, and giving to Portugal all newly discovered lands east of this imaginary line, and to Spain all territory to the west. This was done in the cause of peace, but it led to war grim and

7   B

bitter, for the Pope ignored the Tudor English, and Tudor England would not be ignored.

Chaucer's Canterbury pilgrim, the "shipman," the sea-captain of Dartmouth in Devonshire, was a typical hard and hardy sailorman of his time. He made his living by a coastal trade round England, and from the Spanish coast to the Baltic Sea. He and his like made piratical raids on occasion. To avenge some real or fancied wrong the men of Dartmouth, Fowey, or Plymouth would swoop down upon Brest, burning and plundering, and sooner or later the Frenchmen would come and sack the English ports. They were not above fighting among themselves, for rivalry between the ports was intense, though against the French they would occasionally unite. They were a ruthless breed, and any prisoners who were too poor to be ransomed were flung overboard; "sent home by water," as Chaucer grimly remarks.

Up to the time of Henry VII there had been little change in the character or trading practice of the English sailors, but with the more settled times that came in with the Tudors, the seafaring population became to some extent less lawless. They gradually grew to be less of the pirate and more of the merchant. They were by no means a very important commercial community. They could not be compared with the Mediterranean traders, and the Hanseatic League made the Germans in the Baltic the foremost merchant adventurers of the time. The League was so powerful that it compelled the English North Sea merchants to obey its will. Gradually the English resistance stiffened. A tariff war began. England imposed heavy duties on German goods, and the Germans prohibited the

English cloth trade. In 1533 a commercial treaty was signed at Marienburg with the "Master of the House of S. Mary of Teutonia." Henceforward English merchants were able to settle in the Hansa towns, and sell their cloth. Tudor England was not to be gainsaid. In precisely the same spirit she challenged the monopoly of Spain and Portugal in the New World.

The first challenger sailed from Bristol in 1496, but he was not by birth an Englishman. England has a way of using and absorbing good men wherever they may be found, and John Cabot, another Genoese by birth, was given "full and free authority . . . of navigating to all parts, countries, and seas of the east, west, and north . . . to seek out, discover, and find whatsoever islands, countries, regions or provinces of heathens or infidels, in whatsoever part of the world they be." And the Bristol Merchant Adventurers might well have added "a fig for the power of Spain." John Cabot made a northern landfall, either in Labrador, Newfoundland or Nova Scotia, and though the fishing grounds he discovered were important, and later on played a great part in the development of America, his mind was still set on gold and spices, if a way through to the Pacific could be found. He had once been to Mecca, and had seen the richly laden camel caravans come in from the uttermost regions of Asia. This sight had fired his imagination, and he determined to follow in Columbus' wake. His son Sebastian also voyaged to the Americas, but the Tudor kings were not yet ready to challenge the might of the Iberian Empires, and though a few private voyages of exploration were made, official encouragement was lacking.

Moreover, the interests of Henry VIII did not lie so much in exploration as in the building up of a Royal Navy, by which he too sowed the seeds of England's greatness, and inaugurated a tradition which was to prove England's salvation in his daughter's reign. His father had built the first dry dock at Portsmouth, and in 1546 he created the Navy Board, on which in after years Sir John Hawkins was to serve with such distinction. The Navy Board was charged with the building and upkeep of the Fleet and with providing stores, victuals and pay. The Lord High Admiral, who exercised political and strategical control, had only nominal powers over the Board. Early in the eighth Henry's reign a certain naval architect named James Baker had overcome the difficulty of mounting heavy guns on board ship. From Tudor times and throughout the Stuart era the English won their naval battles by the superiority of their gunnery and their guns. It was in the Netherlands, that country of fortified towns, that the art of making heavy artillery was evolved. These new cannon were excellent for breaching strong walls, and Henry did not see why they should not somehow be used to hull and sink enemy ships. The problem was that they were too heavy to be mounted on the decks or in the aftcastles and forecastles of the light but clumsy ships of the day. Baker had the idea of putting the new heavy muzzle-loading guns in the hold, or rather the lower gun-decks, whence they could fire through gun-ports fitted with water-tight doors, and where they did not upset the trim or balance of the ship. Here was the beginning of the broadside, that simultaneous deadly blast of fire with which the English ships were to punish the galleons of Spain. In this reign ships were designed as much for fighting as for trade, and when the *Mary Rose* was laid down, England's first battleship may be said to have been begun. Another vessel, the *Henri Grâce à Dieu*, popularly known as the *Great Harry*, was the most magnificent and powerful ship of her time. She was a somewhat unwieldy vessel of a thousand tons, with two tiers of guns on the lower decks, and a third tier on her half-deck and forecastle. She carried 700 men, including soldiers. Henry himself stood on the poop of one of his new ships, dressed in a sailor's coat and trousers of cloth of gold, blowing a whistle "as loud as a trumpet." Well he might, for the Royal Navy was born.

In the great treasure-hunt another imperial race did not hang back. The Frenchman Cartier in 1534–5 sailed up the St. Lawrence, and the New-foundland fisheries soon attracted both French and Spaniards. Meanwhile the Spanish adventure still went forward. In 1513 Vasco Nuñez de Balboa succeeded in crossing the Isthmus of Panama, and saw from a peak in Darien the Pacific Ocean, that fabled and mysterious sea. Then Hernando Cortes, who was one of the most daring adventurers of all time, reached Mexico City with a small party in 1519. In 1521 he took it, all Mexico falling into his hands. Exploration and exploitation expeditions were sent out in all directions, and a vast tract of territory was opened up and subdued. Gold and precious stones were there beyond all counting. De Soto extensively explored what are now the southern United States of America, and Francisco Pizarro led the way to the conquest of South America by his extraordinary and romantic adventures in Peru from 1524 to 1527, when he overthrew the ancient civilization of the Incas. Others conquered Ecuador and Chile, and within a very few years the Spanish power had spread all over the west and south of the continent.

The Portuguese again grasped the staff in this great relay race between the seafaring peoples. Ferdinand Magellan is one of the very great names. It was he who forged the connecting link between the New West and the Far East by the passage of the strait that bears his name. It was his comrades who completed his work after his death in the Philippines by making the first circumnavigation of the world. Some idea of the quality of these early navigators and the hardships they endured is perceived from the account of one of Magellan's men :

"Wednesday the twenty-eighth of November 1520 we came forth out of the said strait, and entered into the Pacific sea, where we remained three months and twenty days without taking in provisions or other refreshments, and we only ate old biscuit reduced to powder, and full of grubs, and stinking . . . and we drank water that was yellow and stinking. We also ate the ox hides that were under the mainyard . . . also the sawdust of wood, and rats which cost half a crown each, moreover enough of them were not to be got."

Most of them suffered from scurvy and many died. All seamen of that age frequently endured the same hardships.

Years before this the Portuguese had rounded the Cape of Good Hope again and again, and had pushed on eastwards to Canton. The same year that the Spice Islands were reached from the west by Magellan, Peking, the capital city of Cathay, was visited by the eastwards route, and by 1542 the Portuguese had been to Japan. A Portuguese ship, blown off its course by a storm, found herself off an island south of Satsuma, and the crew went ashore. They stayed among the Japanese islands for some time, making friends with the islanders by selling them arquebuses, so that they could shoot one another more efficiently than with their bows and arrows, and for a while a brisk trade was done. A quarrel with the Jesuit missionaries who followed the traders resulted in Japan being closed to the foreigner for three centuries.

Once more it was England's turn. Shut off from the East and West by the great Iberian Powers, the English determined, before seriously challenging them, to seek the City of Gold and the Earthly Paradise by way of the North. Legends and fables all agreed that this Earthly Paradise was to be sought and found somewhere in Cathay. The marvels related by Marco Polo, and the travellers' tales brought back by the missionary friars inflamed men's minds, and set in motion wonderful stories of that mysterious, rich and beautiful kingdom in the Far East. Amid all the mixed motives of the search, the desire for honour, the lust for gold, the need for spices, the urge to extend the Church of Christ, was the longing to reach that mystical land, where the fruits of the earth were to be obtained without labour, where sacred rivers flowed pure and sweet and lovely, where the sun shone blandly, and torrid heat and bitter frost were unknown.

Like all dreams, it faded, but not before desperate risks had been taken to make it come true. Spain with its Americas barred the westward sea road, Portugal held the eastward. England would go north. What of the ice and snow? English keels would sail those wintry seas. What man can dare man can do. Such was the spirit that led them confidently to attempt the passage round Siberia. The story begins five years before the reign of Elizabeth. It was in 1553, in the last days of the boy king Edward VI, that a Company of Merchant Adventurers was formed "for the discovery of regions, dominions, islands and places unknown." Sebastian Cabot was the first Governor. No doubt he wore a chain of office and a gown trimmed with fur and a square cap. The gowns that are a livery to-day in the great City Companies were the ordinary merchants' dress. The members of the Company were the noblemen and merchants who were willing to put up the money for the trading venture. There is an element of speculation in all business, and these men were legitimate speculators. The merchant's office or counting-house as well as his sale-room was in his own private residence, an inflammable but picturesque, gabled building of timber, like Staple Inn in Holborn. The traders in the smaller towns often went to sea themselves, but the City Fathers of London were men of far too much wealth and standing to do so. They appointed young men of education and business training as "supercargoes." A supercargo attended to all the business side of the voyage, while the master was responsible for the navigation. In a venture like this Cathay one, which was an important expedition, captains were appointed to the ships.

In the Governor's instructions to the Captain-General and the crews of the three ships that set out on the first voyage it was definitely stated that the objective was Cathay. There is much of interest in these instructions, regarding navigation and records to be kept, stewards' accounts, discipline, ammunition accounts, and regulations like the following:

"no blaspheming of God, or detestable swearing be used in any ship, nor communication of ribaldry, filthy tales, or ungodly talk to be suffered in the company of any ship, neither dicing, carding, tabling, nor other devilish games to be frequented, whereby ensueth not only poverty to the players, but also strife, variance, brawling, fighting, and oftentimes murder to the utter destruction of the parties, and provoking of God's most just wrath, and sword of vengeance."

Morning and evening prayer were to be said in each ship every day. "No liquor to be spilt on the ballast, nor filthiness to be left within board: the cook room, and all other places to be kept clean for the better health of the company." The mariners were to wear a uniform, but only on special occasions, "for the advancement and honour of the voyage." Instructions were given for the care of sick, for the safeguarding of the rights of the next-of-kin in the property of or wages due to any that died. Respect for foreign religions, proper treatment of women, and general courtesy were enjoined. The merchants were told to persuade people to come aboard and see and handle their goods; to entertain them well, so that they might bring others; and then is added "if the person so taken (on board) may be made drunk with your beer or wine, you may know all the secrets of his heart."

There were twelve "counsellors" appointed for this voyage, among whom were Sir Hugh Willoughby, Captain-General, in the flagship *Bona Esperanza*, 120 tons; Richard Chancellor, captain of the *Edward Bonaventure*, 160 tons; and the master of the *Confidence*, 90 tons. There were several merchants on board, and a surgeon and chaplain accompanied the expedition. They took with them letters from the King addressed comprehensively "to all Kings, Princes, Rulers, Judges, and Governors of the earth, and all others having any excellent dignity on the same, in all places under the universal heaven."

These three ships, well found in all their gear, cast loose from the quay at Ratcliffe in London River, on 10th May, 1553. They dropped down with the ebb to Deptford, where they lay that night. The ships were towed by their boats, the sailors wearing their sky-blue uniforms. The King was in residence at the Royal Palace of Greenwich. As they passed on down the river the next afternoon the court officials came running out, the windows were filled, and the people thronged the foreshore. The ships' guns thundered forth a salute, and the noise echoed among the hills of the park behind the palace. A roar of cheering came from the sailors as the smoke of the discharge blew away. It was answered by more cheers from the river bank. The voyagers waved their farewells from the poops, the shrouds, the yards and the tops. It was a stirring send-off to a great adventure.

The little fleet made leisurely progress down Thames, and up the Essex coast to Harwich, reaching Yarmouth on the 30th of the month. From Orford Ness the voyage began in earnest. As the lurching vessels breasted the North Sea billows the mariners heard the creak of their halyards, the whistle of the wind in the rigging, the wash of the sea, and the farewell crying of the following gulls. Their hopes were high. Perhaps they would be the first to reach Cathay by the northern sea way, the Englishman's own way.

The ships eventually arrived at the Lofoden Islands off the Norwegian coast at the end of July. They coasted farther and farther north, till in August after rounding North Cape a great storm arose. That night they lay adrift under bare poles, and in the gale and thick weather the *Bona Esperanza* and the *Confidence* lost the *Edward Bonaventure*. They never saw her again, for they themselves were doomed. They sailed east for league after league till they reached the uninhabited shores of Nova Zembla. Here they turned back and went along the Murmansk coast, finding at length a harbour, where they anchored on 18th September. The year was far spent, the weather was very bad, with frost and snow and hail, and they decided to winter there. Long afterwards the two ships were discovered. Willoughby and most of his men were still alive in January 1554, as a will that was found testified, but they all perished of cold and hunger before the long winter lifted from those frozen, barren, uninhabited wastes.

Chancellor, in the *Edward Bonaventure*, had been more fortunate. Alarmed at the dispersion of the little fleet, he betook himself to the agreed rendezvous in Norway near the North Cape, but after waiting there a week, he determined to press on alone. It is said that there is no place on earth where a Scotsman is not to be found, and they must have developed this wandering habit early in their history, for here in this far northern haven, Chancellor met some Scotsmen. They knew the condi-

17

tions of that coast in winter, and with the caution and wisdom of their race, tried to dissuade him from the attempt. Chancellor would not be dissuaded. The Englishman of that day was headstrong, and moreover, Chancellor felt that honour was involved. He pushed on resolutely, loyally supported by his ship's company, and accompanied by the wonder and marvel of the Midnight Sun. At length he penetrated into the great bay of the White Sea, and dropped anchor within it. Far off he espied a little fishing craft, and entering one of the ship's boats, was rowed out to it. By his courtesy and gentleness he quickly made friends with the fishermen and other inhabitants, and word of the strangers' arrival was carried to Ivan the Terrible, Emperor of all the Russias, at Moscow. In due time Chancellor and all his company were invited to Court, and after a long and wearisome journey on sledges they came to the palace of the Tsar. Russia had then no outlet on the Baltic. The opening of a direct sea route was thus an event of the first importance.

Chancellor has left long and interesting accounts of medieval Russia, of the manners and customs of its people, and of the splendours of the Golden Court. He kept a strict eye to business also, his reports on the prospect of trade being very complete. In the spring of 1554 he returned to his ship, finding his guard alive and well, though they had been half dead with cold during the long winter. He reached home safely to find Edward VI dead, and therefore presented the Tsar's letter agreeing to the opening of trade between the two countries to Queen Mary. Mary had married Philip II of Spain, who was only too glad to divert English enterprises away from his possessions in America. He therefore willingly joined the Queen in granting a charter in 1554 to the new Muscovy Company, confirming Sebastian Cabot as Governor, nominating four prominent London citizens to be consuls and twenty-four others to form a Council, granting likewise to the Company full monopoly and jurisdiction.

The *Edward Bonaventure* was fitted out in 1555 for a second voyage. Richard Chancellor was again pilot-general, and agents and factors were appointed by the Company to reside in Moscow and elsewhere. The quest for Cathay was not forgotten. The agents were instructed to find out the best routes by sea or land, and to do their utmost to discover what had become of Sir Hugh Willoughby and his men. As a result of this trading voyage special privileges were granted by the Tsar to the Company, and all went well, save for the hazards of the sea. For Chancellor, returning in the *Edward Bonaventure* at the end of the venture of 1556, with the first Russian ambassador on board, was wrecked on the Scottish coast, the ship going to pieces on the rocks. Chancellor with the Ambassador took to a boat, which was swamped by a great wave. Chancellor was drowned, but the Ambassador was cast up on shore alive.

The pioneers had gone, but the quest went on. The torch was flung to those behind. Stephen Burrough, who had been master of the *Edward* on her first voyage to the White Sea, set forth from London one spring morning in 1556 in a little vessel called the *Searchthrift* to explore those barren shores. At Gravesend, that "good old gentleman, Master Cabota," the Governor of the Company, with a party of ladies and gentlemen, came aboard ship and drank with Burrough success to the voyage. Cabot disbursed liberal presents of money all round to the sailors, who cheered him as he went ashore. At the sign of the "Christopher" he gave a banquet to his party and invited Burrough to join them. The repast was followed by a dance, in which the old gentleman took part, and "which being ended, he and his friends departed most gently, commending us to the governance of Almighty God."

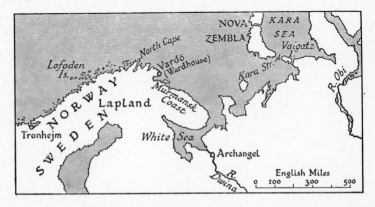

As on all these voyages, they had many adventures with the wild fishers and trappers they met, with the storms and ice and snow they encountered, and with what really terrified them, a monstrous whale breaking surface so close to their tiny craft that they could have prodded him with a sword. By August they had penetrated to Nova Zembla, and then Burrough decided to return, by reason of the terrible north-east winds, the growing ice, and the dark. They wintered at their Norwegian base, and in the following year came home.

The attempts to reach Cathay by the North-East Passage had been discouraging so far, and there were not wanting daring spirits to try the alternative route overland. A Mr. Anthony Jenkinson was conspicuous in this direction. He left Gravesend in May 1557 as captain of the *Primrose*, with three other tall ships, on his first voyage to Russia. By July they had reached the spot where Archangel now stands. Jenkinson embarked in a small boat on the River Dwina, proceeded southwards through the pine forests, and arrived at Moscow on 6th December. He dined with the Tsar at six o'clock on Christmas Day as the chief guest in a hall where six hundred sat down to tables covered with gold plate.

After obtaining from the Tsar letters of recommendation to the rulers of the countries through which he was to pass, Jenkinson left Moscow in April 1558 for the East. He went by way of Nijni Novgorod to Kazan, recently taken from the Tartars, and down the Volga to Astrakhan, then the farthest outpost of the Russian Empire. He and all his company and goods, with some Mohammedan Tartars, set sail upon the Caspian Sea. Unluckily they were boarded by pirates, who demanded to be told whether there were any Christian Russians or other Kaffirs (unbelievers) in the ship. One of the Tartars, who was a Haji, having been to Mecca, spoke up and swore by the Koran that there were not. By this false oath Jenkinson and his cargo of merchandise were saved. He landed on the south-eastern shore and set out to cross Turkestan in September, in company with a caravan of no less than a thousand camels. In one desolate spot the caravan had a desperate pitched battle with bandits, with which great tracts of country were infested. It was not until 23rd December, 1558, that Jenkinson arrived at Bokhara, a very large town with some fine stone houses. He seems to have been especially struck with the "bathstoves." Great caravans used to come in from India, Persia, Russia, Balkh, Tashkend, and Kashgar, but Jenkinson did not think much of their wares. Caravans came in from Cathay in times past, but the route was unsafe owing to incessant wars and banditry. In view of this Jenkinson decided to come home by the way he went, and in March 1559 he left Bokhara in a caravan of six hundred camels. He came through to Moscow safely in September of that year.

He made another attempt in 1561, and this time he reached Persia and had an audience of the Shah, or Sophy, as he called him. Queen Elizabeth wrote to the Emperor of Russia and to the "great Sophy of Persia." Out of a mist of fine words one discerns that the letters were requests for safe-conducts and trading facilities for her "faithful and well-beloved servant Anthony Jenkinson." Jenkinson and others made repeated journeys to Persia and Turkestan. At Jenkinson's first interview with the Shah, he was taken aback at being called a *giaour*, or unbeliever and unclean, and when he left the audience chamber he noted with disapproval that a man followed him with a basket of sand, scattering it in his unclean tracks. Steps were taken to consolidate England's position in Russia, for in 1568 a Mr. Thomas Randolph was appointed English Ambassador in Moscow. When he presented his credentials he handed to the Tsar a present from Queen Elizabeth, "a notable great cup of silver curiously wrought," which in 1935 was shown to Mr. Anthony Eden in the Kremlin.

The attempts to penetrate into China overland

had, like the attempts by sea, proved very discouraging. They were being abandoned, and the
Muscovy Company was concentrating on the Russian
and Persian trade. One final endeavour to force
the North-East Passage was made by Arthur Pet
and Charles Jackman in the year 1580, more than
a quarter of a century after Willoughby's attempt.
The Muscovy Company made a contract with these
two men to try to find the North-East Passage "to
the countries and dominions of the mighty prince,
the Emperor of Cathay." Arthur Pet of Ratcliffe
was to be captain and master of the *George* of
London, 40 tons, with a crew of nine men and a
boy, and a supercargo, and Charles Jackman of
Poplar, captain and master of the *William*, also of
London, 20 tons, the crew consisting of five men and
a boy. Pet was nominated as commander of the
expedition, to carry its flag at his maintop.

In the contract the two captains were enjoined to
hold a daily service of prayer, "so shall you prosper
the better." The route was laid down as far as
possible, and the captains were instructed, if they
reached Cathay, to make for the city of Cambalu
(Peking) and at all costs to establish friendly relations by fair and courteous dealings with the people.
They were to carry letters from the Queen (written
in Latin) for presentation to the Emperor, and to
obtain if possible a letter in reply. In case they
were obliged to winter abroad they were pro-
visioned for two years. If they could do any trade
en route, so much the better, but they should at all
times remember that the land of Cathay was the
chief objective of the expedition. If, however, they
were to find the way barred by land or other
obstacle they were to sail up the River Obi as far

23   C

as possible—"haply you may come to the city of Siberia." The contract was signed, and ended with the words: "The Lord God Almighty send you a prosperous voyage, with happy success and safe return, Amen."

Before they sailed, further detailed instructions were given to the captains. They were to act as explorers, to use the lead along the coasts, taking careful note of the soundings; to keep a log, noting the dead reckoning, set of tides, times of high and low water, currents, strength and direction of winds, and latitude; to take frequent compass bearings when within sight of land, and make a chart of the coast, putting in the physical features, such as altitude, rivers, nature of soil, vegetation. They were told to note the manners, customs, and dress of any people they met, the produce of the country, the commodities available for trade, and the people's needs. The promoters told them that it might be they would have a chance of sailing across to Japan. Here they might find Christians and Jesuit missionaries, perhaps some Englishmen, and they might have added, almost certainly some Scotsmen. It was thought that if the coast beyond Nova Zembla fell away south-east from the Arctic Circle, the expedition might come upon populations less dependent upon furs and skins that would be glad to buy the warm English woollen cloth. The forests inland might also yield masts, pitch, and tar, for English ships, or deal boards for English houses.

Since their numbers were so small, they were warned not to run any unnecessary risks, though they might have to leave one man in exchange for a youth from Cambalu, who was to be brought home if possible. They should also bring back fruits of the country, dried or preserved if necessary, and seeds and kernels of fruits; also seeds of any strange herbs or flowers. The English middle classes were evidently becoming gardeners, for the record speaks of the continual delight in rare flowers. If the mariners should reach Cambalu, a map of the country must certainly be procured, also some old printed book, if any existed, in order to see whether printing had been invented (as some said) before it was known in Europe. Special note was to be taken of the Chinese ships, their size, rigging, sails, armament, whether or no they had guns, powder and shot. Land forces too must be observed, armour, weapons, and cavalry. They must mark the building, fittings and appointments of the houses, the clothing and materials and dye-stuffs, the shops, warehouses, market prices and produce, the supplies of corn, fruit and fish.

The expedition took with them no small store of goods for barter or for sale. Woollen cloth and woollen manufactures formed the bulk of the cargo, though there were specimens of hardware, pewter and glass. The home market for woollen goods had almost reached saturation point, and unemployment was becoming a serious problem. It was, therefore, imperative to find export markets. Everything taken was to be of the best, to uphold the credit of English workmanship. Nor was this all, for provision was made for entertaining on shipboard persons of importance. Perfumes were supplied to be put under hatches "against their coming aboard," and dainties such as marmalade, sweets, sun-dried raisins and barrels of figs, dried fruits, walnuts and almonds, wine, sugar, fine biscuits, and cinnamon water. The venturers were ordered to take a big coloured map of England, and also a large map of London. "And let the river be drawn full of ships of all sorts, to make the more show of your great trade and traffic."

Enough has been said to show the care and forethought expended on all these voyages. The expeditions were well equipped in every detail, and furnished with all that the scientific knowledge of the time could provide. Pet and Jackman and those that sent them did not realize what a risky game they were about to play, but the hazards they did know were no light matter. They were quite undaunted, and set sail on the last day of May 1580 in good spirits and high hopes.

They bore along the Norwegian coast in very foul weather with rain and fog, and on 22nd June they rounded North Cape. The two ships lost each other in the fog. The rendezvous in case this happened was the "Wardhouse," a haven[1] a little east of the North Cape which was used as a base and port of call by all vessels on this route. The *George* put in, and was followed a few hours later by the *William*. Till the end of the month an easterly wind blew, keeping them in harbour, and the *William* was hauled ashore to be caulked, for she was somewhat leaky. The captains and crews filled in their time by writing letters home, which they sent to London by the *Toby*, of Harwich. On 1st July the wind backed to the nor'-nor'-west, and they set sail again east by south, after agreeing that the next meeting-place was to be the Isle of Vaigatch at the entrance to the Kara Sea. They held on easterly, sailing independently. On 6th July Pet in the *George* first met with ice. He sounded fre-

[1] Vardö.

26

quently, logging the results. There was much fog, and the ice began to be very troublesome, indeed, a week later they were alarmed to see ice forming all round them. By great good luck they were able to extricate themselves, and in a few days Pet sighted Vaigatch. In a small island to the west of Vaigatch they found what they were greatly lacking by this time, fuel and water. There was plenty of drift-wood by the shore. Pet pushed through the strait to the south of Vaigatch, and found himself in Kara Bay, with broken ice in every direction. In the evening of 24th July he sighted the *William* across the ice. This caused considerable excite-ment. "Sound a call, trumpeter," said Pet, "and men, shoot off two muskets." In answer up went Jackman's flag to his foretop to show that he saw him. Pet shortened sail, and with only his foresail and maintopsail set made his way as best he could through the ice. The next day, at about five in the morning, the two ships met to the great joy of all.

The *William* had broken her stern post, making the rudder uncontrollable. All hands set to work to lighten her stern and trim her head. A cable was then passed under her stern and attached by the crew of the *George* to their capstan. By turning the capstan they raised the *William*'s stern, and so effected the necessary repairs. The wind was favourable, but the ice was closing all round them. "Winds we have had at will, but ice and fog too much against our wills, if it had pleased the Lord God otherwise." The farther eastward they went into the Kara Sea the thicker was the ice. At last they could go on no more. Pet moored his ship to an ice-floe, and Jackman did the same, but despair of success began to creep into their hearts. They were still in the month of July, but snow began to fall, and high winds made matters worse. They had the boats out, and warped the ships from one huge ice-floe to another, trying to get clear. August came in calm. Imprisoned in the ice, and wrapt in thick mists, they "abode the Lord's leisure." On the 5th a lane opened westwards and homewards. They went cautiously along it, helped by a north-easterly wind. It closed again. On the 11th they made a little progress, forcing their way through. It grew colder, and dark with blizzards. The 13th was the worst day. Ice was grinding against the sides of the ships, the *George* had the shank of her anchor broken, her boat stove in, and her rudder damaged. But 15th August saw them delivered from their danger. The wind was still north-east, and at last they emerged into open sea. The following day found them approaching the strait between Vaigatch and the mainland, and in spite of more ice they came through. On the 22nd Pet lost sight of Jackman in a fog. He never saw him again.

In due time the *George* doubled the North Cape, and during October Pet sailed along the coast of Norway, buffeted by fierce storms. It was not until 9th December that he sighted Buchan Ness on the Aberdeenshire coast. He cruised south-wards, rejoicing in the familiar landmarks, till on Christmas Day he came to anchor off Tilbury in London River. Jackman in the *William* arrived at a haven near Trondhjem in October and stayed there for the winter. In the following February he put to sea. From that time he vanished for ever-more.

The north-eastern ventures were not without

some tangible results, even though the high hopes were dupes. The Muscovy Company had been formed and had opened up a new commerce with Russia and Persia. An impetus had been given to the Baltic trade in masts, tar and pitch for English ships, and there was a new source of supply in the inexhaustible forests of Russia. Yet the last plucky attempt had been a failure like all the others. It was becoming evident that there was no possibility of reaching Cathay by the North-East Passage. Already Frobisher had attempted the north-west route. He had found some ore and pyrites that men thought showed signs of gold. There was no treasure to be found along the coast of Siberia, where the ice and snow had frozen enterprise. Huge distances and the prevalence of banditry closed the overland route. But the lure of Cathay was still potent, and where it seemed that the North-West Passage showed more promise this new north-western adventure was prosecuted with the utmost vigour.

CHAPTER II

THE NORTH-WEST PASSAGE

THE courage of those early navigators among the icebergs of the Arctic seas is the more striking when it is remembered that they had practically no Polar technique such as is known to-day. In these days any ship going on an Arctic voyage is specially built or strengthened for work among the ice. The questions of diet and clothing are carefully studied, the lie of the land, currents, tides are all charted, equipment of all sorts is based on centuries of experience. But these men knew not what they would have to face, what hazards of ice and snow, stormy seas and racing tides, fog and darkness, unknown coasts and savage tribes. Everything was unexpected and strange, and new and unforeseen perils lay in wait for them with every nautical mile they sailed.

The North-West Passage was another forlorn hope. Nevertheless, despite the failure so far to find a north-east route to Cathay, there was a feeling abroad, amounting in many minds to a certainty, that there surely was a way round North America. The experts were perfectly right in both cases. Routes exist, though climatic conditions make them commercially impossible. But in those sanguine days, the impossible was constantly coming true, and it is no wonder that the enthusiasts under-estimated the difficulties. Of all these enthusiasts the keenest and most influential was Humphrey

Gilbert. He was a Devonshire man, educated at Eton and Oxford. No doubt in his early youth his imagination had been fired in that shire of the sea-kings by romantic tales of far-off lands. Millais' well-known picture, "The Boyhood of Raleigh," shows the two half-brothers, Humphrey Gilbert and Walter Raleigh, as eager boys drinking in the story of an old salt whose arm is outflung towards the horizon where ships go down. That picture is a true one, and all his life Gilbert held fast to dreams of Cathay. He was knighted for services rendered in the bloodthirsty Irish wars, he fought in the Netherlands against Alva and the Spanish power, but his dream remained with him, and in 1574 he wrote *The Discourse to prove a Passage by the North-West to Cathaia and the East Indies.* In this he convinced himself and many another, not only of the existence of a way round, but also that it could and should be sailed by English ships. The *Discourse* was published in 1576, and in that same year, largely owing to Gilbert's arguments, Frobisher's first expedition started for the North-West.

Martin Frobisher was a big hefty Yorkshireman, of a good middle-class family. There was no sea-faring tradition in his blood. As a boy he was brought up near Normanton in rural surroundings, where now is a great coalfield. He spent years in the wild wastes looking for treasure, while all the time it was under his feet at home. Martin was born a younger son in 1538. The monastic schools had been abolished, and since the family was far away from the centres of learning he received only a rudimentary education. In any case he was probably not one to profit by it. He had more energy than scholarship in his composition. He was sent to London in 1549 to a rich relative, who promised to make a man of him. This his relative did four or five years later by shipping him on board a small vessel trading to the Guinea coast. Thus Frobisher found his vocation, and rose in time to command a ship of his own. He was a tall man, broad and of immense strength, blue-eyed, hot-tempered and jealous, very tenacious, a martinet in discipline, but having a loving care for his seamen, and as valiant as men are made. Like Drake, he was accused of piracy in his early years, but what is meant by piracy? If by piracy is meant an unofficial undeclared war against what all men recognized as a national enemy, Spain, he was guilty. In fact in 1569 he was arrested at Aldeburgh in Suffolk and taken to London to answer a charge of piracy, a charge that was intended to hoodwink the Spanish Ambassador, for officially peace reigned. Actually, so far from being hanged, Frobisher was taken into the Queen's service, and for the rest of his life he was her man.

The first task she gave him was to go in 1561 to Ireland, where England was engaged in her hopeless attempt to war down the savage Irish tribes with a heavy hand, preparatory to settling the country with (more or less) law-abiding Englishmen. Here Frobisher met Humphrey Gilbert and was infected with the latter's enthusiasm for the North-West, and the prospects of trade and treasure. In Cathay, or better still before Cathay was reached, gold might be won. Frobisher, inspired by Gilbert and introduced by him to Court circles, sought a friend there who might further the project. He found one in the Earl of Warwick, who approached the Muscovy Company on his behalf.

That Company, perfectly satisfied with their trade in furs and tallow with Russia, looked askance at the idea, perhaps not trusting Frobisher; but a certain Michael Lock, a director of the Company, agreed to get the scheme financed, and in 1575 under pressure from the Privy Council the Muscovy Company granted a licence. In the spring of 1576 Frobisher had got together his ships and his crews and was eager to be away.

The expedition was well found. Instruments of various sorts were taken, a globe, an astrolabe,[1] compasses, hour-glasses, maps, a medicine chest full of mellifluous-sounding herbal remedies, food and drink for a year, arms and ammunition. The ships, however, were not imposing. The *Gabriel* displaced 25 tons, the *Michael* 20 tons, and in addition there was a sailing pinnace of six or seven tons. Captain Frobisher was in command, sailing in *Gabriel*, master, Christopher Hall. The master of *Michael* was named Owen Griffin, and the crews of the three vessels numbered thirty-two men and boys.

On 7th June, 1576, they started from Ratcliffe, and under their own sails proceeded down river as far as Deptford. Here they were forced to anchor, the pinnace having been unlucky enough to have her bowsprit and foremast carried away in a collision. The next afternoon the three ships set sail, and a little way farther down dropped their anchors opposite Greenwich, where the Queen was in residence. They banged away with all their little cannon, making "the best show we could," and to their joy they saw as the smoke drifted away the Queen in answer waving her hand from a window.

---

[1] An instrument for measuring the altitude of the sun or stars, now superseded by the sextant.

The Queen, however harassed she might be by ill-health or the crushing load of State affairs, always had time for brave men, and she sent one of her gentlemen-in-waiting aboard the *Gabriel* to command Captain Frobisher to come next day and take leave of her.

After he had kissed the Queen's hand in farewell, Frobisher was rowed back to the *Gabriel* and gave the order to weigh anchor. As the men tramped singing round the capstans, Frobisher stood on the poop of his ship with his long legs apart, while the grey Thames water began to bear him along on the ebb. In his mind were confused thoughts of honour to be gained, treasure to be won, perilous seas to be crossed, with a far-off land as his goal. He was destined to try again and again, others were to follow him, and one day the Passage would be forced, but those pioneers little guessed how fruitless all their endeavours would be.

The first observation of compass variation was taken at Gravesend, and being held up by contrary winds at Harwich, it was some time before they arrived at Fair Isle in the Shetlands. On 11th July they had their first sight of the "Frisland" (Greenland) coast, "rising like pinnacles of steeples and all covered with snow." Frobisher dared not approach the land because of the masses of ice that lay along the shore and the troublesome fogs. They had foul weather, a great storm. The unlucky little pinnace foundered with her crew of four, and the master of the *Michael*, appalled by these unfamiliar terrors, parted company in the mist and darkness and made for home. The undaunted Frobisher, although his mainmast was sprung and his topmast blown overboard, continued on his course north-west. Eighteen

souls on a twenty-five tonner, slowly climbing the
mountainous waves with the bowsprit pointing to
the sky, with a sickening plunge into the enormous
trough on the other side, and the breaking seas
racing over the decks. The men, whipped by the
stinging icy spray, hungry and weary, could hardly

FROBISHER'S
VOYAGES
English Miles
0   100   200   300   400   500

keep their footing in the reeling ship. Towards the
end of July they sighted high ground. Frobisher
named it Queen Elizabeth's Foreland. It is now
known as Resolution Island, off the east end of
Baffin Land. Gradually the sea grew calmer, and
Hall hoisted out a boat and began to take soundings
alongside a huge iceberg. Here they had a new and

terrifying experience. With a mighty roar the berg "calved," falling asunder into two parts. Hall went ashore on an island, but fear of fog coming down prevented him from prospecting for any length of time. However, under instructions from Frobisher, he brought back to the ship such specimens as he could find of flowers and grasses, and one man found a heavy black stone, like a piece of coal in appearance. Frobisher did not think this find to be of any importance, but he kept it, and it was destined to alter the whole significance and scope of subsequent expeditions.

Coming round the north side of the Queen's Foreland, Frobisher sailed up a wide channel for league after league in a westerly direction. At last he thought himself to be on the track of the passage through to Cathay, and optimistically he named it "Frobisher's Straits," following Magellan's example when he discovered the strait into the Pacific. This gulf, for such it was, is now known as Frobisher Bay. When he had sailed a hundred miles or more up the "strait" Frobisher went ashore in his only boat with Hall and eight men. They found a place where a fire had been made, they were attacked by "mighty deer," most probably moose, and then from the top of a hill Frobisher saw floating in the sea what he took at first to be porpoises or seals. On coming nearer he realised that they were men, Eskimos, as they are now known, in tiny one-man boats made of skins.[1] Before he could descend the hill, he found that some of the Eskimos by creeping in behind some rocks, had almost cut him off from his precious boat, and it was only by hard running

[1] The native name of these boats is kayak, and they are laced up in a watertight fashion round the waist of the occupant.

that he saved it. Later he managed to win the Eskimos' confidence. He had them aboard his ship, where they brought him some salmon, and stood eating raw fish and blubber in the faces of the disgusted seamen. The effect produced on the Englishmen by the Eskimos was a feeling of intense curiosity mingled with disgust. They were curious because they had never seen or heard of men like these. They were deeply interested in their kayaks, their larger canoes, their dog sledges, their arrow-heads of bone, their clothes of skins, the tents, everything that was theirs. They were so oily, fishy, and smelly. Eating their food raw was a disgusting habit, the interiors of their tents were beastly, they were probably man-eaters. Such things had been heard of. The Englishmen took a dislike to this strange people. They gave them no credit for their many good qualities. But they wanted some of their skins. The people of fashion in London would give good money for a sealskin. Bells and mirrors were traded for seal and bear skins, but the natives proved treacherous and untrustworthy as indeed Frobisher feared. He went ashore one day and saw their tents, of which he did not think much, and took aboard the ship an Eskimo, to whom he gave a bell and a knife. Probably he wanted a guide, but at all events he did not like the look of the man, and he told five men to land him on a rock and not on any account to go near the beach. Wilfully the men disobeyed, lured by the hope of more skins. Boat and all disappeared and were never seen again.

This was an irreparable disaster. With five men gone and the only boat, nothing more could be done. Winter was coming on, and one morning snow a foot thick lay on the hatches. Frobisher could not go ashore, but he made up his mind to capture a native as a hostage and as a specimen. He rang a bell, signing that he would give it to the man that came to fetch it. Not one dared approach near enough. Frobisher flung the bell towards them, but purposely threw short, so that it fell into the sea. He rang another louder and more alluring bell. Eagerness overcame caution. One of the Eskimos could stand it no longer. He came alongside, nearer and nearer, and stretched out his hand to clutch the coveted toy. And Frobisher, leaning overside his little ship, dropped the bell, and grabbed the man by the arm. Exerting all his magnificent strength, he lugged the unfortunate Eskimo, kayak, paddle and all out of the sea on to the deck. The poor wretch bit his tongue in two in his mortification at being taken captive.

On 26th August they started for home, one little ship, with captain, master, and twelve men and boys, having set out with three ships and crews of thirty-two. They were like to lose another hand, for on 7th September arose a very terrible storm, and a man was swept overboard. He hung on to the foresail sheet, and Frobisher grabbed him and hauled him aboard. That feats such as these should have been possible throws a startling light on the low freeboard of Frobisher's tiny vessel. Early in October the *Gabriel* arrived in London, and then began the excitement about the piece of black ore that she had brought home.

Frobisher thought that the chief result of his voyage was the high hope of a passage through to Cathay by the discovery of his "strait". He recked little of the black stone. But Michael Lock, Frobisher's backer, when he saw it thought otherwise. He jumped to the conclusion that it contained gold. Gold, in the minds of all men at this date, was more important even than Cathay. The golden treasure of the Indies was rapidly depreciating the currency and raising the cost of living in Spain. The same thing was beginning to happen in England. Yet the cry was all for gold and yet more gold. Elizabeth and her ministers wanted a new source of supply, forgetting or rather not knowing that in the long run the gold would be of no use to them. For the present, gold was the sinews of war.

Lock had the lump of rock assayed by three of the expert metallurgists of the City of London. All reported that it was nothing but iron pyrites. Disappointed and ready to be deceived, he gave it to an unscrupulous Italian assayer named Agnello, who saw what was expected of him, and duly reported that the ore contained a little gold. Everyone wished to believe it, and consequently everyone did. "Whereupon preparation was made for a new voyage against the year following, and the captain more specially directed by commission for the searching more of this gold ore than for the searching any further discovery of the passage." The Cathay Company was formed in March 1577 to trade in the North-West. The Queen invested a thousand pounds and lent a tall ship, the *Aid*, of 200 tons. The rest of the fleet consisted of those two "small barks" the *Gabriel* and the *Michael*. The provisions taken comprised five months' supply of biscuit, flour for a year, beer for six months (one gallon per man per day), five tuns of wine (malmsey and sack), beef, and salt to preserve it, pork, peas, stockfish (frozen), butter, cheese, oatmeal, rice, honey,

39 D

salad oil, vinegar, brandy, raisins, almonds, liquorice,
candles, coal, and wood, and all manner of stores
and tackle. The names of the backers, who were
the members of the Cathay Company, included
besides the Queen, many members of the Privy
Council, a number of City of London merchants
(among whom was Anthony Jenkinson), and a few
Bristol men. Lock was the Governor of the Company. The valuable and expensive *Aid* was to load
the gold, and the ships with the archangels' names
were to carry out the exploration and push on if
possible to the Pacific Ocean. A few natives were
to be brought back, and the five lost Englishmen
rescued. Frobisher was as keen as anyone about this
last part of the programme.

Frobisher as "general" sailed in the *Aid*, whereof
Christopher Hall was master, with George Best as
the general's lieutenant. One hundred men in all
was the *Aid*'s full complement, of which a dozen
were gentlemen, and a score or so were soldiers.
There were a few miners, and the rest were "suffi-
cient and tall sailors." Mr. Edward Fenton was
captain of the *Gabriel*, and Mr. Gilbert Yorke
captain of the *Michael*. There were on board these
two ships 18 and 16 persons respectively, making a
total of 134, but for some reason Frobisher was not
allowed to take more than 120 altogether. Some,
therefore, had to be discharged at the last moment.
The expedition left Blackwall on Whit-Sunday,
26th May, 1577, amid the cheers and tears of fathers
and mothers, sweethearts and wives, and dropped
down with the tide to Gravesend. On Monday
morning "aboard the *Aid* we received all the
Communion by the Minister of Gravesend, and
towards night we departed." They took in more

40

victuals at Harwich. The Queen, making one of her tours round the country, was staying with the Earl of Warwick in Essex. Frobisher therefore rode in from Harwich and kissed hands in farewell.

Early in June they reached the Orkneys. Best took a party on shore at St. Magnus Sound to stretch their legs. The inhabitants promptly fled, thinking the visitors were pirates come to plunder, a not uncommon occurrence. Best halted his party and went forward alone to explain. This accomplished, some business was done in local produce. Hall noted their one-roomed stone cottages with no chimneys and a fire of peat in the middle. On the practice of the whole family sleeping and eating on one side of the house while the cattle were stalled on the other his comment was: "very beastly."

Then on 8th June the good ships spread their sails to a "merry wind," which unfortunately soon shifted against them. As they struggled north-westwards they fell in with three English fishing boats homeward bound from the Icelandic fishing grounds. To them the crews gave their letters for England, and tacked on over the wide North Atlantic for twenty-six days, seeing no land, but coming across much driftwood and whole trunks of great fir-trees, which they supposed to have come from Newfoundland. They sighted Greenland on 4th July. They thought wistfully of English summer-time, of bird song and the fragrance of English lanes as they "tasted the most boisterous Boreal blasts mixed with snow and hail," and saw in the distance the icefields. The ice-bound coast and the high snow-covered mountains, dazzling white and gleaming under the infrequent sunlight, with the danger of sudden fogs, made a landing here im-

possible, and they sailed west along latitude 60°
for Meta Incognita, the Unknown Goal, the name
that was given to the land on the south side of
"Frobisher's Straits." Ere they reached it a fierce
storm broke upon them, and the tiny *Michael*,
buffeted by the waves and lashed by the winds, had
her topmasts carried overside and her rudder split.
The ships took in their sails and hove to, among
the vast icebergs, till the weather improved.

They made a happy landfall at Hall's Island and
pushed on up the "strait." Frobisher went ashore
in a small rowing pinnace at the place where the
fateful lump of alleged gold ore had been found. Not
far away a plentiful supply of the rock was discovered. The search had taken some time, and it
was not until ten o'clock at night that the general
returned to the anxious ship's company, which
welcomed him with a joyful volley. On 19th July
Frobisher with a strong party of armed men landed
on Hall's Island to look for natives. Leaving the
boats well guarded, they climbed to the top of a
high hill. There they made a cairn of stones, planted
a flag and sounded a trumpet. Kneeling, they said
a few prayers and named the hill Mount Warwick
in honour of the Earl, who had a large interest in
venture. Some Eskimos appeared and followed
them down to the shore. Having seen the company
into the boats, Frobisher and Hall, unarmed, met
two Eskimos, also unarmed, and began to trade.
Suddenly, on a prearranged signal, each of the two
Englishmen grabbed his man, intending to carry
him on board as a hostage and push off in the boats.
But the Eskimos were too slippery. Like eels they
eluded the Englishmen's grasp and dashed for their
bows and arrows. Frobisher and Hall ran for dear

life to the boats, the former picking an arrow out of his buttock. Their men fired a caliver at the Eskimos, and Nicholas Conger, a Cornishman and a great wrestler, ran out, caught and threw one of them, and took him alive. A sudden storm had sprung up, so that they could not get back to the ships. They rowed to another small island, where they stayed till next morning, cold, wet, and hungry.

While they were engaged in this not very creditable escapade the ships were having their own troubles. They were occupied as best they could in dodging mountainous bergs, of which the sea seemed full. With a high wind and little sea room they were constantly tacking. "But God was our best steersman," remarked Best, adding naively that Jackman and Dyer were also expert. Fortunately it never grew dark, being light all night, and they were thus able to see their peril. "Every man had enough to do with his hands to haul ropes, and with his eyes to look out for danger." Nor was this all. In the *Aid* the flues of the galley fire became red hot and set the ship in a blaze. Prompt action and "God's help" were needed to extinguish it. "But the next morning, as God would, the storm ceased," and Frobisher and his party came aboard.

Coasting along the shore prospecting in the *Michael*, Frobisher spied two tents of skin and whalebone. The occupants fled as the party landed. The Englishmen left some trading trash, taking one dog in exchange, and also left some pens, ink and paper, on the chance that his missing men might be somewhere in the vicinity. For in the tents ("defiled most filthily with their beastly feeding") they had found an English canvas

43

doublet, a shirt, a girdle, and three odd shoes of different sizes.

Mr. Philpot, the "ensign" or sub-lieutenant, took a party of gentlemen adventurers and soldiers (marines, they would be called to-day) again to the tents, and surprised the Eskimos, who loosed off their arrows. The English replied with more arrows, wounding three men, who to the white men's surprise flung themselves into the sea and were drowned. The rest fled, except two women, one an aged crone, and the other encumbered with a young baby on her back. The old body was so ugly that she was suspected of being a devil or a witch, and her footgear was stripped off to see if she had a cloven hoof. The test being negative, she was allowed to go. The younger woman was taken, with the idea of her being a mate for the male captive. It was noticed that the baby's arm had been hit by an arrow. The ship's surgeon applied salves to the hurt, but the woman, distrustful, snatched them off, and by continual licking with her tongue stanched the wound. The woman was confronted with the man on their return to shipboard, and the English stood round curiously to see what would happen. After a long silence, the man "began to tell a long solemn tale to the woman, whereunto she gave good hearing till he had finished," and the two then went below to the cabin that had been allotted to them. Although she proved a good housewife, kept the place clean according to their notions, and prepared the food for them both, they never cohabited together, and exhibited the utmost decency and modesty in their dealings with each other. This surprised the crew, who had plainly regarded them practically as animals.

One day the expedition anchored on the north-eastern side of the "strait" in "Anne Warwick's Sound." This was the most westerly point reached on the voyage. Their captive, who went ashore with the party, intimated by signs that the five lost Englishmen had gone off in a canoe. Some Eskimos had come down, and Frobisher endeavoured to explain that he would deliver up his captives in exchange for the missing men. He also left a letter, direct, sailor-like and earnest, with no hint of reproach for their disobedience.

"In the name of God, in whom we all believe, who (I trust) hath preserved your bodies and souls amongst these infidels, I commend me unto you. I will be glad to seek by all means you can devise for your deliverance, either with force, or with any commodities within my ships, which I will not spare for your sakes, or anything else I can do for you. I have aboard of theirs a man, a woman and a child, which I am contented to deliver for you, but the man which I carried away from hence the last year is dead in England. Moreover you may declare unto them, that if they deliver you not, I will not leave a man alive in their country. And thus, if one of you can come to speak with me, they shall have either the man, women or child in pawn for you. And thus unto God whom I trust you do serve in haste I leave you, and to Him we will daily pray for you. This Tuesday morning the seventh of August. Anno 1577.

Yours to the uttermost of my power,
Martin Frobisher."

He got no answer. A few days later the Eskimos attacked the ships, but were beaten off.

Meanwhile the search for gold had not been

45

neglected. On an island in the Countess of Warwick's Sound, plentiful supplies of the wonderful
ore had been located, and all hands from Frobisher
to the ships' boys set to work to dig it out, under
the miners' directions. Frobisher set the pace and
so hard did they work that in twenty days they had
excavated and carried on board no less than 200
tons of the worthless stuff. Best built a fort, known
as Best's Bulwark, for the defence of the diggers,
throwing up entrenchments, and suffering like them
while at work from mosquitoes, "certain stinging
gnats, which bite so fiercely that the place where
they bite shortly after swelleth and itcheth very
sore." On the night of 21st August they finished
their labour. The men were weary, their clothes
and shoes were worn out, the bottoms of their
baskets burst, their tools broken, legs and backs
were strained, and several men had ruptured themselves; and all for iron pyrites.

It was high time to be going. At night ice began
to congeal and freeze about the ships' sides. On
22nd August they made a bonfire on the highest
point of the island, marched round it with their
ensign displayed, fired a volley in honour of Anne,
Countess of Warwick, and went on board. Frobisher
was determined in accordance with the spirit of
his instructions to leave the further exploration of
the passage for another time and to get home safely
with the "gold." On the 24th they left the Queen's
Foreland astern, and soon ran into fog and snow
and storm. On the 30th, by "a surge of the sea"
the *Gabriel*'s master and boatswain were both swept
overboard. The boatswain clung to a rope with
one hand and with the other caught hold of Smith,
the master, but was forced to let go. The boatswain

was hauled aboard, but the master, who had just before told his captain of a presentiment of his end, was borne away by a huge wave and drowned. In the fog and storm the *Aid* lost the two little ships, which made their way independently to Bristol and Yarmouth. The *Aid* was in trouble. When the sea went down, the crew discovered that their rudder was split almost in two. A dozen of their best men went overside into the icy water to repair the damage, and were hauled into the ship half dead with cold. Eventually Frobisher found himself near the Scilly Isles, and with a contrary wind preventing him from rounding Land's End, made his way to Padstow and Milford Haven, whence he took horse and rode to London for orders.

The Privy Council gave instructions that the precious cargo of rubbish should be solemnly locked up in Bristol Castle. The *Michael* however, had come into the Thames, and her cargo was safely stowed away in Sir William Winter's house on St. Katharine's Hill. Frobisher had only lost two men, Smith of the *Gabriel*, and one heroic soul "that died at sea, which was sick before he came aboard and was so desirous to follow this enterprise, that he rather chose to die therein, than not to be one to attempt so notable a voyage." It was not really so notable. Frobisher had made no fresh geographical discoveries, and his "gold" was dross. A furious dispute about this gold raged in London. The recognized assayers of the City persisted "upon gage of their life and goods" that the rock was worthless, that it contained no gold. The charlatans said it did. Unfortunately Lock and Frobisher did not know the difference between professional and charlatan. Nor did they know the difference between gold ore and iron pyrites. So bemused also were the Council and the City merchants that State help was given again, and fresh money was surprisingly subscribed. Men believe what they want to believe. Frobisher probably cared little whether the rock contained gold or not. He was to command another and greater expedition to the North-West, and nothing else mattered much.

The search for the passage to Cathay was again an ostensible reason for the third adventure, but it was altogether overshadowed by the quest for gold. Connected with the quest was the proposal to found a mining camp for a year in those inhospitable lands near the location of the "mine." For this purpose a barrack was taken to sea, a huge timber frame house in sections. Captain Fenton, who had commanded the *Gabriel* in the last expedition, was appointed to take charge of the party to be left behind, with Captains Best and Philpot as the other officers. A hundred volunteers were enrolled, consisting of thirty miners (probably Cornishmen), forty seamen to man the three small ships that were to remain, and thirty others. These others were gentlemen volunteers, soldiers for guards, carpenters, bakers and all necessary trades. There were fifteen sail in all. "In the *Aid*, being Admiral, was the General, Captain Frobisher; in the *Thomas Allen*, vice-admiral, Captain Yorke; in the *Judith*, Lieutenant-general Captain Fenton; in the *Anne Francis*, Captain Best." The ships' names read like a poem, an odyssey of the North—*Hopewell, Bear, Thomas of Ipswich, Emmanuel of Exeter, Francis of Fowey, Moon, Buss of Bridgwater, Salamander of Weymouth, Denis*, and the faithful *Gabriel* and *Michael*. Christopher Hall, one of the old hands at the game,

48

was chief pilot. Hall ranked as an officer. He was an educated man, who has left full accounts of the first and second voyages and of the customs of the Eskimos, in whom he seems to have been very interested. The best story of the three voyages is that written by Frobisher's lieutenant, George Best. It is distinguished by an occasional vivid phrase, and bears the stamp of a pious, zealous, efficient and modest officer. All the captains, headed by the General, went to the Court at Greenwich to take their leave of the Queen, who received them very graciously. She had always liked Frobisher, and she thought him a proper man. On this occasion she put round his neck a chain of gold, with words of encouragement such as she well knew how to give. Whereupon they all "kissed her hand, took their leave, and departed every man towards his charge."

Frobisher issued his fleet orders. In the first were injunctions to banish swearing, filthy talk, and card play. Matins and evensong according to the use of the Church of England were to be said every day. There were orders, with the appropriate signals, for keeping station, sighting land or a strange sail, for conferences, and for action in case of attack. Signals were made by firing guns, striking sails, or hoisting a flag. Trumpets were to be sounded and drums beat in foggy weather. This was more melodious if less effective than the modern steam siren. Signalling was very primitive. The system of flags of different colours and shapes had not been evolved. There was no code system of flag-signalling, nor a morse code or semaphore. Hence arose the necessity for frequent conferences of all the captains on board the flagship. In action the only method of conveying orders was by small boat. This being slow and cumbrous, naval battles on a large scale tended to degenerate into scrappy, haphazard, individual actions.

The expedition left Harwich on 31st May, 1578. Off Cape Clear a week later the flagship sighted a small vessel which was overhauled and hailed. A feeble shout came in answer, and it quickly appeared that such of the crew as were not dead were wounded and starving. They were Bristol men, who had been plundered by a French pirate and abandoned in this sorry condition. Frobisher, like a good seaman, did all in his power to help. He sent his surgeon on board, with provisions and water. Many of the stricken crew said they had had nothing but olives and stinking water for a week.

The fleet sailed before a favouring breeze for a fortnight out of sight of land. Then came the cry "Land ho!" from the flagship's look-out. Here was the first sight of Greenland's icy mountains, huge peaks whose tops were hid in cloud. This time Frobisher effected a landing, but did not tarry long. With a fair wind behind them the mariners weighed anchor and made for Frobisher's "Straits," on 23rd June. As the last high cliff faded from their view they named it Charing Cross, in the same spirit that the men in the Great War named their trenches Piccadilly and Oxford Street and all the well-known names of home. They met a school of whales. Indeed, the *Salamander* met one of them very forcibly. She was under courses and bonnets,[1] and when she struck the whale, she was brought up all standing, throwing her crew off their feet. She

---

[1] The course was the body of the lower sails. Bonnets were strips of canvas laced to the lower edge of the course in order to gather more wind.

was a stout little ship, and it was the whale that suffered the damage. Then the fog came down, swirling and smoking along the grey seas. In obedience to orders trumpets and drums sounded, muffled in the gloom. A glimpse of Queen's Foreland was seen, and the expedition entered what was believed to be Frobisher's Straits. Ice choked the channel. Great ghostly bergs were floating down, a whiteness appearing in the greyness of the mist, with a cold chilly breath as from a tomb. Now a way would open in front of a ship, then it would close again as the bergs came together with a grinding crash. The *Judith* and the *Michael* were found to be missing. Men thought they had shared the fate of the *Denis*. The crew of this luckless ship saw a mighty berg bearing down upon them. There was no time to get clear. They fired a gun as a signal to the others. Hardly had the echoes ceased to reverberate when with a crash the berg struck the *Denis*, which crumpled like an egg-shell and went to the bottom. Their horrified companions hastily lowered boats and rescued the men struggling in the icy sea. Half of the sectional barracks had gone down in the *Denis*. By great good luck no lives had been lost, but who would be the next to go? Terrible times were to come. A sudden great storm came up from the south-east, and piled up the ice behind them against the current. They could go neither forward nor back. Some hove-to. Others anchored to a berg and rode in its lee. Others, girt about with towering, crashing bergs and grinding floes, made fenders of cables, mattresses, planks. Three-inch planks were shivered and reduced to matchwood. Leaning over the bulwarks they strove to keep off the ice with poles,

pikes, capstan bars, oars, anything they could pick
up. Some dropped overboard on to the ice, and
desperately shoved with their shoulders. Day and
night they laboured, while the stout oak still held
as the squeezed ships heaved themselves up a foot
above their waterline. Frobisher's fleet orders had
banned swearing, but it is hardly to be expected that
English or any other seamen did otherwise than swear
profusely as they shoved and pushed hopelessly (as
it seemed) against the ever-increasing ice. They
were enjoined to pray, and pray they did, fervently.

Four ships, *Anne Francis, Moon, Francis of Fowey*,
and *Gabriel*, were to seaward of the rest and had
more sea room. They were by no means free from
ice, for many huge bergs just slid by them time and
again. One monster was estimated at five hundred
feet high. But by the next day they got clear out
to sea. Best ordered his ship's company (in the
Anne Francis) to kneel round the mainmast to return
thanks for their deliverance and pray for the
succour of their comrades. They believed their
prayer to have been answered when the wind went
round to west-nor'-west and drove the ice seaward
again. The main fleet went down with the tide
and lay offshore to refit.

Undismayed, on 7th July, the fleet tried again,
though navigation was difficult in the dank dark
mists. Doubts began to arise. Could that point be
Mount Warwick? they said. We cannot have come
up so far. Yet what else could it be? The tides,
too, are far stronger than we have had before.
Listen to the flood roaring down. It sounds like the
water rushing over the piers of the Bridge in dear
old London. Frobisher called a conference. Christopher Hall, the chief pilot and most experienced

navigator in the fleet, said frankly that he had never seen that coast before. It is quite clear now what had happened. They were not in the accustomed "straits," but had blundered into what is to-day known as Hudson's Strait, leading to Hudson Bay. Some of the fleet turned back. The rest followed Frobisher in. It is not certain whether Frobisher believed Hall. It may have been a characteristic example of self-will and obstinacy that led him to persevere up the channel, or it may have been his keenness as a navigator and explorer that made him ignore for the moment the mines of ore. Very probably it was a mixture of both influences, and there is little doubt that he must have sometimes cursed the "gold" that so hampered his search for the passage. He found the south side of Meta Incognita more plentiful than the north in flora and fauna, more grass, mosses and flowers, herds of caribou deer, hares, foxes, many more birds, and more Eskimos. With the latter some trade was done in furs and skins and fish. At length he turned back. On sighting Queen's Foreland he perceived a sound running up towards Frobisher's Straits. He sent the *Gabriel* to see if there was a way through. She reported that there was. So the Queen's Foreland was proved to be an island. The fleet sailed through, being nearly wrecked on the rocks in a fog. In the straits Best in the *Anne Francis* rejoined the fleet, and the *Francis of Fowey* and the *Buss of Bridgwater* came in on the following day, the crew of the latter being worn out with work at the pumps.

The weariness, the hardships, dangers and hair-breadth escapes they had all experienced caused at this stage a general dissatisfaction throughout the fleet. When it was seen that Frobisher intended to lead them on through the ice to the mines on Warwick Island complaints grew louder. Some malcontents were even heard to say that they would as lief be hanged for mutiny as perish in the ice. But Frobisher's resolution was iron-hard. He resolved to get through at all costs, and such was the power of his personality and the influence of his splendid body of officers that the murmuring died down and was heard no more.

Then came a blizzard, a gale of wind and snow. The *Anne Francis*, *Moon*, and *Thomas of Ipswich*, seeking sea room, left the straits. The rest, blinded with driving snow, numbed with cold, wet through to the skin, were wondering, if this were summer, what would the winter be like? Frobisher never wavered. He led his fleet through any likely gap in the ice with such skill and daring that on 31st July they anchored in the Countess of Warwick's Sound. In his ship, the *Aid*, men were standing by ready to let the anchor go, when they struck a nearly submerged floe with such force that the flukes of the anchor were driven into the ship's bows below the waterline. They had all they could do to keep her from sinking. In the Sound they discovered those trusty ships *Gabriel* and *Michael*, which they had given up for lost.

On this great occasion when the fleet had "recovered their Port," Mr. Wolfall, the chaplain, preached a notable sermon. He seems to have been a good, likeable man, who gave up the enjoyment of a comfortable living at home to come out and stay for the year in camp with the mining party, to minister to them and "to reform the infidel." It is to be feared that no infidels were reformed, but he was a source of strength to his countrymen.

The miners were set to work on the island. Meanwhile the great question was: could the house be built? The bills of lading showed that only the east and south sides had survived the hazards of the voyage, and many planks of that portion had been damaged by having been used as fenders against the ice. The carpenters stated that even if they had the timber it would take eight or nine weeks to erect barracks for sixty men, let alone a hundred, and there were only twenty-six possible days left. This estimate was probably exaggerated, but there was certainly no timber, and it was agreed by the general and his council that there could be no camp this year.

All this time Best in the *Anne Francis* and the two other ships had been trying to reach the main body. They had been badly bruised by the ice. Moreover, the ropes were often frozen so hard that a man could not handle them without cutting his hands. The men badly wanted to go home. Best however was made of the same stuff as his leader. He refused. They would put together the sections of a pinnace he had on board, and join the general in that. The carpenter shook his head. There were no knee-timbers to strengthen the boat, and no nails to join the planks. Best found a smith in the ship's company, a smith without the tools of his craft. A gun-chamber was taken for an anvil, a pickaxe for a sledge-hammer, two pairs of hand bellows instead of a smith's bellows. For iron for making the nails Best was forced to break up fire-shovel, tongs, and gridiron. When the pinnace was finally assembled, the carpenter, his craftsman's pride outraged, shook his head again. "She only hangs together by the nails. I wouldn't trust myself

in her, not for five hundred pounds, I wouldn't."
The crew looked doubtfully at the knee-less pinnace.
Best came forward. "You all know how important
it is for us to join the general. Who says the boat is
safe?" Whereupon John Gray, master's mate of
the *Anne Francis*, said, "I'll go in her," and other
volunteers followed. After all, they said, with luck
and great care, she might do.

Best and his party pushed off. They rowed
ninety miles before Best saw the smoke of a fire and
a flag being waved on Warwick Island. When
within hailing distance, "What cheer?" they cried.
"All's well, all's well," was the answer, and cheer
after cheer echoed among the rocks and hills, and
caps were flung into the air.

The ships were well laden with ore. Rumour
flew round that the fleet was going home. The
masons built a house of stone and lime to see how
it would stand the winter. The timber sections
were buried for use the following year. Communion
services were held on the various ships. Frobisher
wanted to push on to discover more of his passage
but the opinion of the council and his own better
judgment were against him. Winter was coming
on, snow was falling, darkness setting in, and ice
forming rapidly. Moreover, the beer was all gone.
The casks had been stove in by the weight of coal
and timber that the stevedores had stowed above
them. They would have to drink water! Frobisher
gave way, not without some impatience. On 31st
August the fleet departed. *Anne Francis*, *Buss of
Bridgwater*, and *Michael* stayed behind to finish
loading water and stores. Best's ramshackle pinnace
could not reach the ship on account of the drift ice,
so it was towed in the wake of the *Michael*. As they

came alongside the pinnace collapsed. The men scrambled aboard, but their kits were lost. On 28th September the fleet passed between Scilly and Land's End, and so went up channel to London.

The results of the great adventure were meagre. Frobisher had been into Hudson's Strait leading to Hudson Bay, though he did not know it. He was no nearer the North-West Passage. And as for the ore, nobody wanted it any more. Nobody believed in it now. The Cathay Company was wound up. Many of the subscribers had not paid up their shares, and the seamen had to wait for their pay. Frobisher, the leader of the enterprise, for a time was "on the beach."

In 1861 Mr. C. F. Hall, of Cincinnati, U.S.A., landed on Countess of Warwick's Island, known to the Eskimos in their tongue as White Man's Island. He saw the stone house. He found the "mine" whence the iron pyrites had been so laboriously dug. He learnt the fate of the five lost men. They had discovered the house, dug up the buried timber, made some sort of a boat and set out for home. They were drowned or perished of cold and hunger amid the ice and snow.

The North-West project had been overshadowed and hindered by the not unnatural desire of the promoters to get immediate dividends. For a few years little was heard of it. But there was bound to be a revival of the scheme. Influential people still believed in its practicability. Humphrey Gilbert and his brother Adrian were eager to put it again to the test. Walsingham, the Secretary of State, was sympathetic. Such was the enthusiasm for geographical exploration and for fresh openings for trade that, at the very time when the Spanish menace was looming darkly over England, backers were readily found for another voyage. The Gilberts had the man for it ready to their hands.

The brothers Gilbert lived in what is surely one of the most beautiful places in the world. Greenway Court on the Dart, near Dartmouth, stands high above the river, where the steep wooded hills sweep down to the water's edge. Above there is a wide reach like a lake at high tide, where at low tide herons stand and fish and men net salmon. All round are green heights with trees hanging over the water, save where a little creek runs up to the village of Stoke Gabriel. Hard by is Sandridge, where in 1550 John Davis was born. The Gilbert boys, with their half-brother Walter Raleigh and their neighbour Davis, must have explored together every reach and creek of this lovely river between Totnes and Dartmouth. The friendship begun in boyhood lasted all their lives. Davis probably went to Totnes Grammar School and certainly took to the sea at an early age. By 1579 he had become well-known as a sea captain of scientific attainments and proved capacity. For the next six years he was ashore and often at Sandridge, where he married a Miss Fulford. The Gilberts had left Greenway. However, Adrian was living close by, and Humphrey had bought Compton Castle, near Paignton. Davis therefore saw much of his friends.

Davis was a man of very different character to Frobisher. Though his courage and resolution were not inferior, he had a much gentler and more genial nature than the tall fiery impatient Yorkshireman. He did not possess Frobisher's reputation as a disciplinarian, and in a tight place Frobisher might have been the better man, but whereas Frobisher was admired by his men, Davis was loved. Davis was far better educated, and a more scientific navigator. He combined his knowledge with the qualities that made a brave and determined explorer. He never betrayed the confidence of the patrons and merchants who trusted him. John Davis approached very near to the ideal Elizabethan sea-captain. Many men shared his high qualities, but few united so many in one person.

A strong supporter of Davis in his forthcoming enterprise was a certain Dr. Dee,[1] a philosopher and man of science who lived at Mortlake in Surrey, near London, and who had one of the finest private libraries in England. In the early days of 1584, Adrian Gilbert and John Davis took the long miry road on horseback to London from Devonshire to consult with the doctor and to study his charts. With him they met Mr. Secretary Walsingham, and the plans were then laid. Financial backing had to be obtained, and here Mr. William Sanderson came in. He was a London merchant of great wealth who was introduced to Adrian and John by Sir Walter Raleigh. Sanderson was a member of the Fishmongers' Company. He decided to support the venture, became the largest subscriber and sent a relative, Mr. John Janes, as supercargo. The West Country, particularly the Merchant Adventurers of Exeter, roused by Adrian Gilbert, also liberally financed the expedition, which was under Sir Francis Walsingham's direct patronage. Two ships were fitted out, pleasantly named *Sunshine* and *Moonshine*. The *Sunshine* of London, 50 tons, belonged to Mr. Sanderson, and the *Moonshine* of

---

[1] Dr. Dee had helped in the promotion of the voyages of Frobisher and Drake.

Dartmouth, 35 tons, was probably the property of the Merchant Adventurers of Exeter. There were twenty-three persons in *Sunshine*, nineteen in *Moonshine*. In *Sunshine* four out of the twenty-three were rated as musicians. No well-found expedition out of musical Elizabethan England was ever without its fiddlers and trumpeters to play while the officers dined.

Sunshine and *Moonshine* left the flourishing port of Dartmouth on 7th June, 1585. As they passed the castle and the church of St. Petrox the ships lifted to the Channel swell. Davis's heart was lifted up too, for at last he was away on the voyage for which he had so often longed. The wind was contrary, and after a brief stay at Falmouth he was compelled to harbour in the Scilly Isles for almost a fortnight. Here he was not idle. He and the master and Janes went about in a boat making an exact chart of the islands with the rocks, the harbours and the soundings. When they got under way again the men had some sport with a school of porpoises. The master harpooned one, and they had porpoise stew, which "did eat as sweet as any mutton." Encouraged by this, they tried again the next day, but the porpoises made off with their harpoons and spoilt the sport. The master tried to get one with a pike. The porpoise broke off the head of the pike and got away. He aimed a futile blow with a boathook and then gave it up. Whales too they saw in plenty, for the whale had not yet been hunted almost to extinction in the North Atlantic.

By 19th July they were approaching the ice-fields. The sea was calm. There was a thick fog. Through the dark gloom of the clinging mist came a mighty thunder, like the sound of great waves

60

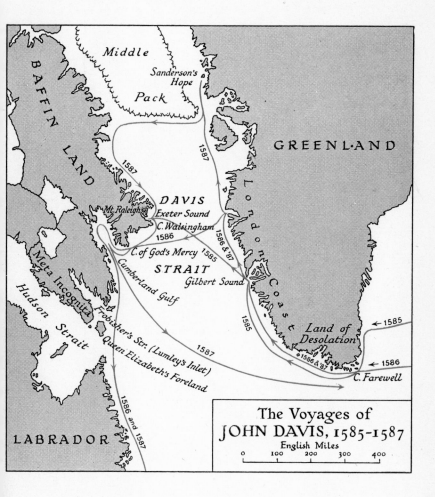

Middle

Sanderson's
Hope

Pack

BAFFIN
LAND

GREENLAND

1587

1587

DAVIS
Exeter Sound
Mt.Raleigh
C. Walsingham
1586

London Coast

C. of God's Mercy   1585

1586 & 87

STRAIT

Gilbert Sound

1585

Cumberland Gulf

1585

Meta Incognita

Land of
Desolation

Hudson Strait

Frobisher's Str. (Lumley's Inlet)

1585

1587

1586 & 87

1586

Queen Elizabeth's Foreland

C. Farewell

1586 and 1587

LABRADOR

The Voyages of
JOHN DAVIS, 1585-1587
English Miles

0   100   200   300   400

breaking upon the shore. The *Moonshine*'s boat was ordered out to take soundings, but could not find bottom even at three hundred fathoms. Davis, his master Mr. Easton, and Mr. Janes went forward in a boat to investigate this mysterious noise. Instructions were given that at every turn of the hour-glass (i.e., every half-hour) a musket shot was to be fired, so that the exploring party should not get lost. They found they were close to a field of pack ice. The alarming noise was nothing but the grinding together of large ice floes. They loaded their boat with lumps of ice to be used as drinking water, and returned to the ship.

Next day the fog rolled away. Hanging in the sky was a huge white cone, and below this mountain peak a belt of cloud. Below this again were the cliffs, and ice running out for miles into the sea. It was the south-east coast of Greenland, and Davis called it The Land of Desolation. When the wind blew off the land or the ice it was somewhat chilly, but off the sea the air was warm. The clothing for Arctic work in those days was English woollen wear. The men's rations were similar to those in Frobisher's expeditions, but breakfast does not seem to have been a regular meal. Davis ordered extra rations on account of the trying weather: "every mess, being five persons, should have half a pound of bread and a can of beer every morning to breakfast."

On 29th July as they coasted along they discovered that the ice had disappeared. They had rounded the southernmost point of Greenland and were sailing north-westward. The wind falling contrary, officers and crews went ashore. Here they met some Eskimos in their kayaks and Davis, wishing to make friends, bade the musicians play some country dances such as all the men would know, and they danced, to the silent wonderment of the natives. Next day the Eskimos came round the ships in their kayaks and invited the English on shore. They were most friendly, and a brisk trade in skins, furs and clothing was done. The Eskimos do not seem to have left such an unfavourable first impression as they did on Frobisher's men. Probably Davis and company knew what to expect.

During the brief summer this part of Greenland has a beauty of its own. The deep blue sea runs up into innumerable fiords, and the soil is covered with mosses, grasses and wild flowers. The men noticed a flower like the English primrose, and a juicy sweet berry that reminded the Devonshire men of the whortleberry "back along in old Dartymoor." They saw no rivers, but only pools of snow water. There were shrubs of birch and willow, and a plentiful supply of spruce fir cast up as driftwood. They saw vast numbers of seals, and had some exciting moments hunting polar bears with muskets and boar spears. Bear steak was voted good. Altogether they thoroughly enjoyed themselves.

On 6th August they sighted land free from ice in 66° 40′ latitude on the western side of what came to be known as Davis Strait. They anchored in "Totnes Road," under the shadow of "Mount Raleigh," and named the inlet Exeter Sound. The foreland to the south was called Cape Walsingham. Here rations were increased at the men's request. The new scale does not strike one as being very appetizing. Each mess of five men had four pounds of bread a day, twelve quarts of beer, and six Newfoundland stockfish. On meat days an extra allowance of peas was issued to save the butter and cheese, which were running short.

The ships penetrated into Cumberland Sound, but did not reach the head of the gulf. The weather began to break up, and on 26th August they sailed for home, reaching Dartmouth a month later.

No time was lost by Davis in getting another expedition financed. This time the West Country merchants were more than ever to the fore, particularly the Merchant Adventurers of Exeter and Totnes. The Exeter folk owned the *Mermaid*, 120 tons. *Sunshine* and *Moonshine* were fitted out again, together with a ten-ton sailing pinnace, *North Star*. On 7th May, 1586, they again left the blue waters of the Dart. They waved a farewell to their friends on the quay, took a last look at the clustering houses straggling uphill, and crossed the harbour bar. They sailed northwards round Ireland. A month out from home the little fleet was divided. Captain Pope in *Sunshine*, with the pinnace *North Star*, was instructed to seek a passage northward between Greenland and Iceland. Davis in *Mermaid*, accompanied by *Moonshine*, held on his old course to the west coast of Greenland. He landed at the same place, and the Eskimos recognized some of the old hands that had come the previous year. The natives were eighteen in number and very friendly. Davis gave them a knife apiece. In consequence, on the next few days they turned up in their kayaks forty, fifty, a hundred at a time. While a pinnace, brought in sections in the *Mermaid*, was being assembled, a brisk trade was done in seal and deer skins, fish and game. The landing party split up into two boatloads and went in search of the Eskimos' tents. Strict orders were given against firing muskets, or doing anything to frighten or injure the people. Ten miles beyond the snow mountains Davis found a stretch of country like Dartmoor, but saw nothing there but a few eagles, ravens, larks and linnets.

The Eskimos seemed so friendly that Davis organized a sports meeting. The Englishmen and the Eskimos sat round together in a half-circle. The Eskimos smelt strongly of fish and oil, but the English were not too fastidious. They too might have offended delicate modern nostrils, for there were no opportunities for baths in small crowded ships. The Englishmen rigged up poles and a cord for the high jump, and the natives at once saw what was intended and tried their skill. The English were easily best at this game, for the Eskimos were very short, stocky and clumsy. It was the same with the long jump. The English could not make the natives understand how to run races, and when at last they did persuade them to run, they would not start together, and they either stopped half-way, or went on running long past the winning post. Races were therefore a failure, but the Eskimos thoroughly comprehended wrestling. The West Country wrestlers met their match. The Eskimos were very strong and cunning, and there was great excitement and shouting on both sides when in the first bout, after some minutes of heaving and straining, the wrestlers fell to the ground with the Eskimo on top.

During this period of friendliness, which unfortunately was not to last very long, the Eskimos showed the English their fire-raising trick. They twirled a stick dipped in oil in a hole made in a piece of board, and in a few moments had their precious flame. The English in turn demonstrated their magic, with flint and steel and tinder box. One of the greatest inventions of the nineteenth century was that of the match and matchbox. It brought a more striking revolution in the art of living than almost anything else. Lighting a domestic fire on a damp morning when the tinder would not catch must have been a tedious business, but getting the galley fire to burn at sea in a leaky ship with everything sodden and damp was far worse.

The sailors' comment on the Eskimos generally was "very simple in all their conversations, but marvellous thievish." They would steal anything. Any article made of iron they found quite irresistible. The thieving became so serious that the two ship's masters begged Davis to leave these new-found friends. Davis saw the humorous side of it. He merely laughed, and told the angry officers that the men must be more careful of their things. He had to change his tune when the Eskimos began to sling large stones at the *Moonshine* and knocked out the boatswain. He jumped into his boat and chased them away with a few rounds of caliver[1] shot. Some of them came back later. The master of the *Mermaid* recognized the leader of the rascals who had stolen his anchor. The Eskimo was immediately made prisoner as a hostage for the anchor, but the *Mermaid*'s master never got his mudhook, for a favourable breeze sprang up and they sailed away, Eskimo and all. "At length he became a pleasant companion."

A cold spell set in, with mighty bergs, thick fogs, and the ropes and sails coated with ice. The men began to fall sick, and respectfully urged that a

[1] Caliver—a hand-gun.

course be set for home. Davis heard them with sympathy, but personally he was determined to go on. In the circumstances, and considering that the *Mermaid* was not such a handy ship as the *Moonshine* and was costing the owners £100 a month to keep in commission, he decided to send the *Mermaid* home, to clean and re-victual the *Moonshine* and go ahead in her. He sailed into Cumberland Gulf once more, and then steered a southerly course along the coast of Labrador apparently to Newfoundland. Here was well-wooded country. The mariners replenished their stores with "pheasants"[1] and partridges which they shot in great numbers with bows and arrows. They were not far from the Grand Banks, the famous fishing grounds. As fast as they cast the line overboard they hauled up cod. Some fish had been put on the beach for curing, and five men were sent to fetch them. To the rage and grief of Davis they were ambushed by Indians from the woods near the shore, and shot down with arrows. Musketry fire from the ship drove off the Indians, but two of the five were slain outright, two grievously wounded, and the fifth escaped by swimming with an arrow through his arm. After a mighty storm off the Newfoundland coast, Davis reached his loved West Country at the beginning of October.

Meanwhile the *Sunshine* and *North Star* had been to Iceland. They did not go very far up the north coast of Greenland. They rounded Cape Farewell and went up the west coast. The crews taught the Eskimos how to play football at one spot where they touched. The play seems to have been rough. The Eskimos were sent sprawling by the English charges

---

[1] There are no true pheasants in the New World.

ere ever they reached the ball, but this was before the days of Association rules. Unhappily the little *North Star* was lost with all hands in a storm, but the *Sunshine* "came into the river of Thames as high as Ratcliffe in safety God be thanked." Heartfelt thanks indeed were raised at every safe arrival into port of little ships out of the lonely tempestuous seas.

Davis, ever optimistic, was pleased with the results of his journey. He had explored a vast extent of coastline. He was confident that one at least of four openings would prove to be the passage. The *Sunshine* had brought home a good cargo of skins, and the *Moonshine* a fair sample of the cod-fishery. Davis wrote at once to Sanderson in London, who was sympathetic, but the Exeter merchants were disappointed. They had expected better results. To them the passage to Cathay appeared to be no nearer than before, and for the third voyage most of the backing came from London. Davis repeated Frobisher's experience. Pure geographical research could not be afforded. The voyage had to be made to pay, not with spurious gold any more, but with fish.

There were this time three small ships, the *Elizabeth* of Dartmouth, and the faithful *Sunshine* of London, and also a clinker-built[1] twenty-tonner, the *Helen* of London. At about midnight on 19th May, 1587, the song of the men tramping round the capstans woke some of the burgesses of Dartmouth, and the fleet put to sea. The "clinker" was an unlucky ship from the start. First her tiller broke, then her foremast went by the board. The owners had said she was a good ship, but the crew found

[1] A clinker-built vessel is one in which the outside planks overlap each other.

that at sea she was like an ox-cart. In a light breeze she could not sail and had to be towed. However, she was at least not leaky. The carpenter reported her as sound and staunch as a cup.

On 14th June, Greenland was sighted, and the carpenters were landed to assemble a small pinnace. It was ready to be launched when about two o'clock in the morning the Eskimos came down and removed the two upper strakes for the sake of the iron in the planks, ruining the boat for any serious work. The *Elizabeth* fired a gun to scare them off, but they got away with the spoil. It was a pity, for the pinnace would have been useful to the fishermen. Davis intended to send the *Elizabeth* and the *Sunshine* fishing, while he himself went exploring in the *Helen*. Before they parted company Davis heard serious news. The *Helen* was leaking after all, and three hundred strokes of the pump were needed to clear her. What was to be done? Davis rose to the occasion. He determined "rather to end his life with credit than to return with infamy and disgrace, and so being all agreed, we purposed to live and die together, and committed ourselves to the ship."

Davis sailed up the west coast of Greenland, which he called London Coast, till he reached 72° latitude. The sea seemed open to the north and west, and when the wind changed to the north, he named the point farthest north Sanderson's Hope, and sailed into the west on 30th June. The little company of adventurers looked backward over the deep blue sea at the grandeur of the scene. Gradually the lofty cliffs, the mighty snow mountains, and the vast gleaming glacier faded from their sight. They turned towards the west in hope.

Soon their course was checked and their hope frustrated. They had reached the great "middle pack" of ice, eight feet thick, and stretching north and south for a hundred miles or more. It was drifting slowly southwards with the wind behind it. Davis with the wind against him could not double it to the northwards, and was therefore constrained to coast along it to the south. He tried to get through a lane in the ice, but only just retreated in time to avoid being caught. Eventually he skirted the pack to the southward, and Mount Raleigh on the west side of the strait was sighted about the middle of July. Davis explored part of Cumberland Gulf. The ship was becalmed in a very hot spell of weather. The master with some of the sailors went ashore to exercise the Eskimo sledge dogs which they had acquired and which were so fat with being on shipboard that they could only waddle along with their tongues hanging out, gasping in the heat. When the wind came again, Davis proceeded south, passing the mouth of "Frobisher's Straits," which he renamed "Lumley's Inlet." Davis, like other geographers of the time, was under the impression that Frobisher's Meta Incognita was a part of Greenland, and thought he had discovered something new.

As Davis passed by the opening of what was later known as Hudson Strait he was fascinated by the sight of the meeting of the tides, where the flood broke with a roar and a whirl of foam. He wrote in his log book: "To our great admiration we saw the sea falling down into the gulf with a mighty overfall, and roaring, and with divers circular motions like whirlpools, in such sort as forcible streams pass through the arches of bridges." By

15th August he had sailed along the whole of the Labrador coast to Newfoundland. He found no trace of his ships in the fishing grounds, and he set out for home, reaching Dartmouth in the middle of September.

Davis wrote at once to Sanderson from Dartmouth. "The passage is most probable," he said, "the execution easy, as at my coming you shall fully know." It is to be hoped that the fishing repaid the expenses of the expedition, for it was not everyone that shared Davis's optimism. From a geographical point of view he had accomplished much, though the discovery of the passage was as far off as ever. He wrote a little book in which he eloquently set out the arguments in favour of the passage and the advantages to be gained thereby. Among the latter he indicated not only the certainty of a great trade with China and India, but also the evangelization of the natives. The Protestants were singularly unsuccessful in this task. They barely obtained a convert. This was largely because the Elizabethan voyages were nearly all either warlike or exploratory. The colonising attempts were failures until after the Elizabethan period had passed, and for evangelization some element of permanence was necessary.

Perhaps the greatest commercial result of Davis's voyages was the impetus they gave to the establishment of the English in the fisheries of Newfoundland and Labrador. Since the discovery of Newfoundland by John Cabot in 1497 the Portuguese, Spaniards and French all fished regularly on the Grand Banks. By 1517 there were about fifty Spanish, French and Portuguese ships employed in this trade. The English made an attempt to colonize Newfoundland in 1536 and landed 120 men, but famine overtook the unfortunate pioneers. In 1583 Sir Humphrey Gilbert claimed the Island in the name of Queen Elizabeth.

Davis had to abandon his hopes, though not his beliefs. Although others in later years again attempted the North-West Passage, the famous year of 1588, the year that followed his last expedition, saw the climax of the long struggle with Spain. Exploration had to wait. England had sterner work to do.

CHAPTER III

TO THE EAST ROUND AFRICA

THE lucrative trade to Guinea and the West African seaboard which led men step by step to the gorgeous East was carried on by the English in defiance of the Portuguese prohibition, and in bitter competition with the French. It is a story of every man's hand being against his neighbour's. Men literally had to fight for their trade. The Portuguese, in attempting to maintain their monopoly, fell foul of the English ships. Later the same Englishmen traded with Portuguese. In the same way no Englishman quite knew whether Spain was an enemy to be fought or a friendly nation with whom business could be done. Frenchmen were either plundering the English or being plundered by them, or else arranging a temporary alliance on the spot against their common enemy Portugal. The English were not sure whether their exploits would be applauded or whether they were running the risk of being hanged as pirates on their return. The safest thing for them to do, on coming home laden with African produce, gold, ivory, pepper, millet, was to keep their mouths shut. If they had on board some French wine or cloth so much the better if they still said nothing. Wherever the English attempted to trade in Africa they were liable to meet with resistance and hard knocks, whether from the Moorish rovers of Tunis and Morocco, Frenchmen at the same game as themselves, the negro inhabitants, or the ubiquitous Portuguese. It is not surprising that they met force with force. No question of conscience entered into the matter. They commended their enterprises to the blessing of God, and had no difficulty in finding an Old Testament text to justify almost anything.

Just as Frobisher and Davis essayed the Arctic ice and snow with inadequate equipment, so did the trading adventurers in the Tropics. The voyages were undertaken in our winter and spring, but little or no special provision was made against the climate. Instead of white ducks and pith helmets they wore as little as possible of their ordinary clothes, and their accustomed hats or caps. Mosquito nets did not exist. There was no quinine as a protection against malaria. They fell victims to sunstroke and all manner of fevers as they drove their prows up the rivers and breathed the pestilential airs of the swamps and dark jungles. The marvel was not that so many men died, but that any at all returned.

The voyages to the Guinea coast began a few years before Elizabeth's accession. Though interesting in themselves, these voyages are but a preliminary to the more extended journeys which were gradually undertaken as the adventurers became more sure of themselves, and which led them by degrees to India and the East. Every winter from 1553 onwards a little flotilla was despatched from London or Plymouth to return with those two major needs of the age, gold and pepper, as well as "Elephants' Teeth." In 1554 young Martin Frobisher made his first voyage with Captain John Lock, in an expedition financed by his kinsman, Sir John Yorke, and others. The following year the Portuguese became alarmed at these incursions into their sphere, and were particularly active and troublesome. The English complained that a Portuguese vessel was following them round and warning the natives to have no dealings with the interlopers. The negroes did not dare to trade with threats hanging over them. It appears that the Portuguese were enslaving numbers of them, and putting irons on their legs, an evil example that was followed later by the English.

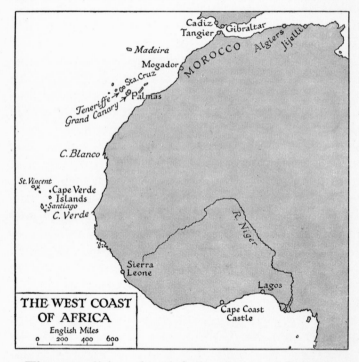

THE WEST COAST OF AFRICA

English Miles

0   200   400   600

The expedition that left London and Bristol and met at Plymouth at the end of 1556 had a full share of adventure. It consisted of the *Tiger* of London, 120 tons, the *Hart*, also of London, 60 tons, and a pinnace of 16 tons. At this time a pinnace was a small vessel propelled by sail or oars, sometimes sailing independently, sometimes carried on board a larger ship. A London merchant, Mr. William Towerson, was in charge. They reached the coast of Guinea on 30th December, 1556. As soon as they had made their landfall they saw three ships and two pinnaces upon the weather bow. The strangers approached them, with pennants streaming in the wind and trumpets sounding. If they proved to be Portuguese the English were determined to fight. When they came within hailing distance the English asked them who they were and whence they came. "Français, français," was the answer. "Why, we are from London in England. Where are the Portugals?" The Frenchmen replied that they had set one on fire a few days back, but that they had done practically no trade in the last six weeks, and might they come aboard and talk things over? They might, and did, and made a proposal to join forces. Mr. Towerson wished for time to consider the matter. They asked him to come to dinner the next day, and bring with him the masters of the ships and his trading staff. Denis Blondel, the Frenchman in command, sent a boat for them and gave them a good dinner. He offered to put himself under the Englishman's command and to help him to get water. They came to an agreement not to spoil each others market, and forthwith began to trade for gold where they could up and down the coast beneath the sunshine and the palm-trees. Five Portuguese ships were reported to be in the vicinity. Partly to impress the natives and partly as a precaution in case they met any Portuguese upstream, the French and English manned their boats with armed men wearing corselets and morions[1] (those that had them), with four trumpets, a drum and fife, silken streamers and pennants. They rowed up the steamy river, past snags and whirlpools, in all this bravery to trade, while the ships lay in the river's mouth. They saw no Portuguese, but a negro chieftain brought word that they were at sea. The next day they went ashore for more barter, and Towerson invited the black headman to dinner. While the trading party was at work in the cool of the evening of the following day, the ships sighted five Portuguese vessels coming up with the wind. The English ships fired guns to recall their men. By the time all were aboard and the anchors weighed, it was dark, and all the night they made themselves ready for action on the morrow.

It was a hot fight. The Portuguese were swift and well-armed. The *Tiger* held her own, but the *Hart* and the pinnace suffered severely, and broke off the action, in fact the pinnace had to be broken up afterwards. As for the Frenchmen, they were badly shot up, with half their men sick or dead, and they would do no more. During the night the Portuguese very fortunately disappeared. The *Tiger* and the *Hart* went on their way along the coast, picking up nuggets and gold dust, pushing at times up the rivers fringed with black ooze and bordered by the dark silent forest.

Off Cape Coast Castle they saw all five Portuguese ships riding at anchor in the roads. They also saw two more tall ships newly arrived from Portugal. Whereupon they decided that the district was more than usually unhealthy, and made for home. But

[1] Steel helmets.

their adventures were not yet over. On 23rd May, when nearly in sight of the Lizard, they met a Frenchman of about 90 tons, apparently a pirate, for he approached with determination. Seeing that the English ships were slow and weakly manned after a long voyage, he came up as if to board them, and men in armour shouted to them to strike sail. Not they. "We sent them some of our stuff, crossbars and chainshot and arrows, so thick that it made the upper work of their ship fly about their ears, and we spoiled him with all his men, and tore his ship miserably with all our great ordnance; and then he began to fall astern of us and to pack on his sails and get away; and we seeing that, gave him four or five good pieces more for his farewell; and thus we were rid of this Frenchman."

The confusion between legitimate trading, acts of war, and warfare bordering on piracy of which most of these voyages were composed is illustrated again by the last voyage of Mr. William Towerson to the Guinea coast in 1577. At the end of January three ships and a pinnace left Plymouth Sound, the *Minion*, "admiral of the fleet," *Christopher*, and *Tiger*. One day out they met with two ships of Danzig, coming from Bordeaux laden with wine. At this time a state of war existed between England and the Government of France, which was torn by religious faction. England was supporting the Protestant Huguenots. Towerson had no doubt at all that the French wine was lawful prize. His only problem was how to deal with it. He could either take the ships to Spain and sell the wine there, or to Ireland with the easterly wind, or better still, if the wind shifted, take them back to England. All these alternatives meant the risk of losing the Guinea voyage, for the season was well advanced. Besides, wine was less profitable than gold and ivory. In the end they took aboard as much wine as they could conveniently carry, incidentally helping themselves to anything else they wanted. Then they let the unfortunate Danzigers go.

After this they made for the Canary Islands. They anchored off Las Palmas in the roads and fired a salute. England and Spain were at peace. A very uneasy peace, it was true, and in the Americas Drake was busy breaking it. The Spanish Governor invited the English captains on shore and received them in friendly fashion. Two days later a Spanish fleet bound for the Indies arrived, and salutes were fired by both the Spaniards and the English. The Spanish admiral sent his pinnace to invite Towerson to dinner. When Towerson had returned to his ship, a gentleman came across to command the English to strike their flag in the presence of the General of the fleet of the Emperor of the Indies. Towerson would do no such thing and kept it flying. Spanish soldiers in the ships began firing their arquebuses at the flag. Towerson announced that if they did not stop that firing, he would put his biggest shot through their sides. This superb piece of impertinence was successful. The Spanish admiral sent a courteous apology, and said that the demand to strike the flag was made without his knowledge. The Englishmen then proceeded on their voyage.

After three or four weeks of trading they fell in with five Portuguese ships, which were patrolling the coast. A desultory fight took place, and at night the antagonists separated, with little damage done. The next encounter was with their commercial rivals the French. They found three French ships lying at anchor. On seeing them the Frenchmen weighed and ran for it. The English came up with one, boarded and took her, and gave chase to the other two, who escaped. They took fifty pounds weight of gold out of the captured Frenchman. The English offered the ship, empty save for its victuals, back to its rightful owners. She was so leaky that they would not have her, but asked to be taken aboard the English ships. Therefore the victuals were removed, the prize was sunk, and the men divided among the *Minion, Christopher,* and *Tiger.* There was no ill-feeling. It was only the luck of the game.

All the month of May they remained on the coast. The white heat haze lay over the water up to the still forests, where the silence was broken only by the occasional chattering of monkeys, or by the scream of a parrakeet. Men began to fall sick and die. On 7th June they sighted five Portuguese, King's ships on patrol. The English by now were very short of food and drink. It was proposed to attack the Portuguese and seize victuals from them. The suggestion was negatived. It was all very well to fight Portuguese if they fired first, but to go in and attack them in their own territory might mean being hanged for piracy, for officially there was peace.

They set sail for home. They were favoured with good winds, but by the time they reached Spain there were not more than six mariners and six merchants hale and sound in the *Minion* and *Christopher.* The *Tiger* had been abandoned long since. They thought of making for the harbour of Vigo in Spain, but were too uncertain of their reception to venture in. The men were too weak to handle the sails. Within sight of home they were forced to lie with no sails set, till one morning the *Minion* put an old bonnet on her foreyard, "which by the good blessing and providence of God brought us to the Isle of Wight."

Ten years previously George Fenner had sailed for Guinea with three ships and had had a great fight with "seven Portugals." He had called at the Cape Verde Islands, where one of his ships, the *Mayflower*, had been suddenly and unexpectedly attacked by four galleys. Fenner's own ship was the *Castle of Comfort*, and there was also with him a small vessel called the *George*. The *Castle of Comfort* was off Terceira in the Azores on 8th May, 1567. The next morning Fenner saw one of the King's galleasses and two caravels bearing down upon him. A caravel was a vessel of Portuguese build and rig, with a square foresail on her foremast, and two or three lateen-rigged mizzen masts. They were usually about fifty or sixty tons, sometimes as much as one hundred. The galleasse was a brave sight as she came threshing up, the monotonous chant of her rowers an undertone to the pealing trumpets, and her pennants fluttering in the breeze. Of four hundred tons, she was formidably armed, with brass cannon, some of them throwing a shot as big as a man's head. and having three hundred fighting men upon her decks. As soon as she came within range the galleasse opened fire with her bow guns. Turning she gave the English ship her broadside, and going about fired her huge stern guns. A duel continued until nightfall, and all night the weary Englishmen laboured to mend their ropes and strengthen their bulwarks. The next morning their anxious eyes beheld four more great caravels, all well appointed and full of men, come to take a share in the unequal battle. The galleasse and a 100-ton caravel made ready to board the *Castle of Comfort*, the galleasse coming upon the larboard side, and the caravel on the starboard. Fenner and the master prepared to give them cold comfort. Guns were loaded with crossbars, chain-shot, and hail-shot. Both broadsides thundered. Havoc was done in the closely-packed ranks of their enemies, and the galleasse and the caravel fell astern for a space. Up came the other five, fired, and fell astern. The little nimble *George* drew the fire of the five caravels. The two big Portugals hammered away at Fenner all the next day. That night the men in the *Castle of Comfort* toiled to repair their ship, to give rough attention to the wounded, and to cast the dead overboard. The *Mayflower* had been well away to leeward, and could not come to their succour. Next morning with much shouting and cheering the Portuguese attacked again, to board or sink the stubborn English ship. Its diminished company stood together and cheered too, daring the Portuguese to board. They dared not. "At night they forsook us with shame, as they came to us at first with pride." The English, smoke-blackened, thirsty, half-dead with fatigue, stopped their shot-holes and their leaks, and that done, flung themselves down anywhere to sleep.

Then they went home. Off the Lizard they met a Portuguese ship, and what transpired shows how confused was the international situation. Neither English nor Portuguese thought of fighting. They spoke each other. Fenner offered to sell them five negroes he had. This black bargain was struck with forty small cases of sugar. While the boats were engaged in transferring the goods, Fenner espied two ships that looked like pirates. In alarm the Portuguese offered him ten more cases of sugar if he would stand by them. He agreed, and the pirates did not venture nearer. He bade farewell to the "Portugal," sailed on past the Start and Lyme harbour, up the Solent safe into Southampton.

The international situation became less perplexing as the years passed. Open war developed with Spain and Portugal, and the Azores became a regular hunting ground for the English privateers. The tale of how the Earl of Cumberland sought treasure there is typical of the men and the times.

George Clifford, third earl of Cumberland, was born in 1558, the year of Elizabeth's accession, and died in 1605, two years after her death. He was a great *entrepreneur*, an organizer of a number of speculative expeditions of a privateering nature, but in spite of huge and valuable captures, he ran through all his fortune before he died. Cumberland did not always accompany the ventures in person. On this occasion he did go, and showed himself a valiant and wise commander. He had been captain of the royal ship, *Elizabeth Bonaventure*, at the Armada fight in the previous year. After the Spanish defeat off Gravelines he carried the news to Tilbury Camp, and made such an impression on the Queen that in 1589 she lent him the *Victory* for his expedition to the Azores. As with the other ventures, he fitted out this enterprise at his own expense. The Queen was a shareholder for the value of her ship. It was a typical example of war carried on as a commercial speculation. Besides the *Victory* of 800 tons, Cumberland had two small ships, the *Meg* and the *Margaret*, and a small caravel. He assembled a gallant company of four hundred gentlemen, sailors and soldiers, and set sail from Plymouth Sound on 18th June, 1589.

On their way out they stopped and searched some French ships, and a few Easterlings[1] bound for their home ports, Hamburg, Bremen, and Lübeck. According to the custom of the time, the flag did not cover the goods, and therefore any goods from Spain or Portugal, with whom England was at war, were lawful prize. Before dismissing the ships they helped themselves to some very valuable consignments of pepper and cinnamon. On 1st August they sighted St. Michael's in the Azores. Approaching at night with a Spanish flag at the maintop, they saw by the light of the moon three large ships and three smaller ones lying in the harbour. Thereupon Cumberland sent in boats well manned. They cut the cables of the three small ships and towed them out. These vessels were laden with wine and oil from Seville, which were transferred to the holds of the English ships. There was much shouting and some shooting from the shore, but in the dark no harm was done. One of the big ships turned out to be the *Falcon* of London, commanded by a Scotsman, probably not the first and certainly not the last instance of a Scotsman commanding a London vessel. The presence of this ship seems curious, considering that England was at war with Spain and, since King Philip of Spain had annexed the Empire of Portugal, with that country also. It serves to illustrate again the uncertainty and irregularity of all this trading and fighting. The expedition learnt here that the West Indian fleet of Spanish

[1] Men from the East, i.e., Hanse traders from the Baltic.

carracks,[1] which they hoped to capture, had left Terceira in the Azores. The English were therefore some days too late, a severe disappointment.

About the middle of the month they reached the island of Flores. Cumberland manned his boats, rowed ashore, and sent word to the inhabitants that he would do them no harm, but that he wanted fresh water and fresh meat, for which he would pay by exchanging some wine and oil and pepper that he happened to have with him. The deal was completed to the satisfaction of both sides. While the expedition was there, a little vessel called *Drake* brought them word that the carracks had put back to Terceira for some more water. Delighted to hear this, the *Victory* and her consorts sailed thither with all the speed they could. On the way they called at Fayal, and by night achieved another successful cutting-out enterprise. Cumberland sent in the *Saucy Jack*, a small vessel that had joined the party, the caravel, and boats. After about an hour's fighting, under fire from the town battery, they towed out six ships. One was of 250 tons, full of sugar, ginger, and hides from the West Indies. Two ships they set adrift, the other four were sent home to England. At this point they were joined by the celebrated Captain John Davis, with his ship, and by another vessel belonging to Sir Walter Raleigh, who had a finger in so many pies.

On the 31st they sighted Terceira, and almost immediately espied a small boat with an improvised sail making towards them. In it were eight English-men, escaped prisoners from the shore, who told them that the carracks had now gone for good. This was the first piece of ill-fortune on what proved

[1] Large armed merchantmen.

to be a somewhat unlucky voyage. Baulked of their prey, they decided to return to Fayal, to see what more they could get out of that unfortunate town. The expedition reached Fayal Roads on 10th September. Some representative inhabitants put off in a boat to the *Victory*. Cumberland demanded to be allowed to occupy the battery. He would do no damage, and they could then treat with him for a ransom for the town. Otherwise, they must "stand the hazard of war." The men in the battery, though not regular troops, refused to evacuate without making a fight for it. Cumberland ordered out all the ships' boats fully manned, and landed his forces about a mile and a half from the battery on the sandy shore, under the slopes of a hill. On this hill some troops appeared against the skyline, and two other bodies were mobilised near the town. They all promptly disappeared in the face of Cumberland's resolute march along the shore. The battery opened fire, but before the English reached it the gunners had also vanished. All this time the ships had been bombarding the town and the battery, and only ceased when the flag of St. George appeared on the sea front.

It was not a glorious victory, but the attackers were out for plunder, and the countries were at war. The town they had taken consisted of about three hundred well-built houses. The English noticed the care taken to preserve the rain-water from the roofs, for fresh water appeared to be scarce. Cumberland issued orders against looting and placed guards outside the churches and the friary, but the order was disobeyed, and most of the private houses were ransacked. It is very noticeable that on these privateering expeditions discipline often broke down when there was loot to be had. These rough seamen were very far from being all heroes and saints, and stories of gallantry and self-sacrifice alternate with incidents which seem, judged by modern standards, very discreditable. They stayed for four days till the "ransom" was forthcoming— two thousand ducats,[1] most of which was found to be church plate. After destroying the battery, and confiscating fifty-eight cannon they found there, they departed, but not before Cumberland had invited all the principal inhabitants to dinner on board the *Victory*. Only four came, their curiosity or desire for a good dinner being apparently stronger than their pride. These four were well entertained, and solemnly dismissed with a fanfare of trumpets and drums, and a salute of guns.

Towards the end of September, after an uneventful cruise, they appeared again in Fayal Roads to pick up an anchor they had left there. They obtained and paid for victuals and water, but before all the necessary water was on board, a sudden storm arose in the night. In the *Victory* Cumberland himself ran to the men's quarters, calling them out to weigh anchor, taking his turn at the capstan, and issuing a ration of wine when the work was safely done. They called next at the island of Graciosa, where they rowed to the shore with water casks, but were met with resistance. However, after negotiations had been opened, they obtained some wine (for the islanders were short of water) on condition that no man from the ships came on shore. In view of what happened at Fayal, this was not unnatural.

There followed a period of rough weather, and

---

[1] Over £500 then, now quite eight times as much.

one evening the English saw fifteen sail of the West Indian fleet go into harbour in Terceira. They went to have a look at the harbour, but it was strongly defended with forts and guns, and the wind had dropped to a dead calm. They ranged about like wolves around a sheepfold, but reluctantly abandoned hope. This was their second piece of ill-luck on the voyage. At St. Mary's Island they again attempted to water, but were met with cannon-shot and musket-shot from entrenchments on the shore. There were two ships lying alongside the quay. The men in the boats began to duck their heads and hesitate with the storm of shot whistling by them, and there were several casualties. The officers urged them to row for the ships. Getting under the lee of one of them they clambered aboard, cast off her mooring ropes and towed her away as a prize. She proved to be laden with sugar. The attempt on the other ship failed, for she was fast aground.

The question then arose as to whether, being short of water, they should go straight home, or whether they should take the coast of Spain on their way and try to pick up something worth having. Seeing that they had missed all the good prizes, it was decided to adopt the second alternative. So, having sent the small ships home, the *Victory* set sail for Spain with a fair wind. Here the luck seemed to turn. Rapidly picking up two small prizes, they sighted a Spaniard of three or four hundred tons. She struck her sail at once to the *Victory*. She was from San Juan d'Ulua in Mexico, with a valuable cargo of hides, cochineal, sugar, china, and silver. A prize crew was put on board. And now their hands were full. With so many foreigners to look after they could spare no more men to man prizes. They shaped their course for England, merrily before the wind, with all the sail they could carry. Some of the company were laying bets that they would see the tilting at Whitehall on the Queen's birthday, 17th November. Others were looking forward to keeping Christmas in style with their prize-money to spend. But a gloom fell upon their cheerfulness. The wind turned easterly, and the vision of England faded. They could not even make the Irish coast, and now the water shortage was serious. The wine had all been drunk, the water gave out altogether. All that the men had was three or four spoonfuls of vinegar with their meals. There was no little excitement when rain or hail fell. The hailstones were gathered up and eaten as if they had been the choicest sweetmeat. Not a raindrop was lost if they could help it. Sheets were hung up by the four corners with a weight in the middle so that the water would run into a jug underneath. Underwear was hung up also, and wrung out or sucked dry. The rain that ran off the decks to the scuppers was struggled for with cans and jars. Like dogs men even licked the decks, the rails, the masts. The prisoners fared no worse than their captors, but there was little indeed for any-body. Many of the sick and wounded died. Day by day bodies were cast overside.

The 2nd December, 1589, was a great day, for a storm arose with torrents of rain, so that every man's cup was filled. And nearly spilled besides, for it was difficult to keep one's footing on the wet reeling pitching decks. The *Victory's* mainsail was torn from the yard and blown into the sea, and most of the other sails were split and rent. The *Victory* shipped it green again and again. Great walls of water came surging over her bows and crashed down upon her decks, flooding them with a sudden foaming swirl. The ship began to leak. She creaked and groaned as if the life were leaving her. She seemed as if she would plunge to her burial in the raging seas, but in due time the storm abated, and the crew, soaked to the skin, praised God for their deliverance, and replaced and repaired their sails. Again the storm arose, and the wind blew. They almost lost their new mainsail, and would have done so, had not William Anthony, the master, himself crawled along the mainyard, which was lowered down to the rails, and lashed the flapping sail to it. He was many times ducked in the sea, but hung on gallantly.

"Port after stormie seas." Early in December they dropped anchor in Ventry harbour on the Kerry coast. All of them, from the Earl of Cumberland downwards, were weak from want of food and drink. Here they obtained fresh water and fresh meat, "whilst the Irish harp sounded sweetly in our ears." They bought some beer, but it gave them dysentery, so they rested content with the sweet fresh running water of the mountain streams. On the 20th they sailed with a fair wind for home, but the breeze died away, and they had to keep a cold Christmas with the Bishop and his Clerks, rocks near the Scillies. Labouring home, they met an English ship, and spoke her. She had news that scores of Spanish prizes had been brought into English harbours, but she carried doleful tidings for the Cumberland expedition. Their ill-luck was still with them. Their rich prize from the West Indies had gone to pieces at "Hell's Gate" in Cornwall. The acting captain and almost all the prize crew were drowned. Much of the cargo had been salved, however, and the adventurers had made a profit on the voyage, in spite of missed opportunities. They anchored in Falmouth harbour, with gladness "setting foot again upon the long-desired English ground."

This expedition was typical of many that were fitted out as speculative ventures, made possible by the rich commerce and treasure of Spain and Portugal which was always on the seas, and by the war, official or unofficial, waged by England against these two countries. Sometimes they were equipped by merchants, such as the Hawkins brothers of Plymouth, or the great London traders. Others who hazarded their fortunes were rich noblemen like Cumberland, men with an idea like Raleigh, fighting sea-captains like Drake. The Queen sometimes lent her ships and sometimes cash, members of her Privy Council such as Walsingham and Leicester were frequently involved. From the point of view of the Government it was a cheap, or rather a profitable way of making war. In the days before there was open war the Government could always, if necessary, repudiate the adventurers as pirates. But like all speculations, if there were sometimes enormous profits, there were also staggering losses, and many a fortune was lost at sea.

One of the greatest hauls of plunder ever taken into England was in the hold of the huge Portuguese carrack *Mother of God* (*Madre de Dios*), taken off the Azores in August 1592. Like some great stag beset by wolves the mighty ship fought her antagonists and shook them off, till at last her flag was hauled down and the pillage and scramble for loot began. Though the expedition that took her was financed by private capitalists as well as by the Queen, the capture could not be called a piratical adventure, for it was a legitimate act of war. However, a great deal of the more portable plunder, such as diamonds and pearls, stuck to the fingers of those that took part in the fight, and never reached the shareholders or the Government.

At the beginning of the year the Queen advanced to the Merchant Adventurers of London the sum of £6,000 against prize money earned by the London squadron in the year 1591. This was on condition that they used the money to fit out another expedition under the direction of Sir Walter Raleigh. They duly helped with the finance of a venture, the plan of which was to lie in wait for the five Portuguese carracks which were expected off the Azores in July. Raleigh left Plymouth early in May with the squadron, but did not intend to take an active part. He returned after a few days, leaving the command in the hands of Sir Martin Frobisher. Frobisher was to cruise off Cape St. Vincent, while Sir John Burgh[1] in the *Roebuck* with a subsidiary squadron was ordered to the Azores. Frobisher nearly caught one carrack, the fastest. He saw the light of her poop lantern on the night of 7th July, but in the morning she was gone, and safe home. One was lost in the Mozambique Channel (they were rounding Africa from the East Indies), and of another no news was ever heard. The *Holy Cross* and the *Mother of God* fell unto the wolves.

The *Dainty*, Captain Thompson, a ship fitted out by Sir John Hawkins, and Her Majesty's ship *Foresight*, Captain Crosse, appear to have taken

[1] Often spelt Burroughs; he always signed Burgh.

French leave of Frobisher, and to have joined Burgh, on whose station the pickings were more likely to be found. The Earl of Cumberland had equipped a complete squadron of seven ships and pinnaces, whereof Captain Norton, in the *Tiger*, was "general." This little fleet also left Plymouth in the beginning of May, and on arrival at the rendezvous at the Azores the captains put themselves under the command of Sir John Burgh, who held the Queen's commission. It was one of Cumberland's ships that first sighted the *Santa Cruz* carrack as she rode at anchor under the island of Flores. The *Assurance* sent her longboat under sail and oar to ascertain who and what she was. The men of the longboat did not take long to make up their minds. They hailed the carrack. "*Santa Cruz* ahoy! Our captain promises to spare your lives if you'll yield your ship and goods into his hands." A scornful laugh came from the upper deck high above, and a voice bade them begone or stay at their peril. Back they went to Norton's ship, and the *Tiger* and the *Assurance* determined, if wind and weather should serve, to lay aboard the carrack. The *Santa Cruz* was not so confident as her spokesman pretended, and hauled herself into a narrow gut between some rocks and the shore, spending the night in unloading some of her cargo. Burgh in the *Roebuck* came up, and it was decided to send a force on shore and attack the carrack simultaneously by land and sea. Half-way through this landing operation a mighty gale of wind arose with torrents of rain. They had to abandon the attempt, but by supper-time on that evening, 22nd June, the storm had moderated. The officer of the watch saw a spurt of flame away in the direction of the carrack. He went along to the cabin to report. The officers left their supper and came on deck. At first they thought it was a signal flare, but as they looked, it spread, and they realized that it was the *Santa Cruz*. The whole ship went up in flames. Sorrowfully they watched the destruction of the prize they had thought was within their grasp, and consulted together how to save what they could. The captains all met, and decided to send their boats ashore to search the island for such goods as the Portuguese had saved from the fire. They made the difficult landing that night, and marched over hill and mountain, through deep woods and stony lanes, till they came to where the Portuguese first landed. There they found silks, taffetas, calicoes, carpets, and quilts of exquisite workmanship, which Burgh took under guard in the name of the Queen and the venturers. The only prisoner they captured was Vincent Fonseca, the purser. They roughly threatened him with torture till in fear he let out the information that in about a fortnight three other carracks were due. After a few days ashore the fleet set sail in search of more booty. Two ships from Barnstaple and Bristol went home, and it was about this time that the *Dainty* arrived. The *Foresight* was already come. The total strength of the fleet was ten, the *Foresight*, Queen's ship, five of the Earl of Cumberland, *Roebuck* of Raleigh's provision, *Dainty*, *Dragon* and *Prudence*.

It was on 3rd August very early in the morning, about forty miles to the westward of Flores, that Captain Thompson of the *Dainty* caught sight of the *Madre de Dios*. The *Dainty* at once gave chase, followed by the rest, but being an excellent sailer, she out-distanced the pack, and exchanged cannon-shot with the carrack. She paid for this rashness by having several men killed and wounded, and by her foremast crashing overside. One wolf was shaken off, but up came the rest of them. About two o'clock the *Dragon* opened fire, at four the *Roebuck* began to fire her heavy guns at a musket's range. When Captain Crosse in the *Foresight* arrived, Burgh hailed him and asked him what he thought of the situation. Crosse replied that if the carrack were not boarded, she would go ashore and set herself on fire as the *Santa Cruz* had done. So the two agreed to lay her aboard, the *Roebuck* at the bow, and the *Foresight* on her quarter. Something went wrong with the manœuvre. The *Roebuck* found herself alongside the *Madre de Dios*, with the *Foresight* alongside her. The *Roebuck* was soon holed below the waterline. She quickly had six or seven feet of water in her, and the pumps were going hard. She was compelled to ask the *Foresight* to sheer off to allow her to get clear. Another wolf was torn.

The carrack then stood in for the shore. Hampton, the chief pilot, warned Crosse that she would escape unless some ship laid her across the bowsprit. The *Foresight*, skilfully handled, was brought up into this position. Her men hacked at the rigging of the carrack and at her spritsail sheet. *Foresight* was under the carrack's lee, and so could not get away, till at midnight the *Assurance* and the *Tiger* came into action and to her rescue. They lay aboard on either side of the carrack. Savagely the wolves howled. They swore to take her, or else burn and sink her. Nigh two hundred men leapt upon her decks, crying "God and St. George for England! a Cumberland! a Cumberland!" The English called upon God, and the Portuguese upon the Mother of God, and the men fell upon each other with clash of cutlass and push of pike. The Portuguese fought manfully, but were overborne at last, the survivors being trapped in corners, and there assailed until they cried for quarter. They were disarmed and stowed below hatches. The Englishmen, as they stood the victors upon the carrack's deck, were staggered by the huge bulk of the ship, bigger than anything they had ever seen, but they could only with difficulty pick their way over the bodies of the dead and dying. There were actually heaps of dead at the helm, which was so big that it needed twelve or fourteen men to work it. One cannon-ball frequently slew four or five men at once, and as fresh reliefs had come up, so they were slaughtered. The sight was a hideous one, and Burgh, moved with pity for the wounded, ordered his men to do what they could for them, and sent his own surgeons to relieve their pain. He also dismissed the captain of the carrack and the surviving members of the crew to their own country, "in certain vessels furnished with all kinds of necessary provisions."

And now ensued an unseemly scramble for loot. The plunder on the orlop, or lowest deck, was by custom considered as "pillage" for the men who had stormed the ship, but the excited exultant men swarmed all over the tiers of decks, plundering the cabins by candle-light, and pocketing diamonds, pearls, rubies, and all manner of precious stones. It was all Burgh could do to prevent the *Roebuck* from sinking, and he did not come aboard the carrack till the next day, by which time the ship had been sacked, and most of the portable valuables had gone. He tried to restore order, but was unsuccessful at first, as the Earl of Cumberland's men challenged his right to command the carrack. He displayed a firm front and eventually took over the ship and cargo in the Queen's name. He brought her, after many adventures with wind and weather, safely into Dartmouth on 7th September.

Crosse had brought the *Foresight* into Portsmouth, and quite illegally he and his men began to dispose of their loot. Gosport was like Bartholomew Fair. The *Prudence* arrived in Plymouth. She had some spices and calico on board, but as it seemed to be mostly "pillage," Drake and his fellow commissioners for the charge of the carrack did nothing in the matter. The *Dainty* was unlucky. At the beginning of the action her foremast went by the board, and she could not and did not come up until the carrack had been sacked. Captain Thompson went to Sir John Burgh and asked for his share, "for other captains have whole cabins-full of jewels and gold." Sir John replied that all was taken over in the Queen's name. "But is there never a chain of gold left," said Thompson, "nor apparel?" "I have something for you," said Sir John, "because you were away," and tossed him the key of an ordinary seaman's chest, already rifled. Nearly all the ships were laden with loot. By the time the *Madre de Dios* reached Dartmouth, the town was agog with excitement, and full of dealers and buyers. The commissioners had a difficult task. The jewels had practically all vanished. The pepper and spices, carpets and silks, drugs and calicoes, ivory and china were valued at more than £140,000, and were brought up to Leadenhall in London. Of the proceeds Raleigh had £24,000, which with his usual ill-luck, found him out of pocket. Cumberland made a profit with £37,000. The London merchants got £12,000, or double their investment. The Queen's share was the pepper, of which there was 370 tons. She was offered £80,000 for the lot, but was advised to hold out for £90,000. This was a good return on an investment of £3,000 in the venture.

The *Madre de Dios*, that great ship, the like of which had never been seen in England, of 1,600 tons, 165 feet long overall, 47 feet in the beam, with four full decks, and three more in poop and forecastle, was dismantled, and slowly rotted away. Her capture made a great impression. It drew men's minds to the great wealth of the East Indies. Why not have a share in it? they asked. A few years later the famous East India Company was founded. It was partly owing to a prize taken at sea that the English embarked on their Imperial career.

.   .   .   .   .

Before the English reached the East round Africa, India had been visited overland by Newbery and Ralph Fitch of London in 1585. They attended the Court of the Mogul Emperor Akbar at Fatehpur Sikri near Agra. Fitch's long account of his travels is very informative and often amusing. "Here I saw a dissembling prophet which sat upon a horse in the market place, and made as though he slept, and many of the people came and touched his feet with their hands and then kissed their hands. They took him for a great man, but sure he was a lazy lubber. I left him there sleeping." In 1579 at Ternate in the Moluccas, Drake had negotiated with the Sultan in the name of the

Queen a treaty reserving to her the spice trade with the island. The Portuguese monopoly in the East Indies was being undermined. This treaty was of considerable importance in the opening up of the East to English enterprise and commerce.

In 1579 an Englishman named Thomas Stevens went to Goa in a Portuguese ship from Lisbon, but the East Indies were not reached by sea in English ships until 1591. The expedition that came through to Malaya in that year did not touch the mainland of India, and was indeed a failure. Three tall ships, *Penelope*, with Captain John Raymond as general, *Merchant Royal*, and *Edward Bonaventure*, Captain James Lancaster, left Plymouth one spring morning in 1590. Two months out near the Equator they captured a Portuguese caravel, laden "with divers necessaries for our voyage." The wine, oil, olives, and capers were, they said, better than gold, for they had many sick with scurvy, and were drenched with rain. The *Merchant Royal* was sent home with a cargo of sick men. One night, soon after doubling the Cape of Good Hope, the *Penelope* with Raymond the leader, was lost in a great storm. The men in the *Edward* saw a great wave break right over the *Penelope*, her light disappeared in the swirl of waters, and that was the last they saw of her. The *Edward* had her share of misfortune. A lightning stroke killed four men outright, and of the whole company of ninety-four, so it is said, there was not one untouched. Some were blinded, others were bruised, but all the injured recovered, "God be thanked." The mainmast was split in two. At the isle of Comoro, off Mozambique, they lost nearly thirty men massacred by the treacherous inhabitants, and at Zanzibar, where they found much good victual, the ship's surgeon died of heat apoplexy. Unfavourable winds blew them northwards almost to Socotra, when "it pleased God to bring the wind more westerly." With this behind them they crossed the Indian Ocean, rounded Cape Comorin, or more probably Dundra Head in Ceylon, and reached Penang in the Malay peninsula, fourteen months after leaving home. By this time, more men having become sick and died, they were reduced to thirty-three men and one boy. Of these only twenty-two were hale and sound, and by no means all of them were sailors. Their spirit was still strong enough to enable them to rob a number of Portuguese ships of their cargoes of pepper and wine and rice and cloth. They could go no farther eastward. Lancaster was for continuing the voyage, but the men, with that independence so characteristic of the age, refused, and he had to give way. However, it was not until March 1593 that they doubled the Cape of Good Hope. They arrived at St. Helena in April. Here they recuperated, not before it was necessary. When they resumed their voyage, winds were contrary. They crossed the wide Atlantic, and after many weeks found themselves in the West Indies. On one of those green islands, set in a turquoise sea, with gleaming white sand below the palm-trees, they hoped to find refreshment and rest. Lancaster and nineteen men landed to try to get provisions and water. When the landing party returned to the shore, the *Edward* had disappeared. Five men and a boy had been left in her. Some of the men had been surly and mutinous, and it seemed as if they had madly cut the cable and made off. Their fate was dubious enough, but those left on shore nearly starved. Lancaster and the survivors were eventually rescued by some French ships, and came safely home in May 1594, after over three years' absence. The significance of this unsuccessful voyage is that it exemplifies the manifold risks and hardships to be endured, the perils of storm and shipwreck, of contrary winds, of starvation, sickness and slaughter, in the long, long journey by sea to India. Yet these pioneers had done their part. Each voyage brought them nearer the desired end. The next to enter the race was the City of London.

Sir Thomas Smythe was at this time the leader among the London merchant princes. He had two houses in the City, in Philpot Lane and Gracechurch Street, where he lived and did his business and where his offices and sale-rooms were. His country house, Brooke Place, was in the lovely valley of the Darenth, in the little Kentish village of Sutton-at-Hone. He was the Governor of the Levant Company. He encouraged sea enterprise and exploration not only for the wealth it might bring, but for the honour and credit of England. It was this man who was the leading spirit in the foundation of the East India Company.

The movement towards direct trade with the East was greatly stimulated by the two successful voyages of the Dutch in 1598 and 1599. John Davis of Arctic fame had been pilot-in-chief in the second voyage. The high price of pepper promised great profits to those who "got in on the ground floor," and in 1599 a number of London merchants, including the Lord Mayor, Sir Stephen Soane, subscribed £30,000 for an expedition. Negotiations with the Government were prolonged, but towards the end of 1600 the Privy Council told the City to go ahead with the plans. The Privy Council recommended Sir Edward Michelborne for the post of general in charge of the fleet. The City would not have him. They said quite frankly that they did not want "gentlemen," but were unanimous in appointing a merchant sailor, one of their own kind, Captain James Lancaster, with John Davis as pilot-major. On the last day of the year 1600 the Charter for the incorporation of the East India Company was granted. For a period of fifteen years certain named adventurers were alone privileged to trade with the East Indies. George Clifford, Earl of Cumberland, and 215 knights, aldermen and merchants, including many members of the Levant Company, were parties to the enterprise. Sir Thomas Smythe was first Governor, and among the twenty-four directors were James Lancaster and John Middleton, the second in command. The total amount subscribed for the first voyage was £70,000. This must not be regarded as the capital of the Company, for as a corporate body the Company possessed no capital. Sums were raised for each voyage and dividends were paid at the end of it. A member was not required to subscribe to every voyage, but all trading to the East had to be done by members only, and under the super-vision of the Company.

With a large sum at their disposal the Governor and directors took care that the expedition should be well equipped. The flagship, the "admiral," was a vessel of 600 tons belonging to the Earl of Cumberland, which they purchased for £3,700. It had been named by the Queen the *Malice Scourge*, but seeing that it was to be employed on a more or less peaceable errand, it was given the less fierce

name of *Red Dragon*. It carried Captain James
Lancaster with the Queen's commission as "general," and 202 men. The *Hector*, 300 tons, was vice-
admiral, with Captain John Middleton and 108
men. The *Ascension* and *Susan*, each about 250 tons,
and a little store ship, the *Guest*, made up the fleet.
In the light of the imperfect knowledge of the time,
both Smythe and Lancaster were careful of the
health and comfort of the men. The meat had to be
salted, but the quality was good. The beasts were
bought alive after inspection and slaughtered in
the Company's yard at Blackwall. The ships were
well armed. They were furnished with provisions
for twenty months, and with the usual merchandise
as well as Spanish money to be exchanged for spices
and other produce. The whole of the subscriptions
was spent on ships and necessaries for the voyage,
and in advances of pay to the sailors. The mercan-
tile information brought back by John Davis from
his voyage to Malaya and Sumatra with the Dutch
was extremely useful, and his skill and experience
in navigation made him valuable as chief pilot.
He sailed in the *Red Dragon* with Lancaster. He
was paid by results. His fee was £500 if the voyage
yielded two shares for one, £1,000 if three for one,
and £2,000 if five for one. Probably Lancaster and
the other officers were remunerated in similar
fashion.

On 13th February, 1601, the fleet sailed from
Woolwich, with a personnel of about 500. At the
end of March they were still in English waters, for
they spent Easter Day in Torbay. That wide and
lovely harbour has now a great population on its
happy shores. Then there were but a few fishing
villages. The voyage was uneventful for many weeks

till near the Equator *Red Dragon* chased and over-hauled a strange sail. She proved to be a Portuguese. Her cargo of wine and oil and meal was most acceptable and was divided impartially among the ships. They crossed the Line on 30th June not very far from the Brazilian coast. Somewhere off South-West Africa the store ship was stripped and turned adrift, her upper works being chopped up for fire-wood. It is curious that sailors of that time, when abandoning a ship for any reason, seldom troubled to scuttle her, but let her drift a derelict.

It was not until 9th September that the men descried far away the pale shape of Table Mountain standing up out of the sea. They put in to Table Bay. Seldom was land more welcome to weary mariners, for scurvy had prostrated the crews. In some ships the merchants had to take the helm and go aloft to take in the topsails. The *Dragon* was the only ship that scurvy had not ravaged. The reason was that Lancaster had provided himself with lemon-juice. He had tried the experiment of dosing the men with three spoonfuls every morning, and keeping them fasting till noon. The *Dragon's* men had to help the crews of the other ships to hoist out their boats, for they were too weak to do it themselves. One hundred and five men died, but the rest and refreshment in tents ashore quickly put new life into the rest. They found that the natives had been roughly used by the Dutch sailors who had passed that way, and Lancaster with his usual wisdom was determined to keep on friendly terms. He established a market under an armed guard. No man, except the traders, was allowed to speak to a native without special leave. The results were excellent. The traders managed to do good business in provisions, flocks of sheep and herds of cattle being purchased for pieces of old iron. However, they found it impossible to learn the language. The "clicks" in the native tongue baffled them completely.

On 29th October they were at sea once more. Scurvy again broke out, so they landed at St. Mary's Island near Madagascar to obtain a supply of oranges and lemons. On the Madagascan coast another regulated market was set up, again with an armed guard. Rice, peas, beans, oranges, lemons, bananas, and poultry were bought, but the natives were hard bargainers, and Lancaster had to establish fixed prices with beads as currency. Their stay on this coast was not so happy as that spent on the white sand where now is Capetown. The chaplain, the surgeon, the master's mate and ten men in the *Dragon* died of dysentery through drinking bad water, and the master and two men in the *Hector* also died. The captain of the *Ascension* took a boat for the shore to attend the funeral of the *Dragon*'s master's mate. The *Dragon*'s gunner was firing minute guns in salute. Unfortunately one of the guns was inadvertently loaded with shot. The shot struck the boat, killing the *Ascension*'s captain and boatswain, "so that they that went to see the burial of another were both buried there themselves." Distressed by these mischances, for weeks they laboured wearily across the Indian Ocean. The spicy breezes blew soft from off the islands, but they went on. After many days, on 5th June, 1602, they dropped their anchors in the Bay of Achin, in Sumatra.

Here they felt that they had reached an objective. The King or Sultan, Ala-u-din Shah, had his court here. He was a hale old man of ninety-three. Captain Middleton was sent on shore to inform him that the great Queen of England had written him a letter. Ala-u-din sent a very courteous reply, saying that he had heard much of the Queen and her victories over the Spaniards, and that he would be pleased to receive the letter. Lancaster, as the Queen's ambassador, determined to present it in person. He came on shore with a suitable escort. Six elephants were provided. Lancaster rode on one elephant. The letter was given a place of honour on another, lying beneath a golden basin in the howdah or "castle" on the elephant's back. They rode in state, swaying up to the palace amid thronging crowds, with blare of trumpet and beat of drum. The King made them very welcome. Lancaster had brought out with him a Jewish interpreter who understood Arabic, so there was no difficulty in conversing. Lancaster handed to the King the precious letter and the Queen's presents, a basin of silver and a silver cup, a headpiece with a plume of feathers (which pleased him most), a fan, a case of daggers, and an embroidered sword-belt. The English mission squatted down on cushions and partook of a magnificent banquet served on gold plate. The King drank arrack, a very potent spirit distilled from rice, but Lancaster asked and obtained permission liberally to dilute his. There followed an entertainment of dancing girls (a great honour this), some wild music, and a very special cockfight. With the old man in a thoroughly good temper, Lancaster requested from him a licence to open a "factory" in his dominions.

Merchants abroad were generally known as factors and the building in which they transacted business the factory. With factors always at the port, goods could be sold when prices were high, and not necessarily on arrival of the ship, when buyers would be sure to hold back. In the same way, spices and other commodities could be bought in a favourable market and stored. Otherwise purchases would have to be made when the ship was loading, and prices would be sure to rise sharply. Permission for a factory was granted after much lengthy negotiation and a treaty was signed. The factors began to collect pepper, which at this season and in this place was unexpectedly dear. The *Susan* therefore was sent to Priaman, on the west coast of Sumatra, where there was a better market.

All this time the Portuguese ambassador had not been idle. He was naturally perturbed at the Englishmen's success, of which his spies brought him full news. Lancaster also had his agents in the Portuguese embassy. The ambassador's intrigues to put a stop to this trading were exposed, and Ala-u-din dismissed him. Lancaster was about to sail for Malacca to see if he could pick up any Portuguese prizes. He therefore asked Ala-u-din to detain the ambassador till he should be gone, so that no news of his departure should reach Malacca. The King laughed. "Well," said he, "you must bring me a fair Portuguese maiden when you return, and then I will." The expedition duly picked up a Portuguese prize. The valuable cargo was removed, and the passengers and crew resumed their voyage. With his usual foresight and wisdom Lancaster took steps to prevent any looting of this great ship. He placed four picked men only aboard the prize to superintend the transfer of the goods. The actual unloading was done entirely by the luckless Portuguese. In October Lancaster returned to Achin. He took his leave of the King, and brought him a present from the prize. The King was very pleased, but jestingly reminded Lancaster that he had not provided the Portuguese maiden. To this Lancaster made the diplomatic reply that there were no Portuguese maidens worthy of such an honour. Ala-u-din gave him a present for the Queen. The old man was, of course, a Mohammedan. He asked Lancaster if he knew the Psalms of David. "The general answered: Yes, we sing them daily. Then said the King: I and the rest of these nobles about me will sing a psalm to God for your prosperity, and so they did very solemnly. And after it was ended the King said: I would hear you sing another psalm in your own language. So there being in the company some twelve of us, we sung another psalm; and after the psalm was ended the general took his leave of the King."

The *Ascension* left for home with the pepper and other spices loaded at Achin, and the *Dragon* and the *Hector* went to call for the *Susan* at Priaman. She too was sent home laden with pepper and cloves. The *Red Dragon* and *Hector* went on to Bantam[1] in Java, the chief export market for pepper in all these islands, and a great resort for Chinese junks. Wishing to make an impression they saluted the King on arrival with all the guns they had. Lancaster presented a copy of the Queen's letter to the young King (he was only eleven years old) and took care to make himself very agreeable to the boy's protector. No difficulty was made about opening a factory. Lancaster left three factors and eight men. The ships were soon fully loaded with

[1] Whence comes the small variety of domestic fowls.

pepper berries in bags. On 20th February, 1603, the adventurers fired their last salute with joy and left for England, "giving thanks to God."

Their joy was premature. They made a good passage across the Indian Ocean, but near the Cape of Good Hope they encountered a terrible storm. For days they ran under bare poles in an enormous sea, range after range illimitable, hills of grey and silver. The *Dragon* suffered severely from the battering of the waves. One mighty sea struck her, and she shivered. It snapped two or three of the iron hooks on which the rudder was hung. The rudder broke away and was lost in a moment. In desperation they unshipped the mizzen mast, and attempted to use it as a rudder, but the seas were too heavy, and the whole stern shuddered as the furious waves shook the pole. The weather abated a little. A rudder was fashioned out of the mast, and hung on the remaining hooks, but the seas unshipped it again. They began to drift far south. Lancaster was urged to abandon ship, but refused. He ordered the *Hector* home. Next morning to his astonishment he beheld the *Hector* still standing by. "These men regard no orders," was his comment. Yet even the foulest weather moderates some day. On 16th June, after three months out of sight of land *Red Dragon* and the faithful *Hector* reached St. Helena, where with rest, fresh water, and fresh victuals the sick men recovered. They had a fair run home. Their perils and hardships were over.

Lancaster was knighted. He had proved himself a very competent commander. Like many a sailor since, he was a prudent and successful diplomat, and withal a good business man. He had deserved well of his country and of the Company.

The results of this triumphant voyage were momentous. Venice gradually abandoned her overland route to the East. London began to take her place as the great market for Eastern produce. The City merchants were encouraged to persevere, and each year an expedition sailed. In 1612 the tenth voyage under Best established permanent factories on the mainland of India, and made a treaty with the Great Mogul. From this beginning the Company went on from strength to strength. In such fashion were laid the foundations of the Empire of India.

CHAPTER IV

WESTWARD HO! AND THE SPANISH MAIN

THE Spanish and Portuguese claims to the monopoly of trade with the New World in the east and west was sooner or later bound to be challenged. It was the desire and need for trade that first led the English to ignore the claims and try their luck on the Spanish Main and in the islands of the Americas. The rough treatment they received turned them from traders into plunderers of the Spanish ships and towns. If they could not exchange goods they would take what they wanted by force. Long before Elizabeth was ready for open war between England and Spain a private war was declared by Hawkins and Drake and others who followed in their wake. That Devonshire worthy, John Hawkins, fired the first shot in the long campaign which lasted with brief intervals for more than a hundred years.

John Hawkins was the son of William Hawkins the elder, Member of Parliament and several times Mayor of Plymouth. William was probably the wealthiest man in the little but growing town. Years before the Queen came to the throne he had made voyages to Guinea and Brazil. His two sons, William and John, carried on the firm. John was born in 1532. Like his father and brother, he was a merchant adventurer sailing in his own ship. He only changed from merchant to fighting man by

Aº Dñi 1595

SIR JOHN HAWKINS

force of circumstances, and all through his fighting and administrative career the business of the firm still proceeded. As a merchant he acquired a reputation for honest and upright dealing. He was careful to get good value for his money, a Devonian characteristic, and a quality very useful in his work as Treasurer of the Navy. In his prime he was a stern-faced handsome man with clear fearless eyes and clean-cut features, and a fair short beard. He had a rough hearty manner, and was "very wise, vigilant, and true-hearted." Like Blake in after years, he was a stern upholder of the honour of England. In 1570 fifty sail of Spanish ships bound for Flanders to fetch Anne of Austria to be King Philip's fourth wife, came inside the Island at Plymouth without lowering their topsails or their flags, as the custom was. John Hawkins, in command of some of Her Majesty's ships riding at anchor in Cattewater, ordered his gunner to shoot at the flag of the admiral as a plain hint. No notice being taken, the next shot was through the Spaniard's sides. The visiting fleet promptly furled their topsails, lowered their flags, and anchored. Their commander expostulated, but on being given twelve hours to leave the port or be attacked, apologized. There followed mutual compliments and invitations to dinner.

Hawkins's first voyage to West Africa and the Spanish Indies was in 1562-3, when he sold to the Spanish planters the negroes he had captured in his African raid. In the following year he set out again. He had three ships with him besides the Queen's ship, *Jesus of Lübeck*, 700 tons, in which he sailed. *Jesus* seems a queer name for a slaver, but nobody saw the incongruity then. Hawkins's sailing orders contain the words: "Serve God daily,[1] love one another, preserve your victuals, beware of fire, and keep good company." One is reminded of the grim Protector's counsel: "Trust in God and keep your powder dry."

It is quite horrible to read of these slaving operations in which Hawkins was engaged. It is, however, impossible to blame him more than any one else of those times. For many years negroes had been imported by the Spanish for their plantations and mines. The blacks were looked upon by the English and Spanish alike as inferior beings, given by God to the elect for an inheritance. Hawkins's second voyage was as successful as the first. He had braved the prohibition and had traded in spite of it. The brothers determined to venture again. A third voyage was financed by the Queen, who lent two ships, *Jesus of Lubeck* and *Minion*, by Sir William Garrard and a few other London merchants, and by the Hawkins brothers, who supplied four more ships of their own, *Angel*, *Swallow*, *Judith*, and *William and John*. The *Judith*'s captain was a young man named Francis Drake, a distant kinsman of Hawkins.

William came down to the quay at Plymouth to see them off, with a crowd of well-wishers, parents, wives and sweethearts. The men cheered lustily as they cast off on 2nd October, 1567. They sailed out of the Sound. The green-clad cliffs of the Hoe and the trees of the Island and Mount Edgcumbe faded into grey. Rame Head was lost in the gathering mist. It was for most of them the last look at English ground.

A storm off Cape Finisterre scattered the ships, but they all made the rendezvous in the Canaries.

[1] i.e., hold a daily service of prayer.

After watering, they sailed for the Guinea Coast, calling at Cape Verde in Senegambia on the way. Here they landed 150 men hoping to secure some negroes, but they got very few. Many of the sailors were wounded by arrows and died of tetanus. Hawkins himself was hit by an arrow. All during December and up to the middle of January of the following year they worked the coast down to Sierra Leone, plying their horrid trade, but they only kidnapped 150 negroes. This was not considered good enough, and the decision was taken to sail along to the Gold Coast, where they might pick up some precious metal to augment their profits on the voyage. However, a negro chief who wanted help against an enemy, sent word that there were plenty of niggers to be had in exchange for such aid. Hawkins sent 120 men, who assaulted a large town of 8,000 people. It was well stockaded and defended, and the attackers were repulsed with loss. Hawkins then assumed command himself, and with the support of his negro ally, took and fired the town. He found himself with 250 prisoners, men, women and children, but that was all, for the chief decamped that night, taking his prisoners with him.

Their ships being crammed to suffocation with over 400 negroes, Hawkins set out across the Atlantic for the West Indies to get rid of them for good hard cash. The King of Spain had by special decree strictly forbidden his Governors to allow any business with foreigners, but the English had a good reputation as traders and the Spanish planters and mineowners wanted the slaves. A friendly trade was done at several places. However, at Rio de la Hacha (in the modern state of Colombia), a place famous for its pearl fishery, the Treasurer in charge flatly refused to allow any trade or even to let the English have any water. He backed his refusal with a company of a hundred men with arquebuses, and a system of fortifications. He doubtless calculated that lack of water would force the English to land their negroes, which could then be picked up for nothing. But to fight for their water was a frequent if disagreeable necessity, and a party of two hundred men carried the barricades and entered the town. The arquebusiers fired one volley, hitting only two of the attackers, and straightway fled. Negotiations followed, and a slave-market was held by night, the Spaniards buying two hundred of the negroes.

Cartagena was the last place they visited, and having sold practically all their living cargo, they turned towards home on 24th July, 1568. Off the west end of Cuba, near the coast of Florida, a hurricane burst upon them. The *Jesus*, an old ship, suffered severely. Hawkins ordered all the top hamper to be cut away. The rudder was nearly lost, and the ship was leaking fast. Without overhaul she could not make the Atlantic crossing, and so, after a second storm had done its worst upon them, they sought refuge in the port of Mexico, San Juan d'Ulua, on 16th September. Hawkins sent a letter to the authorities in Mexico City, two hundred miles up country, to ask for facilities for repairs and revictualling, on payment. He had good hope of his request being granted, for England and Spain were at peace.

The very next morning he had a shock. At the mouth of the harbour lay thirteen great galleons of Spain. Hawkins immediately sent word to the

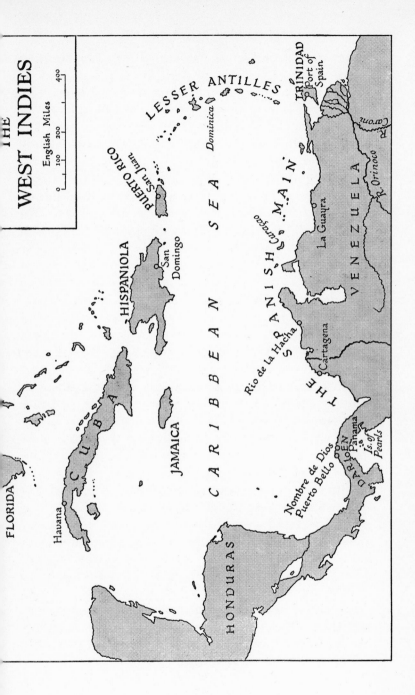

THE
WEST INDIES

English Miles

0   100   200   400

FLORIDA

Havana

C U B A

JAMAICA

HISPANIOLA

San
Domingo

PUERTO RICO

San Juan

LESSER ANTILLES

Dominica

C A R I B B E A N   S E A

THE   S P A N I S H   M A I N

Cumaná

TRINIDAD

Port of
Spain

R. Caroni

VENEZUELA

R. Orinoco

La Guayra

Cartagena

Rio de la Hacha

HONDURAS

Nombre de Dios
Puerto Bello

DARIEN

Panama

Is. of
Pearls

admiral that before he could permit the Spanish ships to enter their own port, they must come to some understanding whereby the English might remain in safety and in peace. Hawkins was in a most awkward dilemma. On all that coast there was no other shelter from the fierce north winds. Moreover, the harbour was so small that all the ships, Spanish and English, would have to lie alongside each other. If Hawkins kept the Spanish fleet outside, which seeing how narrow was the entrance he was well able to do, it would assuredly be wrecked with the loss of a vast treasure. This would greatly embarrass the Queen, who was most anxious for the present to avoid any act of war. On the other hand, if he let them come in, he was out-numbered, and he did not trust their word. However, the second alternative was the only possible one. The risk had to be taken. He received permission from the Viceroy of New Spain (Mexico) to stay at San Juan, so he made the best terms he could. This Viceroy had arrived with the fleet and was on the spot. Both sides swore not to violate the peace. This done, the fleet entered the port, both the English and Spanish firing guns in salute, according to the custom of the sea.

During the morning of Thursday, the 23rd, the English grew suspicious. There was a movement of guns and troops which boded ill. They had reason to suspect that a large body of men were hidden in a great ship of 800 tons, which was moored alongside the *Minion*. Hawkins therefore sent the master of the *Jesus*, Robert Barrett, who spoke Spanish, to the Viceroy to ask what was meant by all this. The Viceroy, seeing that his plot was suspected, apprehended the master, and bade the trumpeters sound a call. Immediately the English were attacked on all sides. Their working parties and sentries ashore were slaughtered almost to a man. Three hundred men from the galleon under suspicion tried to board the *Minion*, but she was too quick, and got clear by cutting the mooring cables at her head. The *Jesus* and the *Minion* drew clear two ship's lengths from the Spaniards, and the fight began. The English guns were splendidly served. They inflicted such punishment on those Spanish ships that afforded them any target in the crowded harbour that within an hour the flagship and another had been sunk, and a third great ship burnt. Early in the fight Hawkins called to Samuel, his page, for a drink. He was brought a silver cup of beer. He drank to all, and shouted to his gunners to stand to their guns like men. As he set down the cup a shot swept it from his hand. Hawkins bawled above the din, "Fear nothing! God, who hath preserved us from this shot, will also deliver us from these traitors and villains!" Soon the guns on shore had shattered the masts and yards of the *Jesus*. Two Spanish fireships blazing furiously, bore down upon them with the wind. Fearfully, without orders, the men in the *Minion* hoisted sail. Hawkins just managed to scramble aboard her. Some of the *Jesus* survivors followed him in a small boat. The rest with all the profits of the voyage were left to the mercy of the Spaniards. The Spaniards had little mercy.

The smaller ships were taken or sunk, with the exception of the *Judith*, which, skilfully handled by Francis Drake, made good her escape and sailed for home. Hawkins seems at first to have resented this apparent desertion, although he himself was involved in the *sauve qui peut* from the harbour. The fact was that both ships had put out to sea, and Drake lost the *Minion* in the night. He saw that the best way of saving his little ship from the Spaniards and the weather was to quit those unhealthy shores as quickly as possible, and he arrived home a few days before Hawkins. For two days the *Minion* remained in the vicinity of the harbour, the Spaniards apparently not daring to molest her. She had only two anchors and two cables left, and the dreaded north wind began to blow. She survived the storm, and when the weather permitted Hawkins set sail, but with all the survivors of the expedition on board, and with very little food, his plight was serious. The crew gnawed at hides, ate rats and the ship's cats, ate even their pet monkeys and parrots, but hunger forced them to land in the Bay of Mexico. Their ship was leaking and battered by cannon shot, they were weak from want of food. One hundred and fourteen men begged to be put ashore, the remaining hundred preferred the hazard of the sea. Of those that landed only one or two after long years saw England again. They were slain by the Indians, died of disease, broke their hearts in the galleys, or were put to death by the Inquisition. Of those who sailed for England, many, very many, never saw that dear land again. Daily, as they toiled slowly home, their bodies were lowered overside, and those that were left grew so weak that they could scarcely work the ship. More dead than alive, they reached Mount's Bay in Cornwall, on 25th January, 1569.

The significance of this adventure lies not in the trade in slaves. That cruel traffic was to endure for many a year yet. One notable fact that emerges from this woeful tale is the power and weight of the English guns, beginning to be felt for the first time. Though greatly outnumbered Hawkins gave as much punishment as he got, and it was the first example of that superiority in gunfire which reached its culminating point in the great fight with the Spanish Armada. In that fight Hawkins lived to take a worthy part. Another fact of great significance was the appearance on the Spanish Main of Francis Drake. He had gone out to trade, and had put his little fortune into the venture. He returned having lost everything. He had, he thought, been treacherously robbed, and his comrades had been slain. He swore to have his revenge on the Spanish power, from henceforth his enemy. He kept his oath. That day in San Juan d'Ulua Spain made an implacable and deadly foe.

Francis Drake was born in a cottage on a farm not far from Tavistock in Devon in or about the year 1541. His father, though probably connected with the lesser gentry and yoemen of those parts, was a poor man with a large family. He was an ardent evangelical preacher of the new Protestant faith that had taken such strong root in England. At this time, however, the bulk of the people were still attached to the Mass, and it appears that Edmund Drake the father found that his zeal had made things so impossible for him that he fled into Kent in 1549 with his young family. Under the Protestant Government of Edward VI he obtained the post of chaplain to the fleet in the Medway. Here Francis, the eldest son, grew up amid ships and sailors. Here also he drank in that Protestant fervour which in a universal though varying degree was so striking a characteristic of the Elizabethan seamen.

Francis very early went to sea. While still a boy he was apprenticed to a ship's captain trading to the Low Countries. He did well, and eventually became the skipper and owner of a small vessel. Soon his native Devonshire called him home. He knew that from Plymouth in the service of his distant kinsmen, the Hawkins brothers, he would have a chance of sailing wider seas. His portraits show him thick-set, short, and sturdy, with fair curly hair and beard, a typical Devonian in appearance. He was by no means the swashbuckler, the sort of vulgar bandit that many picture him to have been. On the contrary, he had an instinctive courtesy and consideration, and was exceptionally humane for the times in which he lived. True he was hot-tempered, overbearing, and when angry, had a rough swearing tongue, but so had Grenville and Raleigh, so had the Queen herself. He was swift in decision and bold in execution, ruthless when he deemed it necessary. He had a boyish gaiety and a fearless way with him. He was at his best when handling incipient mutiny or panic, or extricating himself from a really tight place. He was a dashing, brilliant commander, but impatient of opposition. He was not good as a colleague. Howard, the Lord Admiral, got on very well with him in 1588 because he always took his advice.

Young Francis went with John Hawkins because he had his living to earn and because he wanted adventure. He lost all his money, but he had his adventure. Henceforward he made the downfall of Spain his life's aim.

Queen Elizabeth's position at this time was a difficult one. She was furious at the loss of the *Jesus*, the old ship that represented her investment in the Hawkins enterprise, but neither she nor Burghley wanted war with Spain. Spain was the mightiest power since Rome, England was small and weak. Elizabeth was ready to aid and abet her seamen so long as it could be done secretly, but an open breach she most emphatically did not want, as yet. She, like her subjects, was not disposed to sit down for ever under the ban forbidding all trade with the New World. She was to make this plain later, but again, not yet. Philip of Spain was also patient and restrained. He had ruled in England as consort to Queen Mary for a few years. He knew something of the quality of the islanders. He had trouble enough in the Netherlands, and did not want the English on his back. He could also bide his time. Moreover, Ireland was largely Catholic, and a source of weakness to the English, Scottish Catholics were numerous, and Catholics were still very strong in the North of England. Could not some underhand work be done there? Then there was the Queen of Scots, a Catholic, and a possible focus of nationalism. Philip and Elizabeth spied on each other, wrote letters of protest to each other, and steadily refused to break the precarious peace.

At this moment, it was clear, Drake could look for no official support if he wanted to go a-raiding. This did not deter him in the least. He thought he had as much moral support as he needed. In his view, he was redressing a private wrong, breaking down an outrageous monopoly, and striking a blow at what he already discerned as a national enemy. The Spanish attitude was naturally altogether different. They set his actions down as rank piracy, an offence against God, Holy Church, and man. Francis Drake cared not at all. He was as confident as the Spaniards that God was on his side. God would help him to recover his property and avenge his dead comrades.

He set to work methodically. Hawkins and others backed him, and in a tiny ship of twenty-five tons he slipped quietly out of Plymouth on a cruise of investigation. He reached the Spanish Main unobserved in 1571. He was determined to find out all about the loading and sailing of the treasure ships for Spain. It became clear that the gold and silver and jewels from Peru were taken by sea to Panama and landed there. From this port the treasure was carried by mule train under armed guard across the Isthmus to Nombre de Dios, stored there in the treasure house, and in due course shipped to Europe when the galleons arrived to fetch it. Francis had no intention of trying to capture the Spanish fleet. That was an impossibility. His audacious proposal was to raid the treasure house itself in Nombre de Dios. The plan was kept a profound secret. To his contemporaries it would have seemed about as mad as if to-day a small party of gunmen were to try to overpower the detachment of His Majesty's Guards and rob the Bank of England. He explored the coast for a quiet spot as a base and a hiding-place, and found one. It was a little sandy cove on an uninhabited shore, where springs of fresh water came tumbling down the hillside, and beyond the palm-trees was a bushy thicket whence birds like pheasants called. He named it Port Pheasant, and buried some stores there. Before leaving for home he snapped up a few small coasting vessels wherewith to pay his expenses. Instead of heaving his prisoners overboard like a real pirate, he set them all free. Drake always did this. It earned him a reputation for humanity in those rough times. He reached home in safety, and at once made all preparations for this characteristic, reckless, light-hearted adventure.

The risks were tremendous. Drake had two small ships, the *Pasha* of 70 tons which he commanded himself, and the little *Swan*, in which he had carried out his voyage of exploration. This was in charge of his brother John. His crews consisted of seventy-three men and boys, all but one, Tom Moon, under thirty years old. This band of dare-devils was crammed on board these two little ships with as much ammunition, food, water, and beer as they could carry.

Francis Drake and his men left Plymouth on 24th May, 1572. They had a fortunate voyage to that home of romance, the Spanish Main. Drake found Port Pheasant, but someone had discovered his cache. His stores were gone. Nevertheless, it was too good a spot to abandon, and he determined to make a base there. He ordered his lads to fell trees and build a big stockade thirty feet high. For his purposes it was necessary to be as mobile as possible and to be independent of winds. He had, therefore, brought out from home three dainty pinnaces in sections, which were put together here. They could be rowed if the wind failed. While his boys were busy at this job a man named James Ranse, a wandering English trader and rover, turned up with his ship. He asked leave to join Drake, who did not in the least want to be bothered with him. However, he was better as an ally than if he went blundering about by himself and perhaps giving the alarm. So they drew up a deed of partnership, with Francis in sole command. The ships were left behind with twenty Devonshire men and some newcomers under Ranse. Twenty of Ranse's party were ready in a boat he had recently captured, and Drake with fifty-three of his merry men manned the three pinnaces. Silently they slipped out and crept westwards along the coast, with Nombre de Dios as their objective. They put in at an island that Drake called the Isle of Pines, and there they saw some black fellows loading timber on to two small ships that had come from Nombre. They were Cimaroons, neither negroes nor Indians, but a cross breed between the two. The word means "wild men from the hills," and wild they were, to the Spaniards. They were runaway slaves or their descendants, and they bore to their late masters an implacable deadly hate. They would kill any Spaniard, man or woman, at sight, and were dangerous neighbours, for they constantly raided the plantations and settlements. These particular men had been kidnapped from their tribe in some Spanish reprisal and "marooned" upon this island to work. Drake promptly earned their gratitude by offering to set them ashore on the Main, gaining at one stroke guides, allies and spies. The English always called them Maroons.

For five days they stole along the coast. Quite close to the town a landing was made and arms were issued. There were a few swords and arque-buses, and some pikes with tow attached to the heads. These were to be lighted when the signal for attack was given, to cause surprise and alarm. Some were handed bows and arrows, with tow on the arrowheads. Flaming arrows dropping into the town or among the troops might easily start a panic, especially with plenty of yelling and shouting, and trumpets blaring and drums throbbing. Two trumpeters and two drums were taken.

At night they re-embarked, and hid behind the arm of the bay. Zero hour was fixed for dawn, but the strain of waiting began to tell upon the lads. "Thisyer town be so big as Plymouth," muttered one. "And full of they Spanish soldiers, sure 'nough," replied his neighbour. Drake, ever vigilant, observed these fidgets and the general uneasiness. Without waiting for the dawn, he gave the order to proceed as soon as the clear white light of the moon began to appear. They dashed round the point, rowing hard, made fast by the fort, and leapt out. There was but one gunner in charge, and he ran for the town to give the alarm. Twang! went a bow, and an arrow whizzed over his shoulder. The wretched man ran as he had never run before. In a few moments a bell clanged madly from the church tower, and drums and trumpets called the little garrison to arms. Drake and company paused to seize crowbars and tumble the guns of the fort off their carriages, then raced for the town. Drake had detailed his brother John and John Oxenham to go round to the eastwards of the market-place and attack it from that side, while he advanced up the main street. The pikes flared, the flaming arrows soared and fell. With trumpet braying and with roll of drum the yelling, shouting Englishmen ran on. They were met with a sharp volley of musketry. Drake, leading, was hit in the leg by a bullet, and the trumpeter fell dead. Drake took no heed but carried on. Oxenham and John Drake with sword and pike took the Spaniards in flank, and the cheering English hustled them out through the landward gate, slammed and bolted it.

In the yard of the Governor's house was stacked a huge pile of silver bars. Aghast at so much wealth, the breathless, exultant lads stared, but Drake ordered them away. "Sink the silver," he said, "come where gold and jewels be to." He led them down towards the treasure house on the quay. They had to be quick, for they could not hold the town, and the Spanish were rallying. Drake told his brother and Oxenham to run on and break the place open. Even as he spoke, they saw as the day dawned that his tracks were full of blood. He dropped where he stood. They forgot the treasure. They bound up his wound, and despite his protests tenderly carried their much loved captain to the boats.

They made off, and landed on an island near by. In due course there came a Spanish officer with a white flag, ostensibly to parley, but actually to see and hear all he could about the numbers and resources of this audacious rover. Drake was in a bad temper. He told the envoy that, God willing, he meant to reap some of the golden harvest they sent into Spain to trouble the world. Then he relented, invited the Spaniard to dinner, and regaled him with Canary wine he had taken from a Spanish ship. The spy enjoyed his dinner and the wine. But it was evdently time to be going. Ranse thought the game was up, and that the coast would henceforth be too unhealthy. The partnership was therefore dissolved. Ranse took himself off, and Drake his wound nearly healed, was once more alone with his lads from Devonshire and his dainty pinnaces. He was by no means daunted. He had his plans, but they must wait awhile.

Drake went to Cartagena, the capital of the Main,

and a fine well-built city. One night he took his boats into the bay, cut out and boarded a ship from Seville, and when day broke towed her amid cheers and laughter across the mouth of the harbour. Bells clashed from all the steeples, and shots from the forts plumped harmlessly into the sea. Still shaking with laughter, Drake set the Seville men ashore on an island to their surprise and joy, and towed the ship back to the Isle of Pines to be ransacked.

For Drake's future plans the pinnaces were more than ever necessary. But how was he to man them properly? Skeleton crews had to be left with the *Pasha* and the *Swan*, and there were not enough men to man three pinnaces and two ships. The *Swan* must go. But the *Swan* was John Drake's darling command. Some way had to be devised to scuttle the *Swan* without hurting his feelings. Drake took Tom Moon, the carpenter of the *Swan*, into his cabin and into his confidence. He told him to go down secretly in the middle of the second watch, and with a great spike-gimlet bore three holes as near to the keel as he could and wedge a board down over the holes so that no one should see or hear the water welling up. Tom was horrified at the idea of sinking such a good stout ship. "What will Master John and the crew say? They will kill me." But in the end, when Drake had convinced him of the absolute necessity, he obeyed. The next morning John was puzzled to know why his ship seemed so low in the water. He sent the steward below to investigate. There was a splash and a cry. The dripping steward reappeared with the news that there was six foot of water in the hold. All hands went to the pumps and worked incessantly until three o'clock in the afternoon. The *Pasha* provided reliefs for the weary men of the *Swan*, but the water poured in as fast as it was pumped out. It was all very mysterious, but with such a leak there seemed nothing to be done but to abandon ship. John Drake was offered the *Pasha*, and Drake would go in a pinnace till something suitable was captured. The *Swan* was set on fire that night. In this characteristic and considerate fashion Francis Drake got his way.

With the *Pasha* and the pinnaces Drake crossed the Gulf of Darien. Another base was established and hutments were erected. The larboard and starboard watches took it in turns to work on refitting the ships and pinnaces. The watch off duty held archery competitions or played skittles, bowls, and quoits. Drake was busy with his plans. Baulked once at Nombre de Dios, it was no use trying there again. He had made up his mind to get some of that treasure somehow. Instead of seizing it at the port, he would attack it on the way by swooping down upon the mule train from Panama. The Maroons brought him news. The rainy season was due, and the mule tracks would become impassable. No more convoys would set out until the dry weather came. Something would have to be done meanwhile. Take to the sea again, and keep the Spaniards guessing.

Up and down the coast they went, plundering small ships where they could. They had to be careful where they landed, for everywhere the Spaniards were on the alert. Rain and sea water spoilt much of their food, they were often cold and wet. A pinnace's crew said they were willing to follow him anywhere in the world, but this weather was detestable, and they were eighteen men with only a gammon of bacon and thirty pounds of biscuit left. At that rate they would soon all be dead. Drake said he had a piece of bacon too, with forty pounds of biscuit for twenty-four men. He did not propose to die, but to trust in Providence and tighten his belt. The weather soon abated, and they boarded a Spanish ship of ninety tons, finding therein all the victual they needed.

They had been successful in these crazy adventures for so long that some of them grew careless. John Drake in his pinnace attempted to board a Spaniard and was shot dead by an arquebus bullet. Then fever broke out in the camp. Man after man sickened and succumbed. Francis Drake had his young brother Joseph die in his arms. The ship's surgeon could do nothing. He concocted a strange and weird medicine, tried it on himself, and died of it. When the plague had run its course, Drake had only forty-one men left, some of them sick. They all revived sufficiently to take another frigate.[1] Some Maroons were with them in camp, and Drake had difficulty in preventing them from slaughtering the prisoners.

Presently news came that the Plate or Silver fleet had arrived at Nombre de Dios, and the dry weather was here at last. A mule-train might start any day. The time for action had come. Drake left a strong guard over the ship and the pinnaces. Allowing for the sick men, he had only eighteen to spare for the great adventure. He took thirty Maroons with him, and together they entered the green wilderness of the forest. Soon they left

[1] Not the frigate of Nelson's day, but generally a small single-masted vessel with a dozen or so oars.

behind the low-lying country and the malaria. They came to the foothills af the Cordilleras, daily they climbed higher. The Maroons kept all their hatred for the Spanish, and the English had no trouble with them. On the contrary, they were devoted allies. They acted as bearers, carrying the food and gear, and making huts of palm-thatch at night. The Maroons had some barbaric rags and tatters of the Christian religion, but it had lapsed into fetishism. Drake's Protestant piety was shocked at this, and he did what he could to remedy it. It must have been a queer sight to see this leader of a buccaneering expedition solemnly sitting down in the dim green twilight of the forest, trying to teach those fierce savages the Lord's Prayer.

At the summit of the watershed stood a mighty tree. The Maroons showed Drake a series of steps cut in it, leading up to a prospect platform. He climbed up and fell on his knees as he saw, over the green tree tops falling below him, the mysterious ocean, the Pacific, gleaming wide. He was the first Englishman to behold it. He prayed aloud, lifted up in spirit like Moses on Pisgah's height, "O God, give me life and leave to sail an English ship on yonder sea." Oxenham also came up to look, and made a secret vow.

The mule-trains very sensibly travelled in the cool of the night on the well-worn trail. To avoid confusion, Drake ordered that shirts were to be worn over coats, so that they would be visible in the dark. The men were divided into two parties, one on either side of the track about fifty yards apart, in order that they could fall simultaneously on the head and tail of the mule train. Francis gave orders that no woman or unarmed man was to be touched,

SIR FRANCIS DRAKE

and absolute silence and stillness were to be kept till his whistle blew. The Treasurer of Lima, with his family, was expected to travel with this convoy, which would probably be a rich one.

A ration of brandy was issued while the men were waiting. In the tense stillness a horse's hoof was heard. A rider was coming along the road. The silence and excitement were too much for one of the lads. The brandy had probably gone to his head a little. To everyone's consternation he sprang up. A Maroon flung him down and jumped on him, but the rider's horse shied at the white shirt. The Spaniard spurred on towards Panama, met the convoy and told his tale. The Treasurer trotted back to the town, the treasure was unloaded, and the mules sent forward to test the trap. When at last the whistle blew the adventurers found empty panniers.

It is nowhere reported what Drake said on this occasion, but Robert Pike, the luckless lad whose fault it was, must have heard some choice things about himself and his progenitors. In desperation they mounted the mules, thwacked them into startled action, and entered the town of Venta Cruz. Some soldiers and armed monks showed signs of wanting to fight. They were bundled into a monastery and locked in under guard, while the Devonshire boys ransacked the town for food. Then they went back to the ships. If they were going to try again (and Drake had no mind to give up the attempt) it was essential to keep away for a while and give the convoys a new sense of security. So they plundered the coastal shipping once more, and stayed away from the land. One day a Captain Tétu, a Huguenot privateer from Le Havre, came in with his ship. He seemed ready for anything, and Drake was very shorthanded. Tétu agreed to serve under Drake. The mule trains had resumed their routine marches, and this time Drake determined to strike just at the point when the guards would consider the danger of ambush past—a mile from the very town of Nombre de Dios.

The same dispositions were taken as before. English, French and Maroons awaited the leader's whistle as the jingling mule-bells came nearer and nearer. There was no hitch this time. With a yell they leapt out and dashed for the heads of the leading and rear mules. The guards loosed off their arquebuses, mortally wounding Tétu, and fled. The mules lay down. There were three trains, one hundred and ninety animals in all. Wild with delight, they crammed the silver bars into land-crabs' holes, hid them under bushes, dumped them anywhere, in the hope that they might come back for them. They could only carry the gold. Laden with the precious stuff, they staggered back through the forest to the mouth of the river, where they expected to find the pinnaces. There was not a sign of them. To add to their dismay they saw seven small Spanish vessels offshore. No doubt they had taken the pinnaces. This was a blow between the eyes. Drake was always at his best when confronted with a situation that looked desperate. Recent wild weather had brought down some trees. A rough log raft was made, with a young tree for a mast, another for a rudder, others for poles, and a biscuit-bag for a sail. Drake with another Englishman and two Frenchmen set out on this crazy raft, half under water, to seek the pinnaces along the coast. " Us'll see 'ee safe aboard, spite of all the Spanishers in the Indies." Exhausted with their paddling, burnt with the tropic sun, caked with sea salt, just before nightfall the thirsty intrepid four spied the pinnaces, which the gale had blown out to sea. "All's well," was the cry, and they loaded up and got safely away.

The Maroons were rewarded with suitable presents, and the Frenchmen received their share of the loot. The Plate fleet was in Cartagena. Drake sailed past the harbour mouth with the cross of St. George at his maintop and silken streamers trailing in the sea. The Spanish captains cursed the daring English corsair and the wind that kept them fast in port. They had not seen the last of him. Drake, the Dragon, as they called him, was to be their scourge and terror.

The little band of adventurers arrived at Plymouth on a Sunday morning, 4th August, 1573. The great Church of St. Andrew was filled with townsfolk listening to a sermon. A man rushed excitedly in. "Frankie Drake's come home!" was his startling news. The mayor rose and left the church. One after another the congregation followed. The excitement grew, and the movement became general. In a few minutes none were left, and the parson's sermon died on his lips as the pews emptied. He followed his flock down to the quay.

. . . . .

The sad tale of John Oxenham's vow and its fulfilment is a brief one. He also was from Devonshire. A resolute, reckless, impetuous young man, he lacked Drake's touch of genius. Until he lost it at the close of his life, Drake possessed the touch that commands success. Oxenham never had it. Up in the great tree with Drake, in full view of the Pacific, or South Sea, as they called it, he heard Drake's prayer, and vowed to himself that he would be the first Englishman to sail that fabled ocean. He was the first. He had that honour, though the end of the tale is tragic.

In 1575 Oxenham took with him seventy men in a ship of 140 tons, and landed in the Gulf of Darien where he had been with Drake. He was soon in touch with the Cimaroons, from whom he learnt that since Drake's exploit the mule trains were very strongly guarded by soldiers. He abandoned any idea he may have had of tampering with the convoys, and determined to carry out his plan to attack the shipping on the Pacific side of the Isthmus. He ran his ship aground in a creek, and camouflaged her with branches of trees, just as big howitzers were covered in the Great War. His ship's guns he removed and buried, all except two pieces of small calibre, and some calivers. With these weapons, a little ammunition, and with all his men, he crossed to the other side of the watershed. On the bank of a river running down to the "South Sea" he felled trees and with great labour made a pinnace, a large one, with a 45-foot keel. The party dropped down the river in this, with six Maroons as guides, and passed exulting to the sea. They made for the Isle of Pearls, about seventy miles from Panama, on the direct route from Peru to that place. It was not long before they captured a small coaster from Guayaquil with 60,000 pesos[1] of gold on board as well as provisions. After that Oxenham snapped up a vessel from Lima containing 100,000 pesos worth of bar silver. He transferred the booty to the

[1] A peso was worth about 7s. in Elizabethan money.

pinnace, and returned to the mouth of the river, where he dismissed the two prizes and their crews. Then things went wrong. He ought to have carried the treasure to his ship and made off straightway, especially as he had released his prizes. But he quarrelled with his men. He promised them a share of the treasure in addition to their pay if they made the three or four journeys necessary to carry it. For some reason the seamen did not trust him, and demanded that this share be set aside there and then. Oxenham lost his temper, and said that if they would not take his word, he would get the black fellows to carry the stuff. He got the black porters, but the delay was fatal.

Information of what had occurred was brought to the Governor of Panama by the natives in the Isle of Pearls. Within two days the energetic Governor had fitted out an expedition to recover the treasure, a hundred soldiers under the command of Señor Juan de Ortega. He was hot on the pursuit when he met the two ships that had been captured and released, the crews of which told him that the English had gone up the river. The river fell into the sea by three mouths. Ortega, in doubt which to take, had almost decided on the largest, when one of his negro oarsmen, wise in woodcraft, noticed some hen's feathers coming down one of the other streams. Up this one, therefore, Ortega went. After four days' journey he rounded a bend, and there on the sandy shore lay the Englishmen's pinnace. Six men were in her. They jumped out and fled. One was shot dead as he ran, but the rest escaped. No gold or silver was in the boat, and it was evident that the treasure must be hidden somewhere. With eighty musketeers Ortega followed the fugitives for about a mile and a half and came upon a little hut made of boughs of trees. In it was the missing treasure and also the Englishmen's tools. Ortega was satisfied with the recovery of the gold and silver, and did not feel disposed to penetrate further into the bush in pursuit of the Englishmen. He and his men carried the treasure and the gear back to their boats.

The alarm had been given by the five men who had escaped from the pinnace. Oxenham and his men, all differences forgotten, with a large body of black carriers, followed the Spaniards down to the river and attacked them furiously. The Spaniards were trained troops. They took cover behind trees and beat the English off. The latter lost eleven white men killed and seven prisoners, and fell back hoping to regain their hidden ship in the Gulf of Darien. Ortega returned to Panama with the prisoners and the treasure.

Oxenham and the remnant of his company would have been lucky to have escaped with their lives, but they were too far away from their ship, and another disaster befell them. On Ortega's return the Governor sent a special messenger on horseback to Nombre de Dios to tell the authorities there where the English ship was. Whereupon the men of Nombre manned four vessels, went round to the Gulf, and took away the hidden ship and all her buried guns. Oxenham's party had to take to the hills with the Cimaroons, destitute, ragged, without tools. They were given no long respite. The Viceroy of Peru thought it unsafe to leave fifty Englishmen at large among the runaway slaves. He sent a company of 150 soldiers to hunt them down. The troops surprised them as they were attempting to build some canoes. Fifteen sick men fell into the Spaniards' hands. The rest fled. The soldiers pursued them over the mountains. A Cimaroon betrayed them, and they were all captured and taken to Panama. Oxenham was brought before the magistrate there, who inquired if he had any privateer's licence from the Queen or from anyone else. Oxenham replied that he had none, but that he came on his own account. The whole party was condemned to death, and most of them suffered the penalty at Panama. Oxenham, the master, the pilot, and five boys were taken to Lima to be questioned by the Viceroy. The boys were spared. The three officers were hanged as pirates.

It was a sorry ending to the adventure. From the Spanish point of view justice had been done. Had Drake been caught, he also would have been hanged. But Drake's exploit had been a success, and nothing succeeds like success. All over England the tale went round with cheers and laughter. The taverns of the West Country were full of it. It was carried to the great houses, and from thence to the Court and to the Queen herself. Drake swore he was no pirate, and he undoubtedly believed it. He had gone out to recoup himself for his losses due to treachery. He had done so handsomely, and if he was forbidden to trade fairly, he would take what he wanted. Burghley and the more cautious heads in the Privy Council did not like it, but the country as a whole cared not a jot whether Drake was a pirate or no. He was a man after their own heart. He was the personification of this new spirit of exaltation in England that dared to defy the King of Spain.

CHAPTER V

THE CIRCUMNAVIGATION OF THE WORLD

ROYAL displeasure was certainly not visited upon Drake. The Queen was very probably highly delighted with his exploit. At all events, the next time there is news of him he is found in command of a ship in the Queen's service off the Irish coast. It was not proper employment for him. He had no wish to be harrying the wretched Irish. The Spaniard was his enemy. He longed to be at his own destined work. During these few years, however, negotiations for a settlement and treaty with Spain had been proceeding, and it was considered politic to keep Drake out of the way. His time came at last. In 1575 it became apparent that a treaty was impossible, and soon afterwards the news was brought to England that an English ship belonging to Sir Edward Osborne[1] had been confiscated in a Spanish port and the crew handed over to the Inquisition. Elizabeth was furious. She told Walsingham, the Secretary of State, to seek out Captain Drake and discover what was in his mind. She had an idea that something was afoot, for Drake had been dropping hints which had reached Sir Christopher Hatton as they were intended to do, and Hatton had the ear of the Queen. Walsingham, a grim Puritan, was by now convinced that

[1] This wealthy merchant prince had, when an apprentice, leapt off London Bridge and rescued his master's daughter from drowning. He married her, and rose to be Knight and Lord Mayor.

peace with Spain was impossible, and that war was only a question of time. Burghley, the Lord Treasurer, on the other hand, still clung to hopes of an eventual amicable settlement. The Queen was inclined to agree with Walsingham.

Drake confided to Walsingham his proposal, which was, in short, to sail through the Strait of Magellan, to harry the unsuspecting treasure ships and undefended towns on the Pacific seaboard, and then go north to see if there was any possibility of English settlement on the west coast of North America. Afterwards he might attempt the journey home by way of the Arctic Ocean, or better still come home by the China Seas and open up trade with the Spice Islands. Walsingham told him to set down the scheme in writing and he would show it to the Queen. Drake the reckless knew when caution was advisable. Nothing was safe from the agents of the King of Spain. Besides, the Queen might die, and a Sovereign of different views take her place, in which unhappy event the existence of this document would be highly dangerous for Drake. No. If Her Majesty wished to hear about his scheme, she should hear it from his own lips. This she did. The adventurous daring of the plan captured her imagination, and she told him to proceed. Drake asked for a commission. He was going to run tremendous risks, and he did not want to go a second time with a noose around his neck. Much evidence has come to light in recent years which proves beyond a doubt that he obtained his commission. He also got a ship and a thousand crowns in cash, but he was instructed to keep the matter very secret. He was not to tell Burghley on any account. This was to be the Queen's private speculation, though she would let Leicester in, and Hatton, and of course Walsingham. The Queen gave him a sword, and with it the words of encouragement, "He which striketh at thee, Drake, striketh at us."

Drake began to assemble and fit out his ships and his crews. It was publicly announced that it was to be a Mediterranean expedition, bound for Alexandria to trade. Nobody believed it, but the story served its purpose. It kept the real objective in the dark, and the King of Spain's spies could send him no definite news. Burghley was kept in ignorance, but he did not believe the Alexandria tale for a moment. He obtained the real facts from one of Drake's gentlemen adventurers, Thomas Doughty. It has been suggested that he told Doughty to do his best to hamper Drake in his project. It is more probable that he shrugged his shoulders despairingly and held his peace, for by the time he heard of the scheme it was too late. It is just possible that Doughty's subsequent conduct was due to Burghley's instructions, but it seems very unlikely from what is known of Burghley's character. Almost certainly Doughty acted as he did for reasons of his own. His jealousy and ambition were his undoing.

Drake sailed as "General" of the enterprise in a hundred-ton ship, the *Pelican*, afterwards renamed the *Golden Hind*. Her length at the waterline was about that of a cricket pitch (22 yards) and she carried 18 guns. Her figurehead was a pelican. At the mainmast flew the ensign of St. George, the flag of England. Aft was the Tudor flag, horizontal green stripes quartered with a St. George's cross. The *Pelican* carried ninety men or more, officers, seamen, boys, musicians, and tradesmen such as carpenters, smiths and coopers. The *Elizabeth* of 80 tons was next in size, a Queen's ship, commanded by a young Queen's officer, Captain John Winter, son of Sir William Winter, himself a well-known officer in the Royal service. The *Marigold*, 30 tons, the *Swan* (a 50-ton victualling ship), and a pinnace in charge of Thomas Moon, made up the little armada. The crews, including all officers and boys, totalled 164. Puny as it seems, hopelessly inadequate for the risks to be run, it was one of the most important expeditions that had left these shores up to this time. Guns and ammunition were plentiful and of the finest quality. To support the general's rank, and for reasons of prestige when among strange peoples, all the furniture and equipment were the best procurable. Drake's cabin was panelled in oak. Of oak also were the table and chairs, and his dinner service was of silver. A page, his cousin, John Drake, stood behind his chair at meals. When at dinner with his officers and gentlemen adventurers the general had his fiddlers playing. Trumpeters sounded the call to dine, and his drum beat. Drake always took this drum to sea with him. To-day it hangs on the wall of Buckland Abbey, the house at Yelverton near Plymouth that he bought from Sir Richard Grenville. Quarters must have been very cramped, but as far as was possible the general lived in good style. His youngest brother Thomas sailed with the expedition, and in the *Pelican* were several younger sons of good families, Eliot, Cary, Chester, Fortescue, and the rest. It was becoming the fashion for such young men to cross their Protestant swords with Spain, either in the Low Countries as volunteers with the Dutch rebels, or in France with the Huguenots, or at sea with men like Drake. With Drake's company were two brothers, Thomas and John Doughty.

Thomas Doughty was well-born and well-edu-cated. His courtly manners and erudition had attracted Drake, who loved these things, when they had first met in Ireland. He was a scholar and a lawyer of the Temple, and was evidently a gay and attractive companion, but his character was marred by a streak of deceit. Drake, a single-minded sailor, was for long quite blind to this underhand intriguing quality. He treated Doughty as an intimate friend. It was to Doughty, who was acting as secretary to Sir Christopher Hatton, that Drake first revealed an outline of his plan, so that it should reach the Queen by way of the favoured Captain of the Guard.

On 15th November, 1577, a morning of blue sky with white clouds sailing high, with a fair wind the *Pelican* and her consorts cast off at Plymouth. Amid the cheers of many hundreds of the townsfolk, with trumpets sounding and drums rolling, they left the Sound and put out to open sea. But as so often happened, there was an anti-climax. Long before they had cleared the Cornish coast, the sky grew dull, the sun was obscured, and the sea was rising fast. The wind, which had dropped, now blew hard from the south-west in roaring gusts. They had to put into Falmouth for shelter and back to Plymouth for repairs. For weeks there was foul weather, but on 13th December the sun shone gaily, and a soft air was blowing off the shore. Farewells were said once more, and this time the adventurers were more fortunate. They had a clear run southerly, and on Christmas Day were off the white sandy shore of Morocco. They launched a boat to take soundings. Finding safe anchorage they remained there a week. There was no trouble with the Moors at first. In defiance of Mohammed's prohibition, the English offered them wine, and to their surprise and amusement, the wine was drunk. However, these friendly potations were rudely interrupted. A sailor, John Fry, as was usual, had been sent a little way inland to the Emir as a hostage. The Emir, mistaking him for a Portuguese, and having no love for these people, carried Fry off to the mountains. Drake landed a search party, but not a Moor was to be seen, and Fry was sadly given up for lost. He somehow managed to explain to the Emir that the expedition was not a Portuguese one, but by the time he reached the coast again the ship had gone. It is good to know that he found his way back to England without being sent to the galleys.

By this time everybody knew that they were not going to Alexandria, and the last shred of disguise was cast away. Whether Drake told his crews the full extent of his plan is doubtful. It was fifty-eight years since Magellan had passed through the Strait named after him, and no one had dared to try it since. The passage was uncharted. The wildest stories were in circulation of the dangers from unmanageable currents and terrific storms. The Spanish made no attempt to use the Strait. All traffic between Atlantic and Pacific was carried overland across the Isthmus of Panama, and their ships that sailed the Pacific were all built upon that seaboard. At this stage it is probable that the men were only told that they were bound for the Brazils.

They kept away from the Canary Islands and coasted southwards along Africa to Cape Blanco, where they stayed for several days, fishing and doing a little trade with the Moorish tribes. The fleet picked up a few small coasting craft, with some welcome supplies, and a larger one, a 40-ton Spanish vessel, which Drake thought he could use. He put the crew and some provisions into Tom Moon's pinnace and bade them begone. Tom's men went to the new capture, which was named the *Christopher*, after Hatton, the friend at Court of both Doughty and Drake. The ships were cleaned at Cape Blanco. A course was then set for the Cape Verde Islands. Drake intended to pay a surprise call to see whether there was anything worth taking. He came to the harbour of Santiago and found a Portuguese vessel lying out of range of the shore batteries. He promptly seized her and sailed away, while the guns of the batteries wasted their shot in the sea between. The Portuguese were allied to the Spaniards, and in any case, were near neighbours, a sufficiently good excuse for helping himself to what was almost offered to him. It was a lucky capture. The ship belonged to a native of Oporto who was sailing in her, one Nuño da Silva, and was bound for Brazil with a cargo of wine and cloth. Da Silva was an experienced navigator who knew the Brazils. Drake therefore took him on board the *Pelican* as pilot. He was well treated and dined in the cabin with Drake and his officers. His ship was renamed *Mary*, after Mary Newman of Saltash, whom Drake had recently married. Thomas Drake was sent aboard her, and Thomas Doughty was given the command.

Drake could trust his brother, but of Doughty he was not quite sure. There was a rumour going about that Doughty was not playing a straight game, that he was sowing distrust of the general among the crews. Drake remembered that he had been warned when walking in his garden at Plymouth that Doughty was dangerous. He had dismissed it as idle talk, but he remembered it now. He did not believe it yet, but it would be a good test of fidelity to give him command of the prize, and brother Thomas could watch him.

Trouble flared up almost at once. Brewer, Drake's trumpeter, who had been on board the *Mary*, returned with the news that Mr. Doughty had taken for himself some of the property of the Portuguese prisoners, who had been sent back to Santiago. This was a serious accusation, for by the law of the sea a prize was the property of all. Upon investigation the charge was found to be perfectly true, but the articles taken were trivial enough, and little more would probably have been said had not Doughty, stung by a reprimand, accused Thomas Drake of the very same thing. In Drake's eyes the charge was obviously absurd. He lost his temper rather easily, and this was enough. "With great oaths" he taxed Doughty with trying to undermine his, the general's, authority. He ordered Doughty into the *Pelican*, and gave his brother the command of the *Mary*.

Thinking perhaps that his outburst had been somewhat hasty, and perhaps wishing to give Doughty another chance, Francis Drake went with his brother in the *Mary*, and placed Doughty in command of the gentlemen adventurers and soldiers in the *Pelican*. This, however, gave Doughty an opportunity. No sooner had the fleet fairly left the islands and started on the long voyage across the Atlantic than he mustered all the ship's company,

145

and told them that he was the general's deputy with power of life and death under the Queen's commission. In fact, he was responsible for discipline. He was under a grave misapprehension. The soldiers were supreme in the Spanish ships, but not in one of Drake's. With him the sailor's word was law at sea. He did not know of this speech till later, when he made it quite clear what was the position of the soldier and gentleman, but he soon had more trouble with Doughty. He sent Brewer one day as a messenger to the *Pelican*. Brewer was received with jeers and laughter, and was the victim of some rough horseplay in which Doughty himself took part. This was an insult not to be borne. Drake returned to the *Pelican*, and ordered Doughty overside into a boat, which took him to the *Swan*. He was under arrest in charge of the master, John Sarocold.

All this while, for nearly two months, the little fleet had been tossing on the wide Atlantic. The winds had oftentimes been contrary, the crews had experienced storms and been becalmed, had endured fierce tropic heat, and had welcomed rain to replenish their water supply. They dropped anchor off an uninhabited shore near the mouth of the River Plate, watered and collected fuel. In rough tempestuous weather they pushed on further south, wondering much whither they were bound. Thomas Doughty, who did know, had before his arrest grumbled that there were no prizes to be had on these southern shores, and nothing but storms and dangers ahead. Drake had replied, "We have come for another object than the seizing of ships."

The voyagers found an inlet which they called Seal Bay, where they remained for some while, living well on fresh seal, and salting down the meat.

Parties of Indians visited them. Relations were friendly on the whole, though the men found the inquisitiveness and acquisitiveness of the painted savages rather trying. One day an Indian brave stalked Drake, snatched the cap from his head and ran. A man raised his arquebuse to his shoulder, but Drake bade him lower his weapon and "not kill a man for a cap. Beat him if you can catch him." The Indian returned, evidently prepared to steal something else. Another man made a lunge at him, but only grabbed hold of his girdle of skins, which came away in the seaman's hand. The enormity of his offence was explained by signs to the mystified savage. Whereupon he scratched his leg with an arrow-head till the blood flowed in order to wash out the wrong he had committed. In one of the narratives of the voyage page after page is devoted to a description of these Indians. The adventurers showed great interest in them, and one narrator thought it a great pity that so comely a people should not know the true God. He added that it would glorify God if the English could only take and possess this goodly land, for so His Church would be enlarged. The Spaniards also were familiar with this argument.

With the men refreshed and the ships in good trim Drake went on south. Almost immediately raging winds and mountainous seas smote him again. The fleet was scattered. *Christopher*, *Mary* and *Swan* disappeared. Drake was troubled. He remembered he had been told that John Doughty boasted that he and his brother could raise the Devil. They obviously wanted to wreck the voyage. Perhaps this awful weather was due to witchcraft on their part. In this respect Drake was no more superstitious than his fellows. Men believed as simply in the Devil and his agents as they did in God and His angels, and sorcery and the black arts were very real to them. The *Pelican, Elizabeth* and *Marigold* struggled on southwards, and the *Swan* rejoined. It was an anxious time for the leader. Two ships were still missing and his brother was in one of them. He determined to break up the *Swan* and take her crew in the *Pelican*. In his present mood it was no wonder that he was furious when Sarocold told him of Mr. Doughty's mutinous talk in the *Swan*. He had Doughty tied to the mast, and after this ignominy ordered both the brothers into the *Christopher*. They refused to go. "Very well," said Drake, "rig tackle and sling them aboard."

Drake was concentrating his forces for the dash through the strait, and he was determined to settle this business with the Doughtys once and for all. On 19th June, 1578, the *Mary* rejoined, to Drake's great relief, and she and the *Christopher* were both broken up. The Doughtys were transferred, still under arrest, to the *Elizabeth*. Strict orders were given that they should not be allowed to read or write, lest they should practise spells or black magic. By now the voyagers were not far from the strait, and it was becoming clear what Drake's plans were. They ran into the bay at Port St. Julian, intending to caulk the ships, leaky after the storms, and take in water before making for the strait. They had to fight for their water, for a party of Indians came down to the shore and shot the *Pelican*'s master gunner through the heart with an arrow. Here at Port St. Julian was discovered a fallen spruce fir that had evidently been used as a gallows. Digging round the base, the men found some bones. There was no doubt whose they were. At this very spot in 1520 Magellan had been faced with Drake's problem. His second-in-command, who held with him a joint commission from the King, had mutinied just as Doughty had done. Magellan had hanged him. Everyone knew the story, and Doughty must have felt it ominous indeed.

Here in this desolate place Thomas Doughty was tried for his life. The indictment was for mutiny and treason. The charge of sorcery was dropped, and proceedings were not taken against John. Nuño da Silva, who spoke English, was present at the trial. He testified on oath before the Inquisition in the following year, after he had been set at liberty, that Doughty at the outset challenged Drake to produce his commission. Da Silva said that Drake read the document aloud to the whole company, and then passed it round for all to see. It was evident, therefore, that he was there by the Queen's authority and by that authority had powers of life and death. He could have executed him out of hand, but he saw the importance of carrying the men with him, and of widening the responsibility. He preferred to give Doughty a fair trial. It was not quite what would be called fair to-day, for Drake was both prosecutor and judge, but it was at least as fair as any trials were at that date. A jury of forty was impanelled, with Captain Winter as foreman, and "the cause was thoroughly heard, and all things done in good order, as near as might be to the course of our laws in England." It was obvious that in a perilous undertaking of this kind, discipline must be maintained, and Drake and the witnesses piled up a great body of evidence of Doughty's incitement to disaffection. Drake was astonished to hear from

Doughty himself that he had told Burghley all about the enterprise in spite of the Queen's prohibition. Drake thought that this proved treason as well. The jury found the prisoner not guilty of treason but guilty of mutiny. Drake alone had the right of sentence, but he asked for the jury's support. "They that think this man worthy of death," he said, "let them with me hold up their hands." All hands went up. Doughty was sentenced to die, not by hanging, but by beheading, the death of a gentleman.

There is no doubt that if Drake could have seen any other alternative he would have taken it. Doughty was his friend. But to take him with them, even under arrest, would not cure the trouble. To put him ashore was equivalent to a death sentence unless the place was inhabited, and then he might imperil the voyage. The success of the undertaking was more important in Drake's eyes than the life of any one man, even a friend. Doughty's death became him better than his life. His end was a gallant one. He is said to have made a full confession. He received the Communion kneeling beside his leader. After they rose from their knees, they embraced, and dined together cere- moniously, pledging each other in wine. Once more Doughty knelt before the silent company of adventurers, but alone. The blade fell. As the head was lifted up, Drake said solemnly, "Lo, this is the end of traitors."

Much has been written about the rights or wrongs of this trial, but when all is said, Drake must remain the best judge of what was necessary in a great emergency. On the next Sunday morning the chaplain administered the Communion to the general and every man in the whole company. Drake told him that he himself would preach the sermon. "Nay, soft, Mr. Fletcher," said he, "I must preach this day myself, although I have small skill in preaching. Well, be all the company here, yea or not?" He then said that there must be no more dissension and jealousy between soldiers and sailors. "We must have these mutinies and discords that are grown amongst us redressed, for by the life of God it doth even take my wits from me to think of it. Here is such controversy between the sailors and the gentlemen, and such stomaching between the gentlemen and sailors, that it doth make me mad to hear it. But, my masters, I must have it left. I must have the gentleman haul and draw with the mariner and the mariner with the gentleman. I would like to know him that would refuse to set his hand to a rope!' He told them where they were going and what they were going to do. If there were any that had no stomach for such an adventure, they could have the *Marigold* and go home. But they must go home, "for if I find them in my way I will surely sink them." This offer met with no response. He reminded them that "there be some here that have deserved as much as Mr. Doughty." He went on to say that the Queen was a party to the voyage, and showed them the bill for the thousand crowns which she had given him. He added she had sworn by her crown that if anyone in her kingdom sent a word to the King of Spain he should lose his head. Then he made an appeal to them to work with him for the honour and glory of England. "And now, my masters, let us consider what we have done. We have set together by the ears three mighty princes, her Majesty, and the Kings of Spain and Portugal. If this voyage shall not have good success, we shall not only be a scorning unto our enemies, but also a great blot to our country for ever; and what triumph would it be to Spain and Portugal!"

He dismissed them to their duties, and that was the end of indiscipline. The black cloud had lifted. *Pelican*, *Elizabeth*, and *Marigold* set sail for the dread strait on 20th August, 1578.

As they entered the strait Drake felt the need for a little ceremony. He gave the order to strike topsails in honour of Her Majesty the Queen. He also paid a compliment to the Queen's Captain of the Guard, Sir Christopher Hatton, by changing the name of his ship from *Pelican* to *Golden Hind*. Hatton's arms were a "hind trippant or". He paraded the men for these ceremonies, and the chaplain read prayers and preached a sermon. There was, of course, a motive behind all this. On his return Drake's position might well be a delicate one. No one knew how the political situation might change while he was away. Burghley would probably be a powerful enemy, and it would be well to have at least one powerful friend at Court.

The channel was intricate, winding and difficult. The ships' boats led the way, with a leadsman in the bows, taking soundings as they went. Frequently the lead found no bottom and therefore no anchorage. "In this strait there be many fair harbours, with store of fresh water, but yet they lack their best commodity: for the water is there of such depth, that no man shall find ground to anchor in, except it be in some narrow river or corner, or between some rocks; so that if any extreme blasts or contrary winds do come (where-

THE GOLDEN HIND

unto the place is much subject) it carrieth with it no small danger." The ships were sometimes faced with a mountainous wall ahead, which on approach resolved itself into a sharp turning. Shut in among these high hills the wind was tricky and came in gusts from unexpected quarters. The foothills near the shore on both sides were covered with trees. Beyond was a range of mountains with their tops veiled in cloud, and above and beyond them again were huge conical snow-covered peaks, many of them smoking volcanoes. The ships came upon an island where there seemed to be a possible landing place. There were plenty of seals there, and the men killed some, but they were particularly impressed by immense flocks of penguins, "fowl which could not fly, of the bigness of geese." In one day they killed three thousand, and salted as many as possible for eating. Surprising as it may seem, they appeared to like them. At least it was a change from the salt beef ration. They only met one tribe of Indians, who were clad in skins, travelled in birch-bark canoes, and used knives made out of mussel shells.

On 6th September, seventeen days after they had entered the strait, the little squadron won through to the Pacific, the South Sea of Drake's prayer in Darien. The very next day, as if the adventurers were to be punished for their temerity, the sky became overcast, fierce squalls snatched savagely at the sails, and rain fell in torrents. Soon the weather became so thick that Drake, peering through the gloom, lost sight of his consorts for ever. They were all quickly under bare poles. No man saw the *Marigold* again. She must have been overwhelmed and have foundered with all hands. Winter in the

Elizabeth was more fortunate. He lost the *Golden Hind* on 8th October, gained the shelter of the strait, and remained near the western end for three weeks, lighting signal fires on shore. He had had enough of those terrible seas. Nothing would make him venture into the Pacific a second time. Evidently the stories were true, and it was next to impossible to get through in safety. No doubt the *Golden Hind* had perished. The rendezvous arranged in the event of separation was in the latitude of Valparaiso, but Winter would not face it and returned home.

As for the men in the *Golden Hind*, they lived in hourly expectation of death, as the ship plunged and wallowed in the enormous waste of waters. The mighty seas would lift her up and up, her bowsprit quivering at the sky. She would tremble, and slip staggering down the slopes, the wind howling through her rigging. At length there came a lull. Drake anchored off shore, but a sudden fresh squall capsized a boatload of eight men, who were lost. Drake had to run for it again. Once more he found it possible to anchor off an island, and managed to obtain fuel and water and some green stuff wherewith to relieve the scurvy that had broken out. But the storms had not yet finished with him. He was blown away again. The *Golden Hind* drifted like a little lonely waif up and down the vast empty seas. Drake was carried far away to the south, and so was made the great discovery of the voyage. Up till now it had been thought that southwards from the Strait of Magellan stretched a vast southern continent, Terra Australis. No one dreamt that Atlantic met Pacific round the Horn. Yet here he was in open sea over the edge of the known world. On 28th October, the storm having at last died down, Drake with Fletcher the chaplain landed at the southernmost point of the southernmost island. Drake flung himself down on the earth with his arms outstretched as if embracing it. They set up a stone and carved thereon the Queen's name and the date.

Drake sailed northwards up the coast of southern Chile, with its innumerable islands, making for the meeting place, for he had still a hope of finding the foundered *Marigold* and the *Elizabeth*, now homeward bound. Somewhere about latitude 38° he anchored off the island of Mocha, in the hope of obtaining some water, of which he was in great need. A boat's crew went ashore and made arrangements with the Indians, after exchanging presents, to fetch some water on the following day. Drake himself went with the water party the next morning. Two men had waded ashore from the boat, and were trundling some barrels up the beach, when a flight of arrows whirring out of the blue pattered down among them. The two men dropped dead on the sand, the rest hastily unshipped their oars and got under way. Every man had been hit, Drake himself being hurt in the face.

The only thing to be done was to go on to Valparaiso, no great city then, but merely a small settlement. Outside, the adventurers picked up an Indian, fishing in a canoe, and persuaded him to pilot them into the harbour. Their anchor splashed into the water near a ship of about their own size, with the resounding name of *Grand Captain of the South*. Her officer of the watch naturally supposed the newcomer to be a friendly Spanish ship. He hailed the grimly smiling English and asked some of them to come aboard and have a drink. In response to this invitation a boat was lowered. Tom Moon and a party put off and clambered on board in silence. Tom was a man like Salvation Yeo in *Westward Ho!* He could not abide a Spaniard, and had a great contempt for them. Striding up to the nearest, he growled out, "Get down, dog!" in Spanish, and with his fist knocked the astonished man off his feet. The English did not use any weapons, but laid about them with their fists. One Spaniard jumped overboard and swam to land. The remaining few were guarded until the cargo of gold and wine had been transferred to the *Golden Hind*. Meanwhile Drake and his men pulled for the shore in order to help themselves to water, victuals, and anything else that took their fancy. They were heartily tired of salt penguin. Drake's simple Protestantism had scant respect for Roman Catholics or their property. They brought back a chalice for the use of their own chaplain, and a great crucifix set with emeralds as prize. The prisoners were put ashore, the friendly Indian was given a present and landed near his home, and the *Grand Captain* was towed out to sea and there set adrift with all sails set.

Further north, at Coquimbo, near the modern town of La Serena, they again had trouble over obtaining fresh water. It was an ever-present source of danger and difficulty. They only had storage for a limited supply, and the water would not keep sweet for any length of time. It was most annoying constantly to have to fight for it. Drake provided an armed guard over the men whose job it was to fill the barrels. No sooner had they fairly begun than a large body of Spanish horsemen came galloping down towards the beach. Richard Minivy who was in charge of the guard, withdrew all the men to the boat. To check the rush, he fired his arquebuse at the Spaniards, who returned his fire and shot him through the head. Drake naturally did not want and could not afford to lose men every time he got water. Afterwards he made it a practice to take a prisoner where possible, and find out from him where water could be had without molestation.

The voyagers still crept northwards along the coast, close in, watching all the time for a chance of any water, and with eyes wide open for loot. There was a wharf at Tarapacá, empty and deserted save for a sentry asleep in the sunshine beside a pile of silver bars. A boatload landed. They tip-toed up to avoid waking him, but as they stooped to lift the silver he tried to scramble to his feet. A brown hand was on his shoulder, another was placed over his mouth. They apologized for waking him, but since they had done so, they would remove his charge so that, his responsibility ended, he could go to sleep again. Drake was at his old games once more. One day they saw a Spaniard driving some llamas laden with silver. A party promptly landed and intercepted the little convoy. It pained them, they said, to see a Spanish señor obliged to do such work. Might they act as drovers in his place? He could trust them to see that the silver was stowed safely away. Speechless with rage, he watched them drive the llamas down to their boat. They even robbed hen-roosts, for poultry and eggs. Nothing was safe from their marauding hands. They captured and emptied two small ships at Arica. Drake smelt treasure in a ship at Arequipa, but the rumour of his presence had preceded him. He boarded the ship, but the crew had vanished, and so had the treasure. Drake ripped out a string of oaths in English and Spanish, and set the ship adrift on the open sea.

He arrived at Lima in Peru on the night of 15th February, 1579. He had heard that John Oxenham was still a prisoner in Lima awaiting execution. Lima was a large and important town, and to attack it was quite impossible. But he had a daring idea. He entered the harbour in the dark, anchored, and then went round in a pinnace, cutting the cables of the various craft lying there. He hoped that the wind and tide would carry them outside, where they could be held to ransom in order to effect a rescue. Unfortunately the wind died away, and the ships were found to be empty. The vessel that was berthed alongside the *Golden Hind* was from Panama. They seized her with the loss of a man, and her crew took to their boats. The tide took her and the *Golden Hind* out of port, but Drake had to abandon her, for two armed vessels came up as if to fight. They thought better of it, however, and did not come within range. Drake smiled to himself and went north.

Somehow near Lima he had heard that a large galleon named *Nuestra Señora de la Concepcion* had just left for Panama with a cargo of silver and gold from the mines of Peru. He was sure he could overhaul her long before she reached her destination, and he gave chase. On the way he overtook another Spanish ship. Drake's name for a prize was "a little comfortable dew from heaven," and if heaven would let fall its dew upon him, he could not turn aside to avoid it. So he ransacked her. He took some gold and a considerable quantity of food and drink. One of Drake's gentlemen volunteers asked the Spanish captain whose flag it was that he flew from his mainmast. He replied that it was the arms of his most Catholic Majesty the King of Spain. Whereupon he was told to haul it down. Drake interrupted to say it could remain where it was, he was not keeping the ship. While the cargo was being transferred, a mulatto boy clerk was questioned as to whether there was any more gold hidden away. He denied that there was, but a negro said that the denial was false. It is recorded that Drake "hanged" the lad. The word has been misunderstood. What actually happened is clear from the boy's own subsequent deposition before the Inquisition. He was suspended from the yard arm, dropped into the sea, fished out by a boat, and put aboard his ship. This was a rough though not uncommon punishment. Drake, though he could be rough, was only once known to have killed prisoners. At San Domingo in 1586, in a furious burst of rage, he hanged two friars as a reprisal for the murder of his messenger.

Drake crowded on all sail to overtake *Our Lady of the Conception*, which was generally known on the coast as the *Cacafuego*, or *Spitfire*. He promised a gold chain to the man who first sighted her. In the heat of the afternoon of 1st March, 1579, arose the cry of "Sail ho!" The young eyes of Drake's page John had won for him the chain. It was off Cape San Francisco, forty miles north of the Equator, that the *Cacafuego* was overtaken. Here was a high white cliff, clothed with tall trees, and backed by the lofty peaks of the Andes, in full view from the sea. The Spanish captain was a man named San Juan de Anton. The Pacific was considered to be the private ocean of King Philip of Spain, and the *Concepcion*, in spite of her immensely valuable cargo, was unarmed and carried no guns. De Anton's bewildered astonishment was profound when the unsuspected stranger came up and summoned him to surrender in the name of the Queen of England. A voice hailed him in Spanish, "Strike sail, Señor San Juan de Anton, strike sail, or be sent to the bottom." De Anton angrily replied, "Who are you? Come and strike the sails yourselves." Drake blew his whistle, a trumpet sounded. The gunner fired a shot that brought down de Anton's mizzen-mast and a flight of arrows rattled on the Spaniard's deck. A swarm of armed Englishmen clambered on board her. The crew and passengers, having no means of resistance, were quickly made prisoners. De Anton, who was slightly wounded by an arrow, was taken into the *Golden Hind* to have his hurt dressed. Drake put his arm round him and said, "Have patience, for such is the fortune of war," telling him he was to be treated as a guest at Drake's own table while his ship was being emptied. The other prisoners were well treated also, and "were allowed to tell their Christian beads as they were accustomed to do." They ran on before the wind till it grew calmer, and the two ships lay side by side gently lifting to the long ocean swell. An enormous treasure of jewels, pearls, gold and silver was transferred and stowed in the hold of the *Golden Hind*. As a Spanish boy remarked, the *Spitfire* was spitting silver. The English ship was ballasted with it. Before de Anton and the other prisoners were put in possession of their rifled vessel Drake wrote to Winter whom he still believed might be on this coast, instructing him not to harm the *Concepcion* nor her company, and handed the letter to de Anton.

The *Golden Hind* was glutted with treasure. Drake's private wrongs were by now fully paid for in cash, and the insults to the Queen were avenged in a way she would appreciate. The problem before him was how to get his precious ship safely home. Bound up with his problem was the fact that his main work was yet to do, namely, to "find good land for settlement in the Queen's name." He had no thought of returning the way he had come. Even if he had wished to do so, it was out of the question, since, apart from the terrible stormy weather encountered in those latitudes, he would almost certainly be intercepted by an armed Spanish squadron. He must go north. So northwards he sailed, till one day in April 1579 he seized a small vessel of 60 tons, homeward bound to Panama from the China Seas. The captain of this ship, Don Francisco de Xararte, was a nobleman of good family. Drake received him in his cabin with every courtesy, bade him be seated, and then said bluntly, "I am a friend of those that tell me the truth, but with those who do not I get out of humour. Therefore you must tell me, how much silver and gold does your ship carry?" De Xararte answered: "None. The cargo is principally silks and porcelain." Drake then asked, "Do you know Don Martin Enriquez, Viceroy of New Spain?" De Xararte knew the ancient enemy of Hawkins and Drake very well. Drake grimly remarked, "It would give me a greater joy to come across him than all the gold and silver of the Indies. You would see how the words of gentlemen should be kept." De Xararte had naturally no reply to make to this.

When the trumpets sounded for dinner de Xararte was seated at Drake's right hand.

A letter written by de Xararte to Don Martin is still in existence. It gives a vivid picture of life in the *Golden Hind*. "He is called Francisco Drac, and is a man about 35 years of age, low of stature, with a fair beard, and is one of the greatest mariners that sails the seas, both as navigator and as a commander. He carries with him nine or ten cavaliers, cadets of noble English houses. He is served on silver dishes with gold borders and gilded garlands, in which are his arms. He carries all possible dainties and perfumed waters, many of them given him by the Queen. None of his gentlemen took a seat or covered his head before him, until he repeatedly urged him to do so. . . . I managed to ascertain whether the General was well-liked, and all said that they adored him. . . . He showed me the commissions that he received from the Queen and carried." Drake told de Xararte the tale of the execution of Thomas Doughty, "speaking much good about the dead man, but adding that he had not been able to act otherwise, because this was what the Queen's service demanded." The Spaniard noted that Nuño da Silva was seated at dinner, as also was John Doughty, who appeared to be "under surveillance." The young men who dined with Drake formed his council, which he always consulted, "though he takes advice from no one." De Xararte also observed that discipline was strict, and that the arms were perfectly kept. He was told that if the King of Spain would give leave to the English to trade in the Indies and on the Main there would be peace, but if not, the English would come and help themselves in the Atlantic and the Pacific too.

After three days in the *Golden Hind* de Xararte and his crew were given their empty ship in which to sail away, with much bowing and ceremony.

Ten days later Drake called at a small place called Guatulco for water and victuals. To ensure that these were obtained in safety, Drake sent the boatswain, a pock-marked little man with a scanty fair beard, in command of a raiding party to obtain hostages. The English sailors marched into the court of justice, which was sitting, carried off magistrates, witnesses and prisoners, and dumped them all on board while they ransacked the town. They did not spare the church, where, so the Spaniards complained, they broke up some images. The Vicar and Factor of Guatulco were among those who made an unwilling stay in the *Golden Hind*. They both gave evidence afterwards before the Inquisition, as did da Silva, who was put ashore here. The Vicar said that he had refused to eat meat as it was the season of Lent, and was given fish. The Factor described the prayers in the cabin, the sermon, the reading from Foxe's *Book of Martyrs*, and the music and hornpipe afterwards, which the Factor evidently thought was part of the service. When all was done, Drake turned to the worthy Factor. "You will be saying now: This man is a devil, who robs by day and prays by night." "Señor," mumbled the embarrassed Factor, who had been saying to himself that very thing. "Well, I do," said Drake, "but just as your Viceroy, Don Martin Enriquez, is commissioned as Governor and is instructed by the King of Spain, so my Sovereign Lady has sent me here, and the responsibility is hers."

During this spring of 1579 Drake pushed further north-westward along the coast of North America.

It is probable that he never had any serious intention of seeking the passage round by the Arctic Ocean. If he had any such idea he quickly abandoned it, for near Vancouver he turned south once more, to seek a more genial climate. He finally anchored in Drake's Bay, near where the modern city of San Francisco now stands. The Indians came down to the shore with presents of tobacco and skins. The red men made deep obeisance, and the women set up a loud screaming and wailing, tearing at their breasts with their fingernails. Drake and his seamen were shocked when they gradually realised that they were being treated as gods. They promptly held a prayer meeting, judging that their kneeling attitudes would rid the Indians of such a horrible idea. Gods or not, they were certainly not going to run any more risks with Indians, and they built a stockade in which they camped while ashore, and where they could store some of their cargo while they caulked their leaky ship. Relations remained friendly, and one day the whole tribe assembled for a solemn palaver. Drake was present. After some very lengthy and quite unintelligible speechmaking on the part of the chief, Drake was hailed as Great Chief, and a feather head-dress was placed upon his head. It was all very gratifying and amusing. Drake on his part made a speech equally unintelligible to the Indians. He accepted the crown in the name of the Queen's most excellent Majesty, and set up a post on which he carved the date and to which he affixed a sixpenny piece with the Queen's head on it. He had found a goodly land, and he named it Nova Albion, "for two causes: the one in respect of the white banks and cliffs which lie towards the sea, and the other, because it might have some affinity with our country in name, which sometime was so called." No white man had ever set foot on it, no Spaniard could claim it, and the natives were friendly. On his return Drake asked the Queen if he could be Governor of a colony there. The Queen agreed, but the project remained a dream. The expedition never started. Drake was needed to fight the King of Spain, whose purposes were casting a shadow over England. A cross now stands overlooking the Golden Gate to commemorate the first Christian service in the English tongue held on this coast by Francis Fletcher, Drake's chaplain.

It was almost autumn before the pioneers left those happy shores. They wandered wearily over the wide Pacific for two whole months out of sight of land. At length they came to the Pellew Islands, and in the middle of November 1579 to the Moluccas. These islands had been held by the Portuguese, but the Sultan of the Island of Ternate had ejected them, and it was to him that Drake went. The Sultan and his court embarked in great galleys, the rowers keeping time with a gong. As they approached the *Golden Hind*, she fired a salute and the trumpets sounded a welcome. The galleys took her in tow to the inner harbour, while the ship's musicians played. Drake bought sugar-cane, rice, sago, plantains, cloves and pepper. The Sultan announced his intention of holding a durbar. Drake's gentlemen adventurers begged him not to go ashore yet. There might be foul play, and in any case a certain aloofness and apparent inaccessibility were desirable. All went well, however, and those that attended the durbar were lavishly entertained. The end of all this feasting and ceremony was that the Sultan gave Drake as the representative of the Queen a monopoly of the spice trade with the island. In itself the concession was not very valuable. Ternate was a mere speck in the vast East Indian archipelago, but the treaty acted as a spur and an encouragement to others, and was the first step towards the British Empire of the East. After it was all over, Drake sailed away to a little isle to the southward of the Celebes where the crew scraped weeds and barnacles from the hull of the ship. Here in the palm-trees "night by night did show themselves an infinite swarm of fiery worms flying in the air," bats "as big as large hens," and land-crabs, which "dig themselves holes in the earth like conies."

Once more they sailed over uncharted seas. In the night of 9th January, 1580, the ship was running before the wind, when with a shock that threw the watch off their feet, and with a scraping tearing sound, she struck fast upon a reef. By God's special providence, so they said, and by reason of the stout sheathing, the good ship did not spring a leak. But the mariners were in dire peril. They took soundings only to find no bottom where an anchor might be cast to warp them off. There they were, fast on the coral reef on the port side, while the wind blowing from the opposite quarter kept the ship upright. What would happen when the wind dropped? Would she remain on the reef or would she capsize? There were fifty-eight men on board, and their boats held twenty. The nearest shore was seven leagues away, and if cast away there they would have a poor chance of survival. The chaplain administered the Sacrament, and then, on the principle that heaven helps those that help themselves, they heaved overboard some of their guns and their bags and bales of spices. On a sudden the wind dropped. The ship heeled over and slid off into deep water.

They called at Java, and leaving the islands, set out boldly across the Indian Ocean. They did not touch anywhere till they reached the Guinea Coast. This was one of the most remarkable feats of a memorable voyage. Drake's pluck and resolution must have been great, and his discipline wonderful. The mariners sighted no land until on 18th June, 1580, they reached the Cape of Good Hope with the stately Table Mountain rising up over the sea, "the fairest cape we saw in the whole circumference of the earth." On the morning of 3rd November, when the trees of the island were flaming red and gold, the *Golden Hind* entered Plymouth Sound, "her storms forgot, her weary watches past." The bells of St. Andrew's pealed merrily all day.

Boats put out to meet the ship that had gone out as the *Pelican* with a squadron, and returned as the *Golden Hind* alone. Torrents of broad Devonshire talk flowed between the men in the boats and the happy excited crew lining the rails. Drake's first question was whether his wife and the Queen were alive and well. If the Queen were dead, the Catholic party might be in power with a Catholic on the throne, Mary Queen of Scots for all he knew. In this event he would be in as great peril as he was when on the rocks among the islands. In any case, no one could answer for the Queen's moods. Suppose she were to repudiate him? Having a rich treasure, Drake held good cards, but his relief was considerable when a messenger rode down to Plymouth with the command for him to come to London and tell his tale, "with some samples of his labours." Drake loaded seven pack-horses with the pick of the loot, and with a strong guard set out along the miry trail for the capital.

The Queen learnt that her share of the treasure was £160,000 in the values of that day. There was no argument like this, no other was necessary. She made up her mind what to do. Everybody was singing Drake's praises. Ballads and broadsheets about him were everywhere. She would set the seal on his popularity in her own dramatic way. Meanwhile she gave instructions for the plunder to be brought to London, and wrote secretly to Tremayne, a justice of the peace at Plymouth, to hand Drake £10,000 for himself, and to pay off the adventurers and the crew.

The Spanish Ambassador was furious at Drake's return, and more so because he apparently was not going to be sacrificed. The Ambassador brought a formal accusation of piracy and murder against Drake. In the official inquiry that was held the whole ship's company swore that no ships were sunk with their crews, as alleged, that not a single Spaniard had been killed, and only one, de Anton, wounded. Of him the greatest care had been taken. As for piracy, there were two sides to that question. The Queen told the Ambassador that "the use of the sea and air is common to all, as neither nature nor public use permitteth any possession thereof." If the King of Spain tried to close the seas, he must expect the entrance to be forced. The *Golden Hind* was taken to Deptford. On 4th April, 1581, the Queen defied the King of Spain and flouted his Ambassador. She was entertained by Drake to a banquet on board. Afterwards on deck in the presence of the French and Spanish Ambassadors she bade him kneel before her. A stir passed through the multitude of Londoners who had come down the river to see the show. "The King of Spain has demanded your head," she said, "I have here a gilded sword with which to strike it off." But he was struck on the shoulder with the flat of the sword, and arose knight. Mendoza, the Ambassador of Spain, was disgusted that this "master thief of the unknown world," as he called him, should receive a signal honour at the hands of his Sovereign. "Matters may come to the cannon," he said. The Queen rose at him. "Another threat of that kind," she replied, "and I'll fling you into a dungeon."

.   .   .   .   .

Drake had made history. He had done much to help the release of men's minds, and he was bound to have imitators. During this reign only one man was successful in sailing round the world in his wake. He was Thomas Cavendish. Drake's adventure had in it the quality of drama, and is distinguished by his masterful and attractive personality. Cavendish was merely a soldier of fortune. His progress round the world was marked by a trail of wanton destruction. The political situation had changed. There was now practically open war between England and Spain, and King Philip's mighty Armada was being prepared for England's subjugation. Cavendish's privateering expedition was, therefore, justifiable by the laws of war, but his story has not the gaiety and light-heartedness of Drake's. Rather it is a heavy tale of burnings and spoliation, though it is to his credit that he followed Drake's example in releasing and victualling his prisoners. At the same time his voyage was a very great achievement, especially for one so young. At the age of twenty-six he was the general of three ships for this expedition, and before that he had commanded a ship in Sir Richard Grenville's Virginia venture, which began as a colonising voyage and ended in freebooting.

Thomas Cavendish was born in 1560 in Suffolk. He was of good family and some wealth. Englishmen were breaking out of their island cage, and roaming the world over in search of gold, of trade, and of honour. It was becoming the fashion for young men of wealth to fit out an expedition to attack the Spanish in the New World, and Cavendish was eager to cross swords with England's enemy. He bore all the expense of the venture. Three ships formed his squadron, the *Desire*, admiral, of 120 tons, the *Content*, of 60 tons, and the *Hugh Gallant*, a "bark" of 40 tons, all victualled for two years for a company of 123 men of all ranks and ratings.

On 21st July, 1586, a crowd of well-wishers watched the brave little ships go gliding out to sea from Plymouth, that gateway to adventure, till they were swallowed up in the grey Atlantic mists. They ran along the coast of West Africa until they reached Sierra Leone at the end of August. Cavendish landed with about seventy men and plundered the mud-walled town, burning two or three huts and suffering three or four casualties from arrows. This was the first and most inexcusable instance of wanton damage. It is not surprising that a few days afterwards when some men were washing their shirts at the watering place they were ambushed by negroes, and lost a soldier killed by a poisoned arrow and many wounded, before they reached their boats. The adventurers crossed the Atlantic

without incident, and on the last day of October
they saw the glorious natural harbour of Rio de
Janeiro with its fantastic hills. Near here by the
island of San Sebastian they landed and remained
three weeks, setting up a forge, making iron hoops
for their water-casks, and building a pinnace.
Southwards still they went into the country of sea
lions and penguins, and Indians still in the Stone
Age, with flint-headed arrows and stone burial
places on the hill tops, such as are seen on Dartmoor
and indeed all over the wilder parts of England.
On 6th January, 1587, they entered the Strait of
Magellan.

Drake's incursion into the Pacific had thoroughly
alarmed the Viceroy of Peru. He had dispatched
Don Pedro de Sarmiento with an armed squadron
to the Strait of Magellan to intercept the Englishman on his return and take him dead or alive. But
Drake went home the other way. In view of the
obvious need to fortify the strait a party of four
hundred colonists was sent out from Spain three
years before Cavendish arrived. They built a town
with four forts, with a gun in each. They sited it
in the best place in the strait for fuel and water, but
the food supply was altogether inadequate. The
supply from home was soon exhausted, they could
get nothing to grow in that severe climate, they were
constantly raided by Indians. Sarmiento had sailed
for Spain for further supplies, but was taken
prisoner on the way and carried into England. The
wretched colonists died miserably of famine, the
survivors being too weak to bury the dead. Cavendish found only twenty-one men and two women
alive. They were just managing to exist on mussels
and limpets, roots and leaves, and occasionally a

bird if they were fortunate enough to shoot one. Cavendish appears to have done nothing to succour them, save one, whom he took with him. They were Spaniards, and he left them to their fate.

The voyagers had the same experiences in the strait as Drake's men. They watched the green seas racing up the black hill-sides to fall back again in white cataracts of foam. They were oppressed by the huge snow-covered mountains rising tier upon tier above them. They were baffled by the contrary gusts and gales, and drenched with continual rain, "most vile and filthy foul weather." On 24th February they came through to the Pacific. They encountered storms as Drake had done. The little *Hugh Gallant* suffered most. She seemed to be leaking in every seam, groaning and complaining as she rolled in the furious running seas. She survived, and met the others at an island off Arauco on the coast of Chile. Here they found storehouses full of wheat, barley, maize, potatoes and dried fish. They helped themselves to whatever they needed including a supply of pigs and chickens.

The squadron put into a bay near Valparaiso and remained there some time, till on 1st April, 1587, twelve men were lost in action with the Spaniards. The Englishmen were filling their barrels with water at a pit a quarter of a mile inland, when a large body of horsemen swooped down and killed or captured a dozen men. A party of about fifteen English soldiers came running up with their arquebuses and rescued the remainder. After an hour's skirmish the Spaniards retired with many empty saddles. The casualty list is given in the English narrative. It shows that the men came from all over the country, from London, Newcastle,

Norfolk, Gloucestershire, Dorset, Devon and Cornwall.

At Arica the English took one or two small prizes
and burnt an empty galleon, but the town was too
strong to be attacked. The little *Hugh Gallant* captured a galleon of 300 tons, but abandoned her as
there was nothing worth having aboard. The rest
of the squadron took two ships, laden with sugar,
maize, wheatmeal, marmalade (then a preserve
made of quinces) and a number of hen-coops full of
live fowls. The cargo was picked over, the ships
were burnt, and the crew and passengers set on
shore. The town of Paita in Peru was burnt. A
landing was made on the rich and fruitful Puna
Island near Guayaquil. It is about the size of the
Isle of Wight. The inhabitants of the town had all
fled on the arrival of the English, who occupied the
palace of the cacique or overlord of the island. The
cacique was a native, married to a Spanish lady,
and his palace was a magnificent building. Near it
was a great church which Cavendish burnt. There
seems no excuse for this act. It was only possible in
times of religious animosity.

Foraging parties set out all over the island for
fruit, sheep, goats, or anything else procurable. A
company of one hundred Spanish soldiers, with
Indian auxiliaries, landed from Guayaquil, met one
of these parties, and by their superior numbers
forced the English back to their boats after a stubborn fight. The English lost nine killed and three
taken prisoners. The same day seventy armed men
went ashore, and attacking resolutely scattered the
Spanish force. Thereupon they burnt the town and
four galleons building on the stocks, and devastated
the fields, orchards and gardens. After this exhibi-

tion of frightfulness the *Hugh Gallant* was broken up, and the *Desire* and *Content* sailed on northwards.

By 27th July the English had reached Guatulco in Mexico, after burning numerous ships. They sacked and fired the town, church, and custom house. They still went north, burning and plundering. Near Cape San Lucas in latitude 23°, between seven and eight o'clock in the morning, the *Desire's* trumpeter, who was aloft in the maintop, shouted, "A sail, a sail!" Great was the excitement, bustle, and rejoicing. Cavendish ordered the *Desire* to be cleared for action, and gave chase for three or four hours to the enemy vessel. It proved to be a King's ship, the *Santa Anna* of 700 tons. She was a large high-built galleon, and the *Desire* was only 120 tons. But the *Desire* had heavy guns, the *Santa Anna's* were light and few. Yet with more rashness than wisdom, Cavendish laid his ship alongside and gave the order to board. The men began to swarm up the sides of the galleon, but the Spaniard hurled great stones (probably brought up from the ballast) on their heads and they were forced to retire to their own ship with two men killed and five wounded. Cavendish then did what he ought to have done at first. He raked the *Santa Anna's* hull with his heavier guns, and swept her decks with small shot. She was holed under water and had many men slain. After some hours battering, she hoisted the white flag. Cavendish promised to spare the Spaniards' lives, and ordered the captain and navigator to come aboard. The passengers and crew, numbering 190 persons, were put on shore, where there was fuel, fresh water, and food available. They were given a good supply of victuals, some wine, their sails for tents and planks to make a boat, also some arms and powder and shot. Then the English began to load their ships with the *Santa Anna*'s cargo. Cavendish had some trouble with the men concerning the share-out of the pillage, especially with those in the *Content*, which had taken no part in the fight. There was gold to the value of 122,000 pesos, silks, satins, damasks, choice food and wines. When all was transferred, Cavendish set the *Santa Anna* ablaze.

On 14th January, 1588 the ships came to the Philippines after a good ocean passage. Cavendish had taken a Portuguese named Nicolas Roderigo, and Thomas de Essola, a Spanish pilot, from the *Santa Anna* and had brought them along with him. The Portuguese slyly came to Cavendish with the news that the Spaniard had written a letter warning the inhabitants of Manila of Cavendish's depredations and of his proximity. To the English captain this brave act was treachery, and the next day saw the Spaniard swinging from the yardarm. The voyagers touched at Java, where they did some trade with the natives, who were very friendly, and in nine weeks reached the Cape of Good Hope without incident. St. Helena was their next port of call. The island was used by the Portuguese as a re-victualling station, and these Englishmen used it in like manner. Home came ever nearer.

"The third of September we met with a Flemish hulk which came from Lisbon, and declared unto us the overthrowing of the Spanish Fleet,[1] to the singular rejoicing and comfort of us all.

"The 9 of September, after a terrible tempest which carried away most part of our sails, by the merciful favour of the Almighty we recovered our long wished port of Plymouth in England, from

[1] The Armada.

whence we set forth at the beginning of our voyage."

According to a Spanish account, Cavendish "arrived at London with his sails made of green damask and all his sailors dressed in silk, to the general delight of that city." He made his last voyage in 1591. Like the last voyages of Hawkins, Drake and Raleigh, it ended in disaster and death. "Boastful and brave, careless of others, unflinching, unrelenting, unforgiving, Cavendish has yet that intensity and wholeness of purpose which is the pith and marrow of great deeds."[1]

There is a long list of gallant failures to be set off against the conspicuous successes of the Elizabethan adventurers. In 1589 a Mr. John Chudleigh took three tall ships and two pinnaces, with over 400 men, as far as the Strait of Magellan, with the intention of raiding the province of Arauco in Chile. While crossing the Atlantic the smallest of the three, the *Delight* of Bristol, lost the other two and never saw them again. These two, the *Wild Man* and the *White Lion*,[2] reached the strait, but lost the general and a great number beside through sickness. The survivors sailed for home. The *Delight* also reached the strait, but she suffered so many casualties by storm, sickness and other mishaps that she also had to turn back. The *Delight* left Plymouth with a crew of 91 men. Only six were alive by the time she entered the English Channel. She was wrecked and lost on the rocks near Cherbourg.

Yet another attempt at a voyage round the world (perhaps the most interesting of all) is that of

[1] *The English Voyages of the Sixteenth Century* (Walter Raleigh).
[2] The names of some of the ships of this period look like inn signs. The reason is that the names were descriptive of the coats of arms of the owners, just as the inn signs bear the arms of the local magnate.

Richard Hawkins, the gallant, accomplished, and lovable son of Sir John Hawkins. He had sailed with Drake to the West Indies in 1585 in command of a small vessel, the *Duck*, and was captain of the *Swallow* in the Armada fight.

After that memorable event, Richard, like Drake and many others, was eager to take advantage of the victory. At once, with his father's help and advice, he prepared for a voyage through the Strait of Magellan to Japan, China, and the East Indies, a voyage mainly to gain information about new markets. A ship was accordingly built in the Thames of about 350 tons. His father's second wife asked to be allowed to name her. She was a religious-minded lady, and called this new, swift and beautiful ship, *Repentance*. Richard protested that it was an unlucky sort of name to give a ship, but she replied that repentance was the safest ship one could sail in to purchase the haven of heaven. The Queen, however, would have none of this. Going down the river in her barge from Whitehall to Greenwich Palace, she caught sight of the bright new craft at anchor at Deptford. Her bargemen were ordered to row round the ship. "I dislike nothing but her name," said the Queen. "I will christen her anew. Henceforth she shall be called *Dainty*."

The voyage was postponed for various reasons, the *Dainty* meanwhile being sent to Burgh's expedition against the Portuguese carracks. It was not until the spring of 1593 that Richard was ready to leave the Port of London for his home port Plymouth. He had engaged a crew, and had loaded the *Dainty* for a long cruise with provisions for three ships, save for the beef, pork, biscuit and cider, which he knew he could purchase more cheaply in Plymouth.

She was deeply laden and rather low in the water, and was very nearly sunk on her way to Barking, where Richard joined her. The wind freshening suddenly, she had heeled over with her ports open. Water poured in. She was nearly gone, and it was only with great difficulty that she was restored to an even keel. Ships were not infrequently lost in this way. A famous instance was the *Mary Rose*, Henry the Eighth's great ship, which went to the bottom with her captain and crew at Portsmouth on a summer afternoon.

Richard had said farewell, a last farewell had he known it, to his father in London, and thought it worth while to send a messenger on horseback to him to announce his own arrival at Plymouth, which he reached on 26th April. He had only taken thirteen days from London River, an almost incredible speed considering the contrary winds. It was made possible by skilful use of the tides and by the fact that "the *Dainty* was a very good sea ship and excellent by the wind." His other two vessels, both his own property, were the *Hawk*, which he intended to use as a store ship and abandon somewhere off Brazil, and the *Fancy*, a pinnace.

It always seems to have been a lengthy business to get these sailing ships away, but by the end of May Richard was ready to set his sails to a favourable breeze. His ships were in the Sound, he was whistling for a wind. A wind came, but westerly. It grew into a gale. Richard instructed the master of the *Dainty*, a first-class seaman named Hugh Cornish, to bring her into the Cattewater, under the lee of Mount Batten. The *Dainty*, however, broke the fluke of her anchor. Cornish let fall another, but she began to drive. Then the mainmast went overboard. This saved her. If she had driven another ship's length she would have been cast away on the rocks, a fate which befell the pinnace. More time was spent re-masting the *Dainty* and salving the pinnace. Richard had to put his hand rather deeply into his pocket, but he was quite undaunted by delay and misfortune. At length came the time for good-bye to "my friends, and my dearest friend, my second self," his wife.

It took Richard, his officers, and the justices of the town, two days to round up the seamen from the taverns, lodging-houses and ale-houses. This was not unusual. Waiting in idleness breeds trouble. Some were so drunk that they had to be carried aboard, some were in debt and had pawned their clothing and equipment, some had spent their imprest-money[1] and then tried to hide. He got most of them together, and at long last hoisted sail on a sunny afternoon, 12th June, 1593. All Plymouth turned out upon the Hoe to see him off, because of the love which he and his family had always borne for their native town. He sailed in close to the height, his trumpets sounding. The ship's band played popular airs. Then all his guns spoke in farewell. The town band struck up a lively tune, the shore batteries answered the salute. In the bright evening air the cheers of the townsfolk floated out across the water. The light breeze took the sails. The cheering was still faintly in the ears of the sailors as darkness fell upon the quiet sea.

Next morning the wind got up, blowing hard, east by south, with a choppy sea. The *Hawk* had to put back, as the caulkers had left a seam uncaulked. This piece of carelessness was enough to have sunk

[1] A bounty given on enlistment.

179

the ship. The favourable wind continued. In the Bay they sighted a foreign vessel, came up alongside and hailed her. She was from Denmark, homeward bound from Spain with a cargo of salt. She showed her charter-parties and bills of lading, "and then saluted us as in the manner of the sea and so departed." The adventurers sailed on past Madeira, past the tall cone of Tenerife, covered with snow, on to Cape Blanco. The crews, as usual, were divided into starboard and larboard watches. Each of the three days available to each watch was set aside for some duty, such as the cleaning of arms, making of sails and netting, or washing or mending clothes. Their reckoning was badly at fault, for they were nearly aground in shallow water off the Guinea Coast. Fortunately Richard noticed the change in the colour of the water just in time.

When close to the Line the men began to fall sick of the scurvy. The diet of salt meat without fresh fruit and vegetables, together with the foul darkness between decks and the lack of ventilation, made this scourge inevitable. Every day men died. During this period Richard had other anxieties to face. Fire in those days was an ever-present peril. The carpenter had caulked with oakum a seam in the deck which had opened with the heat. He asked leave to make hot a pot of pitch on the galley fire, which was as usual below decks. Not without some misgiving permission was given. The misgiving was justified. The pitch boiled over into the fire with a furious flame. One of the crew with a double pair of gloves caught hold of the pitch pot, but the heat made him drop it on the hearth. The blazing pitch ran in all directions, and in a moment the ship was on fire. Flames roared up to the deck. Death by fire or drowning faced them all. Richard ordered everyone to wet his cloak[1] in the sea, and to try and smother the fire with them. It was a desperate chance, but they succeeded, not without many burns. Many another gallant ship had flared into destruction with less cause.

In thankfulness for their deliverance, they determined to abolish swearing at sea. A cane was produced and handed to anyone that swore. He could pass it on to anybody else he heard swearing. Whoever held the cane at prayer-time received three strokes with it on the palm of his hand from the captain or master. This terrific self-denial was very successful for a time. How long it lasted is not known.

About the end of October, the squadron made the port of Victoria in Brazil. They were in a serious plight. In the three ships there were not more than twenty-five sound men. Fresh food for the sick was urgently needed. There was no choice. They must make the best terms they could with the Governor. Richard wrote a diplomatic letter asking for victuals and offering payment, and sent it ashore under a flag of truce. While the letter was going a few miles inland to the Governor, the crews bought some oranges and lemons from the country folk. The Governor's reply was courteous but firm. Richard was reminded that a state of war existed, was forbidden to come ashore, and given three days to depart. He went.

Richard had in the *Dainty* a plant for distilling water, similar probably to that which can be seen in the *Victory* at Portsmouth. It was extremely

---

[1] Rug gowns, or cloaks, had been provided by Richard for the cold night-watches.

valuable, and eked out the supply of fresh water. The voyagers found some islands where they could water, not far from where Rio de Janeiro now stands. Here they caught fish and young gannets, made salads and found fruits. Nevertheless, Richard had already lost half his crews. He determined to burn the *Hawk*, his victualling ship. When off the River Plate a sudden squall arose, and the pinnace *Fancy* disappeared. Richard gave her up for lost, but years afterwards discovered she had deserted and gone home, in the same way that Winter had done on Drake's expedition.

In due course the *Dainty* came to Port St. Julian of sinister memory, and with a good following wind entered the Strait of Magellan. Here the adventurers' experiences were much the same as those of Drake and Cavendish, except that work was lightened by two days ashore which were spent in wrestling and shooting matches between bachelors and married men. They were almost cast away in the narrow and mountainous part of the strait owing to the sudden and uncertain gusts, but eventually they won through and ran north along the coast of Chile.

They swooped upon the town of Valparaiso, and plundered several ships and the warehouses by the waterside. The result was that they departed with the *Dainty* as well stored and victualled as when she left England. It would have been better to have left the town alone, for warning was sent by a long chain of beacon fires from Valparaiso to the Viceroy of Peru at Lima. He was ready for them. This energetic official had equipped six armed vessels with close on two thousand men, under the command of Don Beltran de Castro. The English caught sight of this formidable armada one morning in May 1594.

As the sun rose higher in the sky, the wind began to freshen and the sea grew rough. The men in the *Dainty* laughed to see the Spanish admiral's mainmast snap. Another ship split her mainsail, another broke her mainyard. Under cover of night the *Dainty* gave them all the slip, and the discomforted Spaniards had to put back to Callao.

Don Beltran was soon out upon the warpath again, this time with two large ships and a pinnace. By now the *Dainty* also had a pinnace, one of her several small captures. She was caught by the Spaniards in the bay formed by Cape San Francisco, in Ecuador. Don Beltran had the weathergage, but contrary to expectation came up on the *Dainty*'s lee quarter. Here was an advantage, a gift to the English, but owing to the carelessness of the gunner the guns to leeward and the stern pieces were unloaded. Don Beltran did not give them another opportunity like this.[1]

The English had but 75 men and boys, the Spaniards, it was said, 1,300. The duel of artillery and musketry continued, with many casualties on both sides, but the English could ill spare the loss. The second Spanish ship came alongside on the weather quarter determined to board. The English fire cleared her decks in a moment, but Richard could not spare a man to follow up his advantage. Don Beltran lay alongside his fellow, put 100 men aboard, and then both ships withdrew. The Spanish resumed the gun duel at a musket shot range. After

[1] Unless the ships were close alongside, the ports of those days only allowed the guns to hull an enemy who was to leeward. The guns on the windward side would be pointing upwards as the ship heeled over in the wind, while to leeward they would be pointing downwards.

both sides had hammered away for a long while the English fire began to slacken. Many were slain and many were wounded. Richard himself was hurt in six places, was in great pain and almost fainting. Don Beltran offered terms *a buena guerra*—life, liberty, and repatriation if they surrendered. The surviving officers came to Richard as he lay weak from loss of blood and recommended a flag of truce. They said truly enough that there were not enough men to resist a boarding party, nor enough to man the guns. Richard absolutely refused to yield. For two days and nights more they continued the unequal struggle. The handful of English were utterly worn out with sleeplessness, hunger, and thirst. But their heavier guns smashed and splintered the Spaniards' sides, while the enemy's light artillery made a small clean hole. Many of the English casualties were due to the men's carelessness in neglecting to wear the body armour carefully provided by Richard. They "esteemed a pot of wine a better defence than armour of proof," or as would be said to-day, "put more trust in the rum ration than in a steel helmet."

The third day, being 22nd June, Richard, being as he thought on the point of death, at last agreed to a surrender on the Spaniard's terms. With sails rent, masts and pumps shot to pieces and eight feet of water in the hold, with few men left unwounded, they could do no more. Don Beltran swore by Almighty God and by his knighthood of Alcantara that their lives would be spared and that they would be sent home. The Spanish swarmed aboard the *Dainty*, crying, *Buena guerra, buena guerra! Hoy por mi, mañana por ti! Fair fight, fair fight! To-day to me, to-morrow to thee!*

Don Beltran de Castro was a grandee of Spain. He received Richard with the utmost kindness and care, and gave instructions that his wounded men should have all they required. In due course the English were taken to Lima. The Viceroy of Peru treated Richard with great consideration, but within a week, despite the protests of Don Beltran, he and his men were claimed by the Inquisition. The Viceroy was powerful enough to throw his protection over Richard, and after being detained for three years in Lima, he was sent in a galleon to Spain. For years he remained in prison at Seville. At length the Count of Miranda, a more powerful personage than Don Beltran, moved by the dishonour to the Spanish name caused by Richard's detention, secured his release after nearly eight years in captivity.

His father was dead. Sir John had gone with Sir Francis Drake to the Spanish Main in the faint hope of rescue. Both these famous sea-captains died at sea on this disastrous expedition. Richard settled down with his loved wife and children in the little village of Slapton in South Devon. He was knighted by James the First, was made Vice-Admiral of Devon, and died in 1622.

He was a valiant and lovable man, the very best type of an Elizabethan seaman and gentleman. The account he wrote of his voyage is of absorbing interest and a revelation of his character. He was most observant. His little book abounds with information about the inhabitants and the flora and fauna of the lands and seas he visited. He has much to say on the construction and management of ships, and matters of discipline. His was certainly a "happy ship." He had a blessed sense of humour.

He staged an "attack" with fierce Indian yells and war-cries on a party of his men who were ashore, to see how vigilant they were. The yelling "warriors" stampeded back into the bush when it was seen that the men were alert. This heartened the shore party immensely. Sick men sprang up and stood to arms. Many were the boasts of the Indians they saw and slew. Richard Hawkins had not the audacity of Drake nor the ruthlessness of Cavendish nor the stern discipline of either, but he had high qualities of his own, and shared with them the great gift of leadership.

CHAPTER VI

OPEN WAR

A N unofficial war had been in progress between England and Spain for many years. The transition between unofficial hostilities and the state of open war was so gradual and imperceptible that it is difficult to say exactly when open war began. No precise declaration was ever made. Elizabeth took her courage in both hands when she knighted Drake in 1581 after he had brought home plunder from the New World, and she consistently helped the Netherlanders with men and money in their revolt against King Philip. But she and her councillors were pulled two ways, between a very real fear of the power and might of Spain, and the thought that perhaps after all the colossus had feet of clay. This last was the view of her seamen.

Philip II of Spain had succeeded to the crown and empire of Portugal, and the Marquis de Santa Cruz, High Admiral of Spain, had defeated the Pretender to Portugal's throne in a naval battle off the Azores in 1582. Philip then became the lord of a vast and fabulously wealthy empire, Spain, Portugal, Mexico, Florida, the West Indies, the whole seaboard of South America, Naples, Sicily, the Azores, Canaries, Cape Verde Islands, Guinea, Angola, Mozambique, Goa, Malacca, Macao, and the Philippines. A great power overshadowed the world. With an audacity hard to realize to-day the English seamen snapped their fingers at it.

The event that more than anything else shook the patience of King Philip was Drake's great raid on the West Indian ports in 1585-6. It was undertaken as a reply to the embargo placed on English ships in Spanish ports. With Frobisher as his vice-admiral and Christopher Carlisle in command of a formidable contingent of troops, Drake stormed and held to ransom Cartagena and San Domingo, the two chief cities of the Indies. That a fleet of twenty-five ships, officered and manned by the best seamen of the age, with regiments of seasoned soldiers, should openly sail from an English port to the West, rob and plunder the Spanish possessions, and come away with impunity was more than even the cautious Spanish King could stand. It was a staggering blow to his prestige. The English were jubilant. Even Lord Burghley had to admit that "Sir Francis Drake is a fearful man to the King of Spain."

For long Philip had turned a deaf ear to the Marquis of Santa Cruz, who had been urging a great attack by sea and land on the impudent and heretical island, and its contumacious queen. Now he listened favourably, and the plan was put in motion. Moreover, the conspiracy known as the Babington Plot had just been unmasked by Walsingham's spies. The plot was a scheme to assassinate Queen Elizabeth, and to place Mary Queen of Scots, who was a fugitive in England from her distracted country, on the English throne. The immediate result was the execution of Mary as a danger to the State. The execution removed King Philip's last anxiety. He determined to strike, but not out of horror at the act. Mary Queen of Scots had been in his way. If he had invaded England

and deposed Elizabeth, the next heir would have been Mary. The accession of Mary would not only have united Scotland to England, but would have meant running a very serious risk of playing into the hands of France. The ancient alliance of France and Scotland still held, and Mary was the daughter of a Guise mother. England, Scotland, and France closely allied would be a formidable combination. With Mary removed his course was open before him.

The cause of the war has already been made clear. It was primarily a struggle for trade across the ocean. The religious element in the clash of the two naval powers must not be neglected, but pious Catholic as he was, Philip would never have sent his armada on a proselytizing mission alone. The armada, it is true, was blessed by the Pope, and set out in a crusading spirit to propagate the Faith. Its defeat averted the establishment of the Inquisition in England. The King, however, would have concluded peace before it sailed, if he could have obtained some compensation for the raids of Drake and the others, if England had given up the fortified cities of the Netherlands that she held, and if the Catholic religion could have been freely practised in England. The Queen would never have given any compensation. The surrender of the Netherland cities would have been a dastardly act, though she pretended to consider it. She would not have greatly objected to tolerating Catholics. That characteristically English compromise between Catholicism and Protestantism, the Church of England, had been generally accepted, but the Catholic and Protestant minorities who stood outside were not persecuted at first. During the early years of the reign, indeed, the Catholics had been let alone. Unfortunately politics had crept in to poison the wells of religious toleration. The Papal Bull excommunicating the queen, and absolving her subjects from their allegiance, together with the alleged political activities of the Jesuit priests, had thoroughly alarmed the English Government. The Babington Plot made matters worse. Priests were banished or if they remained were hunted down and delivered to the rope and the ripping knife. People who harboured them also came under the ban of the law. Philip of Spain not unnaturally thought that the Catholics of England would rise and welcome his invasion. In fact, the Catholics proved most loyal. So long as they kept quiet, the ordinary folk were not greatly harassed. They, like the Protestants, did not relish the idea of England becoming an appanage of Spain.

The Spanish ports were as busy as wasps with the great preparations for England's final overthrow. By the beginning of 1587 everything was well advanced. Ships, victuals, stores, munitions and troops were being assembled, and there could be no doubt where their objective lay. The English Government, Elizabeth and her advisers, partly owing to the chronic lack of money in the exchequer, and partly owing to vague hopes that the danger might somehow be averted through negotiation, were taking no serious or considered steps to meet that danger. They made some plans to resist an invasion on land, but to gain and keep command of the sea did not apparently occur to them. Sir Francis Drake had a word to say about this. "Give me a fleet and a free hand," he demanded, "and I will smoke the wasps out of their nests." Elizabeth, in one of her greater moments, consented. Drake went as General with four Royal ships. The *Elizabeth Bonaventure* was his flagship, the *Lion* was commanded by William Borough, the Comptroller of the Navy, as vice-admiral, Thomas Fenner had the *Dreadnought*, and Captain Henry Bellingham took the *Rainbow*. The Royal ships were equipped and their crews paid by the Government, and the rest of the fleet was made up of ships provided by the merchants of the City of London, who looked to be re-imbursed by plunder.

Twenty-six sail set out from Plymouth Sound early in April 1587. Since the ineffectual peace negotiations were still dragging on, the ostensible purpose of the fleet was merely to "gather information." No sooner were the ships hull down over the horizon but the Queen's messenger alighted from his weary steaming horse with a Royal command to Drake that he should not enter Spanish harbours. To do this would be a *casus belli* not to be mistaken, the negotiations would have to be broken off. Drake was fortunately well away. Elizabeth's seamen had a considerable contempt for her statesmen and their intrigues, and Drake meant to strike a blow that would be felt, to "singe the King of Spain's beard," as he afterwards impudently put it. On 18th April he swooped like a falcon upon Cadiz, the principal naval base and arsenal of Spain. Eighteen tall ships lay in the harbour, fitting out for the Great Armada, the Grand Fleet. They were still in the shipwrights' hands. Including store ships there were some sixty vessels in the Roads. For protection they had a few shore batteries and a fleet of galleys. These galleys were the direct descendants of the triremes or triple-banked oar galleys of Greece and Rome. They were ships of low freeboard, with one bank of oars instead of three. Each carried two hundred slave rowers, five or six chained to each oar. They were independent of the wind, and therefore efficient fighting units in calm waters and inland seas, but of little use in the stormy oceans. They had two or sometimes three masts, each with a triangular sail on a big crossyard. There were no guns on the broadside, and they fought in line abreast, with guns pointing foreward from the forecastle. A breastwork in front protected the rowers, and soldiers ready for boarding filled the fore and after castles.

Before the action Drake called a council of war on board his flagship. As usual, his council found itself faced with a decision. "I am going in to Cadiz harbour. You will follow me." Mr. William Borough, vice-admiral, did not share in the otherwise universal enthusiasm with which the council broke up. He was of the old-fashioned school of war, and was deeply disturbed at this travesty of what should have been a weighty deliberation. He shook his head at this preposterous plan of action. Drake took no heed of him whatever. With the wind and the tide he dashed in. Exchanging a few shots with the shore batteries, he ran past them, and met six galleys coming up line abreast. The English saw the glittering armour of the soldiers, the open gun ports in the forecastles, heard the rumble and splash of the oars, the shouts and cracking whips of the overseers on their platforms, and the regular grunt of the rowers as they tugged at their oars. Drake led his fleet in line ahead, and just before the galleys came within effective range, he turned and poured in broadside after broadside as his ships slipped past. His fire did tremendous execution in the crowded galleys. Two were holed under water and almost sunk. Leaving the galleys to lick their wounds, the English went on to sink a 1000-ton galleon of Ragusa. They repeated their manœuvre with four more galleys that came foaming up from within the shoals. Drake had everything of value removed from the shipping and then set it ablaze. He took the *Merchant Royal* of London into the inner harbour and fired an immense galleon of 1,500 tons, which was to have been Santa Cruz's flagship. When night came on ten thousand tons of shipping had been destroyed, and Drake had not lost a man. All night the white houses of Cadiz were lit up by the blazing ships. Next morning the wind dropped with the English fleet still in the harbour. Here was the galleys' chance. Up they came, their oars threshing the water. They were outgunned. The English shot went rending and tearing through their sides, crashing along the banks of oars and hurling the wretched slaves off their seats. The Spaniards launched fireships, but in the faint breeze they were easily evaded. The following morning a wind blew off the land, and Drake stood out to sea.

The news of this wonderful exploit went ringing round the world. Its moral and material effect was enough to delay the sailing of the Armada for a year. Drake's method of defence, which was attack and *toujours l'audace* had been proved to be absolutely right. If he had been allowed to keep a fleet in being he would have remained off the Spanish coast, and such was the power and terror of his name that the Armada would probably never have sailed. Its supplies would have been confiscated, and its squadrons defeated in detail. As it was he stayed there till June. He captured Sagres Castle near Cape St. Vincent, and used the harbour as a temporary base. From this he harried, burnt, and plundered the Spanish shipping, both coastwise and homeward bound from the Indies. He appealed for reinforcements to hold this base, but the landsmen at home had not his vision, and the support did not come. He sailed for the Azores for a little more "comfortable dew from heaven," and to make a trifle more for the Queen, the London merchantmen, and for himself. He found a huge Portuguese carrack crammed with merchandise from the East Indies, and came home at the height of his glory with a prize worth a million sterling in the money of to-day.

Drake begged the Queen and Council to let him carry on in the same way and baulk King Philip's enterprise. "Stop him now and stop him ever!" But there were no funds to keep a great fleet at sea for long periods, and moreover the Government at home was obsessed with the idea that it was necessary to keep an unceasing watch near England's shores to guard the land from invasion. Howard and Drake tried hard to convince the members of the Council that command of the sea was all-important. Without it no invasion could be stopped, with it no invasion could happen.

Spain suffered another disaster. The brave, experienced, and energetic Marquis de Santa Cruz, High Admiral of Spain, died. He had felt keenly the humiliation of Cadiz and of Lisbon, where he had been obliged to refuse battle to Drake when he appeared off the mouth of the Tagus. To the surprise of the whole world King Philip passed over the renowned captains of Spain, and appointed to the supreme command of the Great Armada Don Alonso Perez de Guzman, Duke of Medina Sidonia, a country gentleman of the bluest blood of Spain, with no experience of the sea. The only explanation of this act is that by choosing a figure-head from a noble house, jealousy and rivalry between the fighting men might be avoided. The same system prevailed in England. Charles Lord Howard of Effingham was the Lord Admiral of England. He had none of the sea-knowledge of men like Drake, Hawkins, Frobisher and Fenner. Indeed Drake, who was incomparably the greatest seaman of his time, might reasonably have expected the command. It was he whom the Spaniards feared, his was the brain behind Howard. But Howard, by reason of the prestige his birth gave him, stilled all jealousies. He proved himself greatly superior to Sidonia in his tact, his willingness to take and act on good advice. Moreover, he was in himself a far more competent commander.

The Spanish preparations were resumed, not only in Spain and Portugal, but under the Duke of Parma in Flanders. The invading force was to come from the Belgian ports. Out of a total of 30,000 foot and 1,800 horse Parma had 16,000 of the invincible Spanish infantry, the best in Europe. The Armada was intended to brush aside the English navy, go on up Channel, and join forces with Parma, who would ferry over his army in a flotilla of flat-bottomed boats to the Thames estuary. All this was to be done under cover of the Armada. The weakness of the plan lay in not first making sure that the English fleet was destroyed.

It was an impressive display of naval might that Spain was making ready. The most powerful of all her fighting ships was the galleass, four of which sailed up the Channel with the Armada. The galleass was built to overcome some of the faults of the galley, which, as has been said, could only fire from the bow and stern. It had rounded bows, was very broad in the beam, and had tumble-home sides, that is to say that the width was less at the bulwarks than at the level of the main gun deck. The greatest width was a little above the waterline, a method of construction which gave greater strength and by which the heavy guns were carried more readily. On the main gun deck the heavy guns fired through ports in her side. Lighter guns were placed in the fore and after castles, to fire ahead and astern, and to command the waist of the ship in case she was boarded. The galleass had three masts, the fore- and main-masts being square-rigged and the mizzen-mast carrying a triangular sail. The rest of the motive power was provided by about fifteen great oars on each side, with five men to an oar. The oar deck was below the main deck. Each vessel carried 300 rowers, so as to supply reliefs. The galleass was speedy, mobile, and very formidable in ordinary weather.

The galleon, a type of ship that made up a considerable part of the Armada, was not so big and alarming as is popularly supposed. Many of them were under 500 tons, few if any were more than 1,000 tons. They gave an impression of huge bulk because of their high bulwarks and their great poops and forecastles. Not only did the after- and fore-castles provide quarters for officers and soldiers, but they commanded with light guns and arquebuses the waist of their own ship if they were boarded, and the waist of a grappled enemy which could be swept before boarding. Their main gun deck armament was light, for the Spanish still relied on fighting hand to hand, and not on gunnery. The English, much more heavily gunned, refused to play the Spanish game. They darted in like a boxer on his toes, firing a deadly broadside and sheering off again. The galleons of Spain were not handy ships in rough weather or indeed in any weather. They were overmasted, and therefore strained and leaky. The high superstructures caught the wind. They could not sail near the wind like the English, with their lower poops and forecastles and their shapely hulls. The English were equal in tonnage and numbers and far superior in guns. They had more efficient crews and but few soldiers. The Armada carried an army of 19,000 soldiers and only 8,000 sailors, besides gentlemen volunteers and slave rowers. There were numerous armed store ships and tenders as well as the galleons and galleasses. In the Armada the soldiers were supreme. The sailing-master was under the orders of the soldier commandant, and had no responsibility for discipline. The mariners, who did all the work of the ship, save gunnery, which was a special craft, were wretchedly treated. They had no proper quarters, and were exposed at all times to the weather. Big guns were despised by the soldier-officers, as being the weapons of men afraid to use the pike and sword. Many of the troops were untrained pressed men, unlike the veterans of Parma. It is therefore remarkable that discipline was as good as it was, and that the Armada put up so good a fight.

In the English fleet there were thirty-four ships of the Royal Navy, many of them, like the *Ark Royal*, *Triumph* and *White Bear*, being of great size, equal to the biggest galleon of Spain. Even more in favour of the English than better ships and better guns was their superior moral. Howard wrote: "There is here the gallantest company of captains, soldiers, and mariners that I think ever was seen in England." There were of course plenty of gallant men in the Spanish fleet. In the English Navy, however, there was a spirit of common fellowship, for which Drake had worked so hard, and for the sake of which he had executed his best friend.

In giving some description of the doings of Elizabeth's captains who fought in 1588 it is convenient to deal with Howard and Drake in one narrative. Howard as admiral and Drake as vice-admiral and chief of staff worked together in perfect harmony, and the story of one is the story of the other. The tale of the deeds of the other captains will be told separately.

The contemporary portrait of Lord Howard of Effingham shows him to have been tall, dignified, richly dressed, with dark eyes, a short trim grey beard, a close-fitting cap concealing his baldness, and the firm decisive mouth that so many of these famous Elizabethans possessed. He was at this date fifty-two years of age. It has been frequently stated that he was a Catholic, but whatever he may have been under Queen Mary in his young days, he now conformed to the Church of England, for it is recorded that in 1588 he and Drake took the Sacrament together in the Church of St. Andrew, Plymouth. He was a grandson of the second Duke of Norfolk, and a cousin of Queen Elizabeth. Though no stranger to the sea, "he had skill enough to know those who had more skill than himself." Early in 1588 he went on board his flagship, the

An Elizabethan Galleon.

AN ENGLISH GALLEON OF ELIZABETHAN DAYS

Ark Royal, 800 tons, at Chatham, and there for some time, to his great discontent, he stayed with his fleet, "to keep Chatham church," as he said. He wrote to Walsingham: "if it were not for Her Majesty's presence I had rather live in the company of these noble ships than in any place. *And yet would I be glad if there were something to do.*"

In January of that year Drake had hoisted his flag at Plymouth in the *Revenge*, 500 tons. He had there the nucleus of a fighting fleet, four Royal ships and five well-equipped vessels from London. Drake was far from happy. He was fretting to be allowed to sail with the whole fleet, and attack and sink the enemy as soon as or even before he left harbour. The only way of dealing with the peril that the Queen's Government could conceive was to split up the available ships into three or four squadrons and station them at various points round the coast. They would thus run the risk of accepting defeat in detail. These dispositions stung Drake to a passionate letter of protest, in which he pointed out that if the Spanish fleet were defeated, Parma's plans would be ruined. He hoped "that the Lord of all strength will put into Her Majesty and her people courage and boldness; not to fear any invasion of her country, but to seek God's enemies and Her Majesty's where they may be found . . . with fifty sail of shipping we shall do more good upon their own coast than a great many more will do here at home; and the sooner we are gone the better. . . ." On 13th April he wrote direct to the Queen herself:

"If your Majesty will give present order for our proceeding to sea, and send to the strengthening of this fleet here four more of your Majesty's good ships and those 16 sail of ships with their pinnaces which are preparing in London, then shall your Majesty stand assured, with God's assistance, that if the fleet come out of Lisbon, as long as we have victual to live withal upon that coast, they shall be fought with, and I hope, through the goodness of our merciful God, in such sort as shall hinder his quiet passage into England; for I assure your Majesty, I have not in my lifetime known better men and possessed with gallanter minds than your Majesty's people are for the most part, which are here gathered together voluntarily to put their hands and hearts to the finishing of this great piece of work; wherein we are all persuaded that God, the giver of all victories, will in mercy look upon your Majesty and us your poor subjects, who for the defence of your Majesty, our religion, and native country, have resolutely vowed the hazard of our lives. The advantage of time and place in all martial actions is half a victory. . . ."

Drake was summoned to London and saw the Queen herself. She insisted on a strong squadron under Lord Henry Seymour being left at the eastern end of the Channel to keep an eye on Parma and his transports, but Howard and his ships were released from the Medway and sailed to the West. Drake was appointed vice-admiral, second-in-command to Howard, but with the main responsibility for success or failure resting upon his broad shoulders.

On Thursday, 23rd May, 1588, Drake's squadron, thirty ships in triple line ahead with light craft thrown forward, put out to sea to meet Howard as he came down Channel. The cheering crews of both squadrons manned ship, and with drums beating and the trumpets' brazen note the two fleets met. As they dipped their flags and lowered their topsails, the guns thundered a salute. A pinnace put off from the *Ark Royal*, carrying the Queen's commission and the vice-admiral's flag to the *Revenge*. Drake ran the flag up to the masthead, and went about as he followed Howard into Plymouth Sound.

Drake loyally accepted the position. The Spaniards knew that El Draques, the Dragon, was their real enemy. But Howard was a man of courage, ability, and good sense. The two men respected each other. A fortnight later Howard wrote to Walsingham: "I must not omit to let you know how lovingly and kindly Sir Francis Drake beareth himself; and also how dutifully to Her Majesty's service and unto me, being in the place I am in; which I pray you he may receive thanks for by some private letter from you." Three months after this Drake in his turn wrote to Walsingham:

"I assure your Honour that my Lord Admiral hath so sufficiently instructed himself daily, as I faithfully believe his good Lordship will thoroughly satisfy her Majesty and your Honour what is now best to be done."

A few days after Drake met Howard at Plymouth, the Great Armada weighed anchor at Lisbon, sailed down the Tagus and put out to sea. They had with them the prayers and blessings of the Pope and of half Christendom besides. The men were told it was a crusade against the heretic, and that the main object of the adventure was to "serve God our Lord." Each man in the vast fleet had gone to confession and received communion. General orders forbade bad language and quarrelling on board. Mass was to be said each day in every ship. The Armada, hugging the coast, reached the Bay of

Biscay. Then wind and storm, which were to save them from the shoals at Gravelines only to hurl them northwards into irretrievable ruin, broke loose and smote the rolling galleons, sweeping them like blown scraps of paper into Corunna and the northern ports of Spain.

Meanwhile, on 30th May, Howard and Drake had gone to sea, short of victual as they were. The promised store-ships had not arrived. Howard had written to Burghley, "God send us a wind to put us out, for go we will though we starve. The fault is not mine. We must do as God will provide for us." His wind came, and they left for Spain, but the same wild weather that scattered the Armada drove them back to Plymouth. The smaller ships crowded into the Cattewater, while the larger tossed violently in the rough waters of the Sound. There was no long breakwater in those days. The Queen's Government was still nervous about letting them go out of call. Howard wrote to the Council:

"The opinion of Sir Francis Drake, Mr. Hawkins, Mr. Frobisher, and others that be men of greatest judgment and experience, as also my own concurring with them in the same, is that the surest way to meet with the Spanish fleet is upon their own coast, or in any harbour of their own, and there defeat them."

Drake guessed that the Armada had been held up by bad weather. Now was the time, he thought, to smite the Spaniards in their ports. He wrote:

"Our staying here in this place shall but spend our victual, whereby our whole action is in peril, no service being done. For the lengthening of our victual by setting a straiter order for our company, I find them much dissatisfied if they stay here; whereas, if we proceed, they all promise to live with as little portion as we shall appoint unto them. Our being on the coast of Spain will yield us true intelligence of all their purpose."

But on 8th July the wind went north. In defiance of the Government's wishes, Howard and his eager officers and men made a dash southwards for Spain. Forty leagues from the coast the wind, again proving the saviour of the Spanish, went round to the south once more. Short of supplies as he was, Howard could not afford to lie off the coast and wait, and back he had to go. Drake marvelled at the inscrutable will of God.

With this southerly wind the Armada was on the move once more. The English system of scouting was extraordinarily inefficient, probably partly due to the difficulty of small cruisers keeping station in bad weather. Belated pinnaces coming in from the Bay reported the dispersal of the Armada, but no word seems to have reached anyone in England that the Spanish fleet had met and re-formed at the Scillies till the news came that it had actually been seen off the Lizard. On Friday, 9th July, 1588, a Captain Fleming burst in with this information, and electrified and astounded the assembled company of admirals and captains at bowls on Plymouth Hoe. For a moment all was confusion and excitement. Sir Francis Drake, who better than any man realized the serious nature of these tidings, coolly picked up his wood, and shouted loudly for all to hear: "Time enough to finish the game and beat the Spaniards after."[1]   The remark steadied the party, but in reality, as all those capable sailormen knew, there was no time to lose, and none was lost. The situation looked ugly. It would take hours to warp out the fleet against the wind. At any moment the Spaniards might be upon them and snap up their ships one by one as they came out. Hastily the crews were drummed on board, and the long task of getting to sea was begun. All that night they toiled at the oars. By noon on Saturday, in rain and mist, they were at sea, and an inshore squadron had got behind the enemy's left wing to windward, just in time. On Saturday night Howard's main fleet worked across the front of the Spanish as they came on up Channel before a light wind. He then tacked westward till he was to windward of their right flank. Rain still fell. Medina Sidonia had thrown away his chance. All through the wet misty summer night the Armada drifted eastwards under light canvas, past Plymouth. During the day and all night the smoke and flame of the warning beacons were streaming over England.

The next morning, Sunday, the 21st, the visibility improved. The sea was calm. The surface was just stirred by the gentle breeze. The Armada lay over mile after mile of sea, with a screen of smaller vessels flung out before it. The *San Martin*, the Duke of Medina Sidonia's flagship, led the first division. The supply ships followed, and then the two rear divisions echeloned outwards in two lines abreast. To the English at their heels it appeared as if the whole fleet was in a crescent formation.

[1] This story cannot be lightly rejected. It dates back for more than three hundred years, and it is entirely characteristic of Drake.

The afternoon sun, veiled ever and anon by cloud, flashed on the winking windows and glittered on the splendid gilt carving of their high sterns. As the day wore on, the sunset fell on their sails glowing with red crosses or pictures of the saints, and on the banners of the cavaliers of Spain, as the magnificent pageant moved slowly on. But the glory was obscured by billowing clouds of smoke, in turn lit up by gun flashes. For the waves became flecked with white in the freshening breeze, and the English ships bowed under a press of sail as they came up within range. Their guns spoke. The English gunners licked their thirsty lips, as through the gaps in the smoke they saw the white splinters flying, and the roundshot crashing and tearing through the Spaniards' hulls. Most of the Spanish shot fell short into the sea. The Spanish ships were top-heavy. In anything of a wind they heeled over so much that their leeward guns sent their shot into the sea, while their weather guns pointed high in air. The English on a more even keel raked the decks or hulled the enemy below the waterline. The gallant captains of the Armada longed to clap the ships together and board the insolent islanders, but they could not, with their foe to windward. Drake had urged Howard to give orders not to close with the enemy, but to fight at long range, and Howard had done so. To lay aboard the Spaniards would have been to play the Spaniards' game. If it came to hand-to-hand fighting, the Spaniards were brave men bravely led, and much superior in numbers. But the soldiers' morale was severely tested by the whizzing splinters and the roundshot smashing between crowded decks slippery with blood and littered with mangled bodies. They gasped and

205

coughed in the acrid black smoke, lurching with the roll of the ship. Death came to them, defence-less, in the dark.

The English concentrated their fire on a few of the Spanish ships, and some of these few were con-siderably battered, in particular the *Rata Coronada* and the *Santiago*. The *San Salvador* was put out of action by an explosion. The *Nuestra Señora del Rosario*, flying the flag of Don Pedro de Valdez, admiral of the Andalusian squadron, was disabled in a collision, her foremast going by the board. Pedro de Valdez could not keep his position, and gradually fell further astern of the Armada as dark-ness came on. The main body of the Armada had not been engaged. Howard called a council of war in the *Ark Royal*, and it was decided to break off the action that night, and follow the enemy up Channel. Drake in the *Revenge* was to lead the fleet by the light of his great poop lantern. In the first dim light of dawn he noticed five ships that had appar-ently become detached from the enemy fleet. Turn-ing aside to see what this manœuvre meant, he extinguished his lantern so as not to mislead the rest. Unfortunately some were misled. The watch-keeping in the *Ark Royal* must have been very bad, for it was quite light enough to see what had hap-pened. However, the *Ark Royal* and two other ships followed the Spanish lanterns, and when day fully broke were close behind them. The English admiral had to wait with shortened sail for the rest to come up.

Meanwhile Drake had discovered the five ships to be harmless Hanse merchantmen from Hamburg. On his way back to rejoin the fleet he came upon the crippled *Rosario*. As soon as he was within hailing distance he demanded her surrender. Don Pedro, who knew that his case was hopeless if it came to battle, attempted to parley. Drake said he was in a hurry to rejoin his fleet, he had no time for talk. If the Spanish admiral would come aboard and yield, he would be well treated. If not, he would find Francis Drake no dastard, and his matches were burning. On hearing that name, Don Pedro yielded with a good grace, and with his staff was received on board the *Revenge*, where he had to stay during several days' fighting. The *Rosario* was sent in to Torbay under escort, where, to the disgust of the sheriff, Sir George Cary of Cockington, the prisoners were landed. He thought that a great deal of trouble would have been saved if they had all been thrown overboard, "made into water-spaniels," as he expressed it. They were eventually housed in the huge tithebarn of Torre Abbey, and Cary had great trouble to obtain funds for their food. The captured galleon was alleged to contain 50,000 ducats, a report which caused much jealousy among some of Drake's fellow-captains, in particular Martin Frobisher, who asserted that Drake had left station to capture the *Rosario* and so line his own pockets.

On Monday night there was a flat calm while the fleets were off Portland. The beacon fires had died down. Men at home in England knew that the danger was upon them at last. All along the coast they listened with a sick fear to the distant rumble of the guns at sea.

In the morning the wind blew fresh from the north-east, and so the Spaniards had the weather gauge. They could make but little use of it against the nimble English ships, and when the wind veered to the south and south-west Howard and Drake led the main battle fleet in a novel formation, line ahead, ship after ship massing their fire on one unfortunate Spaniard. They disabled the *Santa Anna*, and badly hammered the *San Martin*, Sidonia's flagship. They finished the day very short of powder, but some supplies arrived, and from the ports all round the coast ships and men were reinforcing the English battle line. The difficulty in keeping control of so large a force with the primitive and utterly inadequate methods of signalling rendered necessary a reorganisation and decentralisation of the command. Four squadrons were therefore formed, commanded respectively by Drake, Hawkins, Frobisher and Howard himself. Howard still kept general control by councils held in the nearest convenient flagship.

Thursday, 25th July,[1] found the antagonists off the Isle of Wight after a period of calm weather. Light fitful variable winds prevailed that day. It was the day of Saint Dominic, the patron saint of the Duke of Medina Sidonia. Surely Saint Dominic would stretch out his hand and bless the battle. Howard led his squadron against the Spanish centre. The *Ark Royal* outsailed her consorts, and the wind dropped just as she was coming within range. The Spanish were exultant. Their time had come. Boarders would overwhelm the rash English admiral. They attempted to close. The *Ark* quickly launched her boats, which took her in tow. A breeze filled her sails, she slipped away. Up came Drake and Hawkins and the rest of the English hearts of oak, and for five hours the battle raged.

---

[1] Old Style, used by the English, 4th August, New Style, used by the Spanish.

Saint Dominic must be sleeping. "God has deserted us," said the Spaniards, out-ranged and out-gunned.

Friday was another calm day. The fleets drifted idly. The respite was spent by the Spaniards in attempting to make good the damage they had suffered, while the English wrote and prayed for more powder. The *Ark Royal* dressed ship with all her flags and streamers, and Howard, as the Queen's representative, gave in the presence of his captains the accolade of knighthood to John Hawkins, Martin Frobisher, Roger Townshend (one of his staff), George Beeston, and his kinsmen Lord Thomas Howard (the *Lion*), and Lord Sheffield (*White Bear*). In those days knighthood was still an honour of chivalry that a peer of the realm was proud to win.

On Saturday a misty rain came down after a stormy night, during which the English followed the Armada as it neared the narrow seas. All through the murky day they sailed in pursuit, saving their scanty stock of powder and shot. At about five o'clock in the afternoon in Calais Roads Sidonia made the signal to anchor. The English anchors splashed into the sea to seaward and to windward of the Spaniards, just out of range. Sidonia sent a message to Parma at Dunkirk, notifying him of his arrival and urging him to go ahead with his invasion. Sidonia probably felt he had not done so badly. He was in touch with Parma with only two ships a total loss. True, he had not defeated the English, but he might yet do that. But little though he realized it, he had failed. He had not gained command of the sea and he never looked like gaining it. The Duke of Parma may have realized this. He sent word that he was not ready.

The English, however, dared take no risks. Their obvious task was to shift the Armada at once, and to send in fireships was clearly the way to attempt it. The decision to do so was taken at a council in the *Ark Royal*. On Sunday preparations were made. Ships were filled with resin and pitch, while the Spaniards lay with sails furled and flags flying. Mass was said in all the great ships, the last Mass heard by many a devout warrior of Spain. That night with the flood tide sails were set in the eight fireships, and darkly and silently they slipped like torpedoes through the water towards the enemy. Their crews jumped into their boats, and with a roar and a crackle they burst into flame. On they came, the charges in all their loaded guns exploding, the night as light as day. Like a herd of stampeding elephants the galleons, their cables cut, crashed and collided as they struggled out to open sea. The Duke of Medina Sidonia with some ships whose masters had kept cool heads rode at anchor outside the harbour, but the majority drifted helplessly, their anchors gone. The fireships, their task accomplished, grounded in the shallows and burnt themselves out.

In the appalling confusion Don Hugo de Monçada's magnificent galleass, *San Lorenzo*, smashed her rudder and ran aground on Calais bar. So little did most commanders at this date understand the first principles of naval war that Howard, when he saw the galleass stranded, did precisely what Drake was accused of having done. He turned aside from the main battle with four or five more to make her his prize. He sailed in as near as he could in the shallow water, and then with the others manned pinnaces and attacked. The *San Lorenzo* resisted for about half an hour, both sides using muskets, till Monçada was killed. His death caused the resistance to collapse and the English took possession of the galleass. Unfortunately for them, the Governor of Calais claimed the ship, and because two of his officers were roughly handled by the English seamen who had got out of hand, he fired on her and drove the pillagers out.

While Howard was thus engaged, Drake was busy on more urgent affairs. He took command, and with Hawkins and Frobisher, sailed after the main body of the Armada as it straggled towards Grave-lines. Howard followed, and joined in the fight later. The action was confused, and it is difficult to discern any strategical plan. The English continued their old tactics, refusing to close, and using their superior gun power to the full. They cut off the galleons one by one and mercilessly pounded them till two were sunk and two wrecked ashore, and many were crippled with masts overboard, rigging cut to pieces, hulls shot through and through. But in spite of the losses inflicted on it, the Armada as a fleet was still in being and still seemed a danger to the island realm. The Spaniards at this moment hardly realized fully their defeat, or the English their victory. A north-west wind was rising fast. The English kept well offshore to windward, but the wind was gradually edging the Spanish ships on to a lee shore, the Zeeland shoals. Drake knew these of old, and, his powder almost spent, he grimly watched thinking that the Lord had delivered his enemy over to the cruel hungry sands. But the winds of God saved them once again. The north-wester backed to south-south-west. The Spaniards joyfully thanked their saints and made for open sea.

Their peril seemed past. They had failed to join Parma, but could win home and try again. Some of the bolder spirits in the Armada were for turning and giving battle, but though they were overborne, the English could not be sure they had seen the last of the Great Armada. Drake wrote to the Council: "We have the army (armada) of Spain before us, and mind, with the grace of God, to wrestle a pull with him. There was never anything pleased me better than to see the enemy flying with a southerly wind to the northwards. God grant you have a good eye to the Duke of Parma; for with the grace of God, if we live, I doubt it not but ere it be long so to handle the matter with the Duke of Sidonia as he shall wish himself at St. Mary Port[1] among his orange trees."

But if Sidonia had no wish to engage, Howard and Drake could fight no more. Short of powder and shot, the expenditure of which had been unprecedented, short of food and drink, they saw the Armada safely past the Firth of Forth, and withdrew. Wind and storm did their deadly work for them. The Armada, beaten, battle-scarred, and leaky, the men starving, sailed round Scotland, but galleon after galleon drove on to the savage rocks of Ireland. Hundreds were drowned in the wild white raging seas. Those who struggled ashore were slaughtered either by English soldiers or Irish kerns. Only nine thousand men were delivered from the tempest to return home under the shadow of disaster and defeat.

The work of Howard and Drake was done, but they did not neglect that first duty of a zealous officer, the care and comfort of their men. Howard

[1] Puerto Santa Maria, near Cadiz.

deplored the high mortality from sickness (apparently typhus) that was ravaging the victorious fleet. He ascribed it as due to the beer which had gone sour, but it was probably caused by bad sanitary conditions, common on land as well as at sea. "It would grieve any man's heart," he wrote, "to see them that have served so valiantly to die so miserably." His attempts to disinfect the ships by burning wet broom between decks were of no avail. The medical knowledge of the time was so scanty as to be practically useless.

Eight years later Howard was associated with Essex and Raleigh in the great attack on Cadiz. As Earl of Nottingham he died full of years and honour in 1624. He had deserved well of his country, but Drake was the real victor. His name was renowned all over the world, but his brightly burning star was near to setting. In 1589 he was in joint command of an unlucky expedition to Portugal on behalf of Don Antonio the Pretender. The meagre results achieved were set down as partly his fault, and for years afterwards he had no other employment afloat. In 1595 he went at last with Sir John Hawkins to the Spanish Main, but both these old warriors met their deaths from disease at sea. Drake was only eight days ill. He "yielded up his spirit like a Christian to his Creator quietly in his cabin," and was buried at sea off Puerto Bello, with the salute of guns and the mournful trumpets, the beating of his drum, and blazing hulks beside him.

John Stow, the chronicler who died in 1605, gives an appreciation of Drake in the following terms: "He was more skilful in all points of navigation than any that ever was before his time, in his time, or since his death. He was also of perfect memory, great observation, eloquent by nature, skilful in artillery, expert and apt to let blood and give physic unto his people according to the climate. . . . His name was a terror to the French, Spaniard, Portugal, and Indian. Many princes of Germany and Italy desired his picture. . . . In brief, he was as famous in Europe and America, as Tamburlane in Asia and Africa." His fame rests chiefly on his deeds as navigator and corsair, whereas he really was the creator of a new art of war. His work was largely forgotten and had to be painfully relearnt in the seventeenth and eighteenth centuries. He was the first to have a true grasp of the principles of naval warfare. In tactics and strategy he was a daring innovator, and like Nelson he knew when to ignore his orders. Unfortunately he was before his time. Then and for long afterwards his ideas were not fully understood. His endearing qualities, his gaiety and his loyalty made men love him, but his vindictiveness and his highhanded manner caused some of his jealous colleagues to detest him. He and his gentlemen would haul on a rope with the ordinary seamen, who adored him. Hawkins and Drake founded after the destruction of the Armada a fund for disabled men known as the "Chatham Chest."[1]

Hawkins's part in the Armada fight was no small one. He held a commission as rear-admiral, and was a prominent member of Howard's council of war. Besides his actual share in the action, it was due to Hawkins's zeal and vigilance that the royal ships were perfectly equipped. In 1572 he had been appointed Treasurer of the Navy by Queen Eliza-

[1] The original chest is in the Naval Museum at Greenwich.

beth, as being "the fittest person in all her dominions to manage her naval affairs." He was Store-keeper, Shipbuilder, Paymaster, and Harbour Works Commissioner, as well as Accountant. Huge sums of money passed through his hands. His uprightness made him many enemies among the dishonest officials and swindling contractors.

Through him in 1585 the pay of the ordinary sea-man was raised from 6s. 8d. to 10s. per month. The basic pay of a captain was 2s. 6d. a day, but allowances and "dead shares" made it up to much more. A certain number of dead men at 10s. per month were carried on the books of each ship, and this formed a fund for increasing the pay of the officers. Hawkins, with Peter Pett the famous ship-wright, was responsible in 1579 for building the *Revenge* class, *Revenge, Nonpareil, Rainbow,* and *Van-guard,* each of 500 tons, lowering the aft and fore-castles and giving them finer and sharper lines. In the spring of 1588, while he was at work in his office at Deptford, his brother William was day and night superintending the construction of several royal ships. The work was "very chargeable, for that it is done by torchlights and cressets, and in an extreme gale of wind."

In 1588 Hawkins's flagship, as rear-admiral, was the *Victory,* 800 tons. Hawkins's name was only less than Drake's in the estimation of the Spanish. They called him "Juan Achines." He, like Howard and Drake, heartily disapproved of the peace overtures which were continued almost till the last minute. He, like they, suspected the negotiations were a Spanish ruse to gain time. "We have to choose," he wrote, "either a dishonourable and uncertain peace, or to put on victorious and valiant minds, to make a way through with such a settled war as may bring forth and command a quiet peace." Hawkins was much to the fore in the first day's fighting, the Battle of Plymouth. During this first day there was an explosion in the great galleon *San Salvador*. The upper works of her stern were blown away, and her mizzen-mast went overside. Fire broke out and there were many casualties, but the crew with admirable discipline set about salving her. During this operation she lagged behind the rest. Hawkins cut her off, and by hard work at the pumps she was kept afloat and taken to Weymouth.

At dawn on Thursday, 25th July (O.S.) off the Isle of Wight, Sir John Hawkins (he had just been dubbed knight) espied another galleon that had lagged behind. She was the *San Luis*, 800 tons and 38 guns, and Hawkins resolved to cut her off. The wind had completely dropped and he lowered his boats to tow the *Victory* towards her. This was a rather rash attempt to make a good prize, for there were three galleasses within sight. Being by their oars independent of the wind, the galleasses came up, towing Don Alonso de Leyva in the *Rata Coronada*. The *Victory* would have had a bad time had not the Lord Admiral in *Ark Royal* and Lord Thomas Howard in *Golden Lion* been towed to her rescue. As the wind rose, other ships were drawn in, and the battle became general.

Until 1590 Hawkins was in harness, bearing on his shoulders all the burden of Admiralty, but in that year he had leave to quit his London house in Mincing Lane and go with Frobisher to the South Sea once more. At Flores in the Azores they picked up some prizes and brought them home to Plymouth. Hawkins told Elizabeth that "Paul planteth and Apollos watereth, but God giveth the increase." "God's death," said she cruelly (she was disappointed that the results were not more) "this fool went out a soldier and is come home a divine."

In 1595 Hawkins and Drake sailed together on what was to prove their last voyage. The two masterful men held a joint commission, which was in itself a grave mistake. Drake was over-reckless, Hawkins over-cautious, and they could not work together. The expedition was a strong one, six royal and twenty-one other ships, manned by 2,500 men, yet too weak for its immense task. The Spaniards were forewarned and therefore fore-armed, and for years they had been arming and fortifying strong points in their colonial defences. Counsels were divided among the English. First Hawkins gave way, then Drake. Both decisions spelt delay. They resolved to attack Puerto Rico, but unluckily the *Francis*, a small vessel, was cut off and captured by five fast light Spanish craft. The Spaniards thus obtained possession of the sailing orders, and further information would be available under torture. The last faint hope of surprise had gone. As the expedition anchored off Puerto Rico on 12th November, 1585, Sir John Hawkins died after a few days illness. His was a mournful passing. He was a disappointed man, old and weary, worn out in the service of the State, racked with grief for his missing son Richard, his end clouded with failure. Sir John Hawkins was a blunt-spoken man, courageous, resolute, tenacious, an able and upright administrator. He spent himself without stint in the service of the Navy.

Martin Frobisher also won fresh honour and a

knighthood in the Armada battles. He had already made his name as an explorer, but the disappointment caused by his failure to win gold out of the Arctic snows had somewhat overclouded his reputation in the public mind. His quarrelsome disposition did not help matters. After his third Arctic voyage he was unreasonably abused, and his retaliation took the form of an attack on the unfortunate Mr. Lock, the hard-hit backer of his enterprise. Frobisher accused him of falsifying accounts, and called him a bankrupt knave.

Frobisher's first appointment in the campaign of 1588 was the command of some Royal ships in the Narrow Seas, while Drake was at Cadiz in 1587. He had been Drake's vice-admiral in the West Indies in 1585-6, but the Dover Patrol was an independent command. He was on the watch for vessels from the Baltic containing contraband of war, such as hemp, hides, tallow, pitch, masts and spars. His ship in 1588 was the *Triumph*, 1,100 tons, probably the largest afloat on either side. It was on 23rd July (Old Style), when the fleets were off Portland, that Frobisher distinguished himself by a wonderful fight against heavy odds. After sunset on the preceding evening the wind died away to a flat calm. The confused group of ships drifted with the tides, and during the moonlit night the *Triumph* and five others found themselves close in to Portland Bill, isolated from the rest of the English fleet. Sidonia saw his chance. He would attack with his oared galleasses. He ordered Don Hugo de Monçada to move with his four galleasses against Frobisher. This order was obeyed three hours too late, due to some absurd punctilio of honour, but at length the heavy sweeps were put in motion and

he great ships got under way. Too late, for a
fresh north-easter sprang up with the dawn, and
Frobisher regained his power of manœuvre. By
good seamanship he was able to foil the attempts
of the galleasses to run alongside and board. With
his light calibre guns he raked their decks, and with
his heavy shot he smashed the oars. He fought his
ship splendidly throughout the day. More Spanish
ships joined in, but during the long afternoon the
wind went round to the south-west, and Howard,
Hawkins and Drake came to the rescue. The
melée became general. At the close of day Sidonia
broke off the engagement and sailed on up Channel.
Probably this brilliant action earned Frobisher his
knighthood, which he received with the others on
board the *Ark Royal*. He was one of the four
squadron leaders in the ensuing reorganisation.

After the Armada had gone, and the English
had returned from the pursuit, Frobisher and
several other captains foregathered over their wine
in Lord Sheffield's *White Bear* at Harwich. Howard
and all England were speaking well of Drake, and
there was a good deal of jealousy. Frobisher was
particularly indignant about Drake's supposed loot
from Don Pedro de Valdez's ship. All were out for
prize money from Howard downwards, but Frobisher's ill-temper got the better of him again, and
he burst out that Drake was a "cowardly knave or
else a traitor. We will have our shares, or I will
make him spend the best blood in his belly." All
this heat was unnecessary, for in due course Frobisher got his share of prize money—£4,979. He
died of wounds received in 1594 during an assault
on Brest, which had been seized by Spain as an
advanced base against England. "A most valorous

man, and one that is to be reckoned amongst the famousest men of an age for counsel and glory gotten at sea."

There is a host of gallant names in the roll of the captains who served against the Armada, and the list of ships is full of beauty. It is not possible to follow even briefly the fortunes of them all. Richard Hawkins commanded the *Swallow*, the Earl of Cumberland the *Elizabeth Bonaventure*, and John Davis the *Black Dog*, a little dispatch vessel, tender to the Lord Admiral. Fenton, Raymond, and Lancaster were there, and also the Fenners, a Sussex family. Twenty years before George Fenner had distinguished himself in his fight with the "seven Portugals," and he commanded the *Galleon Leicester* against the Armada. Thomas Fenner was Drake's flag captain in the West Indian raid in 1585 and was with him at Cadiz in 1587. A wise and daring sailor, he commanded the *Nonpareil* in 1588, and was one of Howard's trusted advisers. Edward Fenner was in *Swiftsure*, and William in the *Aid*.

Sir William Winter was a veteran officer in the Queen's service who acquitted himself well in the *Vanguard*. This ship fired 500 rounds never out of arquebus range and within hailing distance. Winter had always been in the Royal Navy, and was never trader, slaver, or privateer-corsair. He held an important command as early as 1559, when with fourteen ships he had orders to deal somehow with French naval forces in the Firth of Forth, but not to admit to having any commission. Winter crossed the Frenchman's bows, refusing to stop when ordered, and the French opened fire. It was what Winter had been waiting for. He returned the fire, defeated the French squadron, and said how astonished he was at being attacked by a friendly nation. Elizabeth liked this type of officer. He was Master of the Ordnance, one of the principal officers of the Navy, which he loved. He wrote from the Downs in February 1588 to his colleagues: "Our ships do show themselves like gallants here. I assure you it will do a man's heart good to behold them."

On the Saturday evening, 27th July, 1588, after the fight off the Isle of Wight, three capital ships and thirty-three small vessels from the Narrow Seas under Lord Henry Seymour in the *Rainbow* and Sir William Winter his vice-admiral joined Howard to take part in the Battle of Gravelines. They had been stationed at Dover to keep a watch on the Duke of Parma and his flotilla of transports. Without knowing it Seymour had actually passed the Armada in the Channel. When the change of wind had saved the Spanish fleet from destruction on the shoals of Zeeland, Seymour and Winter were ordered back to the watch on the Flanders ports. Seymour did not forgive Howard and Drake for thus, as he thought, robbing him of his chance of a good and final fight. He felt very sore at being sent back among the fisher folk of Dover, while great things were afoot elsewhere, and he signed a letter to the Queen, "Your Majesty's most bounden and faithful fisherman." He seems to have been a zealous and loyal officer, not above using his hands when necessary. Writing to Walsingham from the *Rainbow* on 23rd June, 1588, he says he is forced to dictate his letter, as "I have strained my hand with hauling of a rope."

The deeds of the sea-captains have been briefly

described. What of the seamen and soldiers, without whose steadfastness all the officers' skill and valour would have availed nothing? They lived in the foul air and dimly lighted darkness of the gun deck, shivering in cold and damp, eating hard salt meat and weevily biscuit, drinking stinking water or sour beer, steadfast in battle, undismayed at death and wounds from shot and flying splinter, and when wounded enduring a rough amputation without anæsthetic or antiseptic. Deaths from gangrene were common. If they escaped those hazards, they would die in hundreds of typhus when the excitement was over. Yet their spirit was high and their resolution undimmed.

On his retirement after the Portuguese expedition of 1589 Sir Francis Drake bought Buckland Abbey, a house at Yelverton, near Plymouth. It had belonged to Sir Richard Grenville. Drake lived in Grenville's house, while Grenville took over Drake's beloved *Revenge* on her next commission. Drake must have mourned her loss, yet have been proud of her last great fight. That story has been magnificently told in verse and music by Tennyson and Villiers Stanford. The attempts to colonize the American continent made by Sir Walter Raleigh and Sir Richard Grenville are dealt with in a later chapter, but the loss of the *Revenge* and the death of Grenville are incidents in the open war with Spain, and as such fall into place here.

The famous family of Grenville was as well known in Cornwall as in Devon, but the little seaport town of Bideford in North Devon was for centuries associated with the Grenvilles. Its houses were and are crowded together on the steep slopes above the estuary of the Torridge, which is still crossed by the

An° · DÑI · 1571 ·
ÆTATIS · SVÆ
· 29 ·

ard Granville, killed
fight near the Azores.
1591.

SIR RICHARD GRENVILLE

same long many-arched bridge over acres of mud, sand, and grey-green marshes. At high tide the brimming river rolls over a waste of sands to the point where Taw and Torridge meet, and to the west blue water winds lazily out to blue haze at sea.

Richard Grenville was the son of Sir Roger Grenville, who was drowned when the *Mary Rose* foundered at Portsmouth in 1545, in the reign of Henry the Eighth. Richard was an extraordinarily handsome man. His forehead was lofty, his nose long, straight, and thin, his mouth firm, with a short trim fair moustache and beard, eyes small, the figure tall and well-made. He was a gentleman of race and breeding, brave, upright, honourable, proud, stern, and quite as hot-tempered as Drake. His character lacked the steadiness necessary for true greatness.

In the last days of August 1591, Lord Thomas Howard, with six of Her Majesty's ships, six victual-lers, a small vessel belonging to Sir Walter Raleigh, and a pinnace or two, were riding at anchor close inshore at Flores, one of the islands of the Azores. Howard's flagship was the *Defiance*. Sir Richard Grenville had the *Revenge*, George Fenner the *Lion*. The ships had been six months out from home, and were foul and slow. There was much sickness among the crews, the *Revenge* having ninety of her company incapacitated. The men were all on shore, recuperating, filling water-casks, and getting new ballast into the ships in place of the foul ballast they had cast overside. To Howard's con-sternation in the afternoon of the 31st there appeared round the end of the island a huge armada of Spanish galleons. It was the treasure fleet they had been waiting to intercept, and it had come in quite

unexpected force. There were said to be fifty-three
sail, but the English had no time to count the
seemingly endless array. They had scarcely time
to embark their men and weigh anchor. Some
slipped their cables. The *Revenge* was the last to
leave, as it took a long time to put her ninety sick
men aboard. Howard and the rest just managed to
get the wind and were under way, but Sir Richard
failed to do so. The master of the *Revenge* urged him
to set his mainsail, cast about, and run for it, trusting
to the sailing of the ship, for the Spaniards were on
his weather bow. Sir Richard stubbornly refused
to turn away from the enemy, saying that he would
pass between their two squadrons. This foolhardy
manœuvre was attempted to the utter astonishment
of the Spaniards. He ran on and on, till the great
San Felipe, of 1,500 tons, with her towering castles
and spread of canvas took the wind from his sails.
The *Revenge* refused to answer her helm and drifted.
The *San Felipe* came alongside and discharged her
broadside into the *Revenge*. She had three tiers of
guns, eleven in each tier, but luckily they could not
all be brought to bear. The *Revenge* replied with
crossbar shot low down in her opponent's hull,
with such effect that the *San Felipe* sheered off. Two
more Spaniards came up upon the larboard side
and two upon the starboard. They attempted to
board with their soldiers, but the English mariners,
sweating and gasping through that summer afternoon and evening, beat them back with pike, cutlass, and musket to their ships or into the sea.

The *Revenge* fought in all no fewer than fifteen
vessels, one after another coming up to take her
place in turn by her side. Such was the force,
weight, and resolution of the English gunnery that

two Spanish ships were actually sunk, and the others suffered severely. All night the struggle continued, and when day broke the *Revenge* was a wreck. The sick men lying in the hold were cold in death, of the hundred or so hale men forty had been slain and most of the survivors were wounded. The last barrel of her powder was spent, her pikes were all broken, her masts had gone by the board, her bulwarks were smashed, she was shot through and through, and there were six feet of water in the hold. Sir Richard himself was wounded in the body and the head. Still he would not yield. "Sink me the ship, master gunner," he cried, "sink her, split her in twain!" The gunner, as brave and stubborn as Sir Richard himself, was for obeying, but the master and some of those yet left alive, protested. If they yielded now they could make honourable terms. They had won enough glory, and would like to live and fight another day. The gunner tried to kill himself with his sword, but was seized and locked in his cabin. The Spaniards granted them their lives. They promised them repatriation, and freedom from imprisonment or the galleys. The *Revenge* afforded a terrible sight to the Spaniards who came to take possession, dead and wounded lying everywhere, and her decks slippery with blood. Sir Richard was borne to the Spanish commander's flagship. He was treated with the greatest courtesy and humanity, but in two days he was dead. Then there arose a great storm, scattering the unwieldy galleons. Many were wrecked on the islands. The shattered *Revenge* herself, with her prize crew, was cast away on the island of St. Michael, and was pounded to bits on the rocks by the raging, pitiless sea.

In the parish registers in Bideford Church is the entry:

"The Lady Mary Grenville, daughter unto the Right Honourable Sir John St. Leger, knight, deceased, and wife to that famous warrior, Sir Richard Grenville, knight, also deceased, being in his lifetime, the Spaniards' terror, was buried in the Grenville aisle in this church the fifth day of November 1623."

The "Spaniards' terror" earned undying fame at his life's end. His contemporaries were not sparing in their praise. Richard Hawkins wrote: "He got eternal honour and reputation of great valour." Raleigh wrote to the same effect. No one would deny him the glory, or belittle his fearlessness. Yet Lord Thomas Howard was right in retreating before overwhelming numbers, and Sir Richard should have followed him. His pride caused the loss of many valuable lives, and of one of the best ships in the Navy.

Another episode of the open war must be narrated, because it affords a good example of the amphibious operation that depends for its success upon a strong and confident navy, and no less on a highly disciplined army. This was the expedition to Cadiz in 1596. Eight years after the defeat of the Great Armada, the Queen and her advisers were still haunted by the fear of an invasion in force. Calais had been taken from the French by the Spanish, who were thus at England's very doors. Actually King Philip of Spain was doing his utmost to protect his ports and garrisons in the West Indies, and his treasure fleets. Yet it is plain that he had not abandoned the idea of the great and hazardous

adventure of a war of conquest. The fact that there
was a powerful fleet of men-of-war in Spanish
ports caused a natural nervousness in England.
The Queen wished to see Drake's exploit at Cadiz
repeated on a greater scale, and Lord Howard of
Effingham, the Lord Admiral, was placed in command of the naval forces. Robert Devereux, Earl
of Essex, the young favourite of the aging Queen,
was in charge of the troops. Essex was a romantic
figure, brave, reckless, and dashing, a survival of
the chivalry of a past age. His energy and endurance were inexhaustible. He had the leader's
power of infecting his subordinates with his enthusi-
asms. Surprisingly wise and far-sighted at times,
he was idolized by the men, who appreciated his
concern for them, and adored his fine clothes and
his gallant, extravagant, light-hearted ways. Withal
he became spoilt by success and lack of discipline.
Essex was now about to reach the zenith of his fame.
He and Howard were really joint commanders-
in-chief, an arrangement not at all to Howard's
liking.

The forces at the Generals' disposal were large.
Eleven Royal ships of first-class fighting value with
some smaller vessels, twelve London ships, and a
squadron of Dutchmen composed the fleet, not
counting the seventy transports which carried some
7,000 well-equipped troops besides gentlemen volunteers. Lord Thomas Howard was vice-admiral,
and Sir Walter Raleigh rear-admiral of the fleet,
which was divided into four English squadrons and
one Dutch, marked by different coloured flags.
Almost every family of note in England was represented in the army, which was officered by veterans
of the Flanders wars. It was a very great effort

indeed, perhaps the smartest, best-disciplined and best-equipped expeditionary force that had ever left England, and this at a time when there was no regular standing army and no War Department.

The actual town to be surprised was kept a secret. It was generally supposed to be Lisbon. The fleet of warships and transports weighed anchor at Plymouth on 1st June, 1596, and all England's hopes went with it. When it arrived off Cadiz, there were in the bay and the harbour twelve men-of-war, twenty galleys, and thirty-six large merchant ships laden with cargoes of immense value for the West Indies. The Duke of Medina Sidonia was in charge of the defence arrangements. He only received warning of the approach of the English on 19th June, four days after they had been sighted off Cape St. Vincent. The warships were drawn up across the narrow part of the bay, and the galleys were thrown forward near the mouth. The merchantmen were in the channel leading to the inner harbour.

When the English sailors and soldiers learnt that there were a number of ships in the bay, they cheered again and again, for they had been fearing as they came along that there would be no "sport." Howard and Essex did not hurry. The wind was light and tricky, and Howard at least was a stickler for formality. He and Essex called a formal council of war. The last attack on Cadiz was conducted rather differently. Drake summoned his captains, ordered them to follow him in, and in they went, there and then. This time there was true deliberation, and two days were thus consumed. After much argument a plan of action was drawn up, but at the last minute Howard hesitated, and

refused to go in with the ships till the town and the
forts were taken. Essex was all for action at once.
He was with difficulty restrained from rashly carrying on without Howard. Raleigh persuaded Howard
to yield his point. As he rowed back to Essex's
ship with the good news he hailed the Earl in
Spanish: "Entramos!" he cried, "We are going
in!" Essex flung his hat high in the air, and it
fell into the sea.

But time had been wasted, and still more was
lost. Howard and Raleigh postponed the attack
until the following day. On the morrow Lord
Thomas Howard and Raleigh led the way. The
English ships engaged the main body of the enemy's
fleet and the shore batteries. It was a hot fight
while it lasted, but once more the superiority of
the English gunfire decided the day. Raleigh
boarded the Spanish flagship, *San Felipe*, whereupon
her crew set her on fire, a roaring tornado of flame.
Four galleys ran aground. From these there were
"tumbling into the sea heaps of soldiers, so thick as
if coals had been poured out of a sack in many ports
at once, some drowned and some sticking in the
mud." One or two more ships were fired. The rest
escaped into the inner harbour.

When the Spanish ships gave way, Essex acted.
He was advised to follow the enemy ships and prevent them and the merchantmen from being
destroyed to avoid capture. He refused. That was
Howard's task. In his view his task was to assault
the town. He may have been right, but whoever
bears the blame, the result was unfortunate. Essex
and Vere, his able second-in-command, landed two
thousand men in boats. The spot chosen was a
sandy bay on the narrow neck of land connecting

Cadiz with the mainland. It was an orderly, disciplined operation, and so impressed the garrison of the fort near-by that they hastily evacuated it. The landing was made without the loss of a man, Essex himself being the first to leap ashore. Half the force was detailed to block the Cadiz road from the mainland, while Essex and the rest advanced with difficulty over the deep sand towards the city, in the blazing heat. Some five hundred Spanish troops were found to be drawn up outside the walls. The English approached close under cover of some dead ground, and charged with a rousing cheer. The Spaniards ran for the gates. Though the English were running as fast as their armour and weapons would let them, the Spaniards banged the gates in the faces of the invaders. Essex and Vere went left and right along the wall. Essex found a weak spot and stormed it with his men despite a desperate defence. The troops fired their clumsy matchlocks once, then went for the enemy with pike and sword, steel clashing against steel. Meanwhile Vere burst in the main gate. The English infantry would not be stopped that day. The town was entered. There was bitter hand-to-hand fighting in the narrow lanes. Men and women hurled great stones down from the flat roofs. There were many casualties ere the city was won two hours after landing.

Howard followed up with more troops in support, but left no general officers with the fleet and no orders. The enemy vessels were in shallow water in the inner harbour and were helpless. While the citadel was being surrendered, prisoners ransomed and released, and order and discipline were being maintained in the city, the Spanish merchants made an offer to ransom their ships and cargoes. On an heroic or stupid point of honour the Spanish military authorities interfered and determined to set fire to every ship, royal or private. The cargoes alone were valued at many millions of ducats, but they all went up in a vast column of smoke and flame. The galleys escaped to sea through a narrow channel. These losses were grave, and the Queen was very angry with her commanders for not having taken steps to prevent the destruction. Like Drake at Sagres, Essex wanted to hold Cadiz as a base for future operations. Like Drake he was disapponted. He was overruled. The city was to be evacuated, but the ransoms had not been paid. Therefore everything of value was salved, and the buildings were given to the flames. The English sailed for home, as the city glowed red and smoke still rose from the smouldering wrecks.

On reaching London Essex found himself the people's hero. The campaign seemed like a resounding success. The country was elated. The prestige of Spain had suffered another blow. The punctual treasure convoys, however, were still coming home, and the King of Spain, old and dying, still hungered for his revenge, as his empire slowly decayed.

Essex buried his reputation in Ireland, and came home to die by the axe. Others carried on the Spanish war. Cumberland commanded in person his twelfth and last expedition. With eighteen sail he left Portsmouth in March 1598. He made for Puerto Rico in the West Indies, a town which had beaten off Drake on the latter's last voyage. He took it after a determined and brilliant assault, and returned home with plunder worth 400,000 crowns.

Other privateers took a lone hand in the game that the Royal ships were playing. A Plymouth man, Captain William Parker, returned in 1601 from a daring raid in Spanish colonial waters. He burnt and sacked St. Vincent in the Cape Verde Islands. On the other side of the Atlantic he plundered a pearl fishery, surprised and captured by night Puerto Bello, which was the new port superseding Nombre de Dios. He took the Governor prisoner and transferred the treasure to his ship's hold. He released all his prisoners without ransom. His feat was reminiscent of Drake, who lay at that very spot in his leaden coffin with the green seas swinging to and fro. Captain Amyas Preston and Captain Summers, "both valiant gentlemen and discreet commanders," in 1595 went burning and plundering at La Guayra, on the Main. They climbed over the high mountain ranges by an Indian trail, and dropped down as if from the skies on the astonished townsfolk of Sant' Iago de Leon, which town they reduced to ashes. After many adventures and losses they returned home with not much loot but a breathless story.

The last battles of the long war were fought and won by the Royal ships under three men of conspicuous ability, Sir Richard Leveson, Sir Robert Mansell, and Sir William Monson. With the coming of the new century the war seemed to be dying of itself, but Spain had yet to make a convulsive effort. In 1601 she threatened Ireland with a new Armada. Faced with this danger Leveson and Mansell wrote, in words which showed an appreciation of true naval strategy: "We propose to keep our poor force as strong as we can in one body, and for no ship to engage herself further than her consorts may be

ready to bring succour; to work like mariners and
men of war for gaining the weather gauge, and
when we have gotten our purpose to entertain fight
with them." The Spaniards reached the Irish coast
and were busy landing troops at Kinsale and
Castlehaven harbours when Leveson dashed in and
destroyed the ships at Castlehaven. The Kinsale
squadron thereupon surrendered. After 1601 there
was no longer any danger of invasion.

In 1602 Leveson was in command of the Channel
Guard with Monson as his vice-admiral. Mansell
was admiral of the Narrow Seas. In June they learnt
that a huge East Indian carrack had taken refuge
under the guns of Cezimbra Castle in a bay south
of Lisbon. Eleven galleys were guarding her.
Leveson and Monson boldly entered the Roads,
raked the galleys with their broadsides, doing great
havoc among the crowded decks, and triumphantly
cut out the prize.

The last action of the war finally disposed of the
galley as a ship of war. Spinola, a gallant Italian
in the Spanish service, attempted to take six galleys
up to the Flanders coast. Leveson, Mansell and a
Dutch squadron searched for him one dark autumn
night in the Downs, found him, and destroyed his
galleys by ramming and gunfire. England thus had
the last word in the quarrel.

In the last stages of the war the two great antagonists, Philip and Elizabeth, both died, the former in
1598, the latter five years later. Peace came with
the advent of James the First. In this peace all for
which Hawkins, Drake and the earlier seamen had
fought, the right to trade with the Indies, was
abandoned. Such a peace, necessary for both sides
as it was, could not last. War broke out again and

again in succeeding years. England was exhausted by the long wars, but her enemy was slowly dying. The empire of Spain was beginning to crumble. The deeds of the Elizabethan seamen had helped to sap its strength and bring about its decay.

CHAPTER VII

LONDONERS AT SEA

THE fact that Plymouth or Dartmouth were the starting places for so many of the Elizabethan voyages, and that so many of the famous sea-captains were Devonshire men, tends to give an undue prominence to the West Country sailors. Without in the least detracting from their fame, it must be pointed out that the Port and City of London had a very great share in the maritime events of the age. Many, if not most, of the expeditions that set sail from Plymouth were largely financed and manned by Londoners, and many were the exploring, trading, and privateering voyages that were due wholly to London's enterprise. London was in the forefront of all the naval actions, and her ships always acquitted themselves gallantly. The Port was proud to take a lead in the matter of ships and seamen.

London had overflowed its walls. There were suburbs along the Strand, over the Bridge at Southwark, and elsewhere. Down river, below the Tower, were maritime villages like Wapping and Ratcliffe and Limehouse, and further down still Deptford, a dockyard town, and Greenwich with its royal palace and park. Scores of church spires broke the skyline of London. Wharves and warehouses were strung along the left bank, low sheds for the most part. There were numerous steps and jetties on both banks, for the river was the highway of the City, and the watermen were a naval reserve. The merchant adventurers who equipped the ships and financed the expeditions were members of one or more City companies, which had their beautiful halls, and traditions which still survive. The merchants lived and had their sale-rooms and offices in rambling gabled timber houses, often overhanging the narrow streets or lanes on which they fronted. The rooms were panelled and hung with tapestries and curtains, and the furniture was good and solid. Sanitary arrangements were primitive. The privies were in the basement, and were cleaned out now and again when the cart came round. Life was carried on amid a perpetual pervasive smell, which sweet herbs did little to mitigate. There was also the smell of humanity infrequently bathed. The seamen who manned the ships lived with their families in crowded rat-ridden tenements jostling each other in the very narrow lanes. The cobbled streets were normally in a filthy condition. Slops were emptied from the upper windows into the street with the cry of "Below!" a cry of warning that was still in common use among schoolboys up to forty years ago. Cats, dogs and kites fed on the decaying garbage. A wind raised clouds of germ-laden dust in dry weather. On wet days a passing horse bespattered the gay clothes of the citizens with foul-smelling mud. It has now become merely a polite formality for the man to take the outside place and the woman the wall, but then it was a real act of chivalry. So was the act of Raleigh, who, as the old story goes, took off his rich cloak with a flourish and laid it in the evil mud, that the Queen might not soil her shoes. These pretty stories are so despised by historians that they are in danger of being forgotten. Even if they are not true in fact (and no one can say certainly that they are not) they are usually true in spirit. A story like this exactly sums up the essential magnificence of Raleigh.

The life at home of the mariners and their officers was much the same in Bristol, Plymouth, and other towns of the period. The fetid atmosphere aboard ship and the primitive sanitation would not be such a great change from their daily life as might be imagined. Plague and sickness took terrible toll of the crews, but disease was constantly sweeping through the crowded cities. Fire was another deadly peril both ashore and afloat. Scurvy and bad food were the peculiar evils of life at sea.

Many and varied were the adventures of the London ships. One of these was the valiant escape of the *Primrose* from Bilbao in Spain after she had been arrested and boarded by Spanish troops. The harvest of 1584 in Galicia and throughout northern Spain had been a very poor one, and by the spring of the following year something very like famine was threatening the northern provinces. There had been good harvests in England, where there was a surplus for export. Spain and England were still nominally at peace. King Philip's Government invited grain ships from England to unload at Corunna and Bilbao. The English merchants, always ready to trade, sent the ships. They had not finished unloading when, by a grave administrative blunder or an act of gross treachery, an order came from the King to the provincial governors to arrest all Dutch, German, and English ships in Spanish ports and to apprehend their crews. This order is extant. It is dated 29th May (New Style, 19th Old

Style) 1585. It speaks of the great fleet that was being assembled at Lisbon and Cadiz, and says that the ships to be seized, with their weapons, tackle, sails, munitions, and victuals, were required for this armada. The Governors were to act "with as much dissimulation as may be."

All the ships at Corunna were taken, but at Bilbao one escaped, the *Primrose*, of 150 tons, with a short crew of twenty-eight. She had been lying in the harbour for two days, and had begun to unload a cargo of foodstuffs, when on Wednesday morning, 26th May, 1585, there put off from the shore a pinnace, carrying the Corregidor or Governor of the Province of Biscay, and six men. They purported to be traders in fruit, bringing baskets of cherries. Foster, the ship's master, was hailed by them in very friendly fashion. He gave them what he thought proper, sailors' fare, salt beef, biscuit, and beer. After this amicable repast, four out of the seven, including the Corregidor, went back in their boat to the town, the three Spaniards left behind spending the day aboard. The Corregidor had discovered the numbers of the crew. Early in the evening he reappeared alongside in the pinnace with twenty-four men. A longboat also came up crammed with more "merchants." Foster did not like the look of this. When the Corregidor and three or four of his men had come aboard, Foster sang out that the rest were to stay in their boats. At that there was a rush. The Spaniards tumbled aboard the *Primrose*, carrying swords, and swarmed over the decks. The master was threatened with a dagger and was ordered to yield in the King's name. He flung the Spaniard's arm from him, and with a shout of "Treachery" leapt to warn his men. The

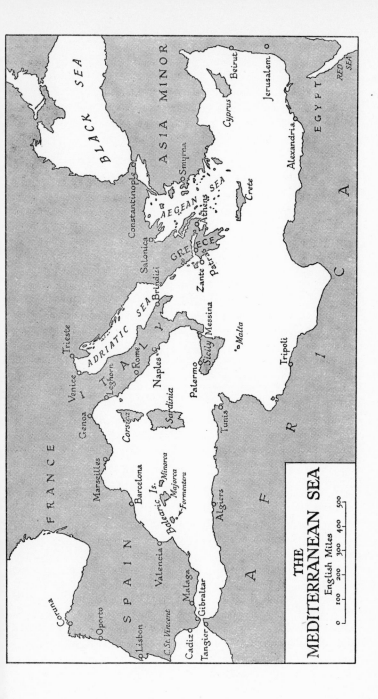

THE
MEDITERRANEAN SEA

English Miles

0   100 200 300 400 500

wary and determined sailors, who had five calivers loaded ready in the waist of the ship, fired them up at the crowd of men above them on the poop, doing great execution. Swearing to die rather than be taken to the galleys or to a cruel death in Spain, the *Primrose*'s sailors seized what weapons they could, boar-spears and lances and short swords. They fiercely stormed the poop, quickly clearing the deck. They bundled the Spanish soldiers overside into their boats or into the sea. One Englishman was killed and six wounded, besides the loss of two who were ashore supervising the discharge of the cargo. Many of the Spaniards were drowned, but Foster rescued four. One of them turned out to be the Corregidor himself. Foster weighed anchor and set sail for home. He demanded of the Spaniard the reason for this treacherous attack. "King's orders," was the reply, and asking for his hose which was hanging up to dry, the Corregidor fished out therefrom the document. Foster showed it to the Privy Council when he reached London. The Queen was furious at the outrage. Mendoza, the Spanish ambassador, was given his passports, and that autumn Drake sailed for the Spanish Main.

Exactly three years before the *Primrose* was attacked, Richard Hasleton, an Essex man, born at Braintree, a picturesque market town many miles from the coast, set out from London to have his fill of adventure. Nothing is known of his early life, nor how he came to follow the sea. Probably ambition drove him to London. He found employment with a firm of foreign merchants. His ship was the *Mary Martin* of London, the owners being Messrs. Eastwoode and Estridge, citizens of London and Limehouse respectively. The master appar-

ently commanded the ship, and it seems certain that
Hasleton was acting as the representative of the
owners, as the supercargo, in charge of all the
commercial transactions of the voyage.

One May morning in the year 1582 the *Mary
Martin* dropped down London River and made an
uneventful journey to the port of Patras in Greece,
then forming part of the dominions of the Sultan of
Turkey. The merchandise carried was sold, and
after a month's sojourn the ship was laden with a
general cargo of local produce. The anchor was
weighed, the sails were set for the adventurous
voyage home. Perils of the deep the ship's company
avoided, the deadlier peril was at the hands of man.
Near Almeria in Spain, on their way to the Straits,
they sighted two great galleys, rovers from Algiers.
Either the master was stricken with panic, or his
judgment was at fault. He commanded the gunner
to run out the guns and open fire, long before the
galleys were within range. The galleys threshed up
and let fly with cannon balls and musket bullets,
killing both gunners and wounding others. They
hulled the poor little *Mary Martin* under water.
She began to founder. As she sank under them,
most of the men leapt overboard, some made for
the skiff trailing astern and cut the painter, others
swam to the galleys, some were drowned. Hasleton
had been hit by a musket ball, and remained alone
on the stern of the sinking ship. Two Moors came
aboard, hoping for loot. One went below, and
went down with the ship, the other came up to
Hasleton, and took hold of him. Quick as lightning
Hasleton's hand flew to his side, drew a dagger and
stabbed the Moor. The water was swirling near his
feet. He slipped overboard, and in spite of his

wound, swam to a galley, and clutched at an oar. He was hauled aboard, stripped, and questioned. Answering nothing, he was beaten and flung into the hold, where he lay for six days, in great pain from his smarting wound. However, it healed, and in due time the galleys returned to Algiers. Here he was taken to the slave market, and with many others was put up for auction. Hasleton was unlucky. Had he been sold to some merchant for use as a clerk or some such employment he would have had a bearable existence and tolerable food. Instead he was sold for 66 doubloons[1] as a galley slave. Ill as he still was, he was sent to sea at once to labour at an oar. For nearly five years he endured this misery, naked, thirsty and hungry always, caked with salt from the sea, sore and weary, sick with appalling smells, sweating in the blazing heat of the day, shivering when cold winds blew, chained to his bench and oar, with the long curling lash on his back if he faltered in his stroke. During his periods on shore, he was lodged in a stable, his bed the cold ground, bread and water his food, and all his clothes a thin shirt and a pair of linen breeches.

Yet his trials were only beginning. In April 1587 his galley was driven ashore in a storm on the island of Formentera, one of the Balearic Isles. Two hundred and fifty Christians and Moors were in her, fifteen only safely reached the shore. One of these was Hasleton, who with two others, managed to break the chains, and cling on to an oar. The Christians hid in the woods, struck off their irons with sharp stones, and gave themselves up to the local authorities, hoping for safety in Christian hands. Hasleton

---

[1] About £4 15s.—say £40 now.

knew no respite. One of the survivors of the wreck told the magistrate that Hasleton was an English Lutheran. This was worse than being an infidel. He was taken at once to the larger island of Iviza, and clapt into jail, heavily chained, and fed for nine days upon bread and water. From there he was sent to Majorca to appear before the Inquisition. From his prison he was brought into a church. The Inquisitor bade him bow down before certain images. He utterly refused to perform this act of "idolatry," as he termed it, and when the Inquisitor handed him a crucifix, bidding him reverently to touch it, Hasleton spat at the Inquisitor. The enraged secretary struck him violently in the face.

Seeing that they had to deal with a fanatic, the Inquisitor adjourned the court. When Hasleton was again brought before him the Inquisitor asked him many questions about the sacraments, confession, images, and other matters, to all of which he affirmed in a most uncompromising manner his Protestant views. The Inquisitor was patient and persuasive, but all to no effect. At last Hasleton asked why he had been kept in prison, saying, "God hath delivered me from the cruelty of the Turks: when I thought to find such favour as one Christian oweth to another, I find them now more cruel than the Turks." The Inquisitor replied that it was because the King of Spain was at war with the Queen of England. "Would you keep me if there were peace?" persisted Hasleton. "Yes," replied the Inquisitor, "unless you submit yourself to the faith of the Catholic Church."

They could do nothing with him, though they tried many times, and in the end they committed him to the dungeon of the castle, thirty feet underground. For a whole year he lay there, on the bare ground, in the dark, exchanging no word with any living soul save when his keeper brought him once a day a little bread and water. But nothing could shake his indomitable spirit. On 1st May, 1588, a little boy, the keeper's son, came to give him his daily ration. He opened the trap door in the ceiling, and let down by a rope the usual basket containing his loaf and jar of water. He said his father had gone to Mass, and then went away, forgetting to haul up the basket. Hasleton waited a moment, then swarmed up the rope, and found himself alone, for it was a saint's day, and everyone was in church. He lay hid till midnight, and wandering about the castle, found three cart-horses tethered with halters and hobble ropes to their stalls. He untied all the ropes, knotted them together, and with this and the aid of a friendly vine clambered over the castle wall, and dropped into the town moat. He swam along till he found a place where he could get out. He walked about the town for two hours, stretching his legs with immense relief, but he did not dare to attempt the gate, which was in any case shut, and he could not scale the walls. So back he went to the moat. He followed it till he came to a water-gate, where the water (the moat being fed by a spring) plunged underneath the wall. Filling his lungs with air, he swam under water and shot through the gates to freedom. By daylight he was six miles away in a thick wood.

Hereabouts Hasleton stayed for a week or more. Horsemen were patrolling the rides, men on foot were beating the undergrowth, he was nearly taken half a dozen times. He was weak with hunger and cold. He existed on berries and roots. He had nothing but a linen cloth about his body, and a cap, which he was obliged to tear in two, to wrap round his bare and bleeding feet. In desperation, very early one morning, he crossed a road, was seen, and gave himself up to a party of fifteen men, armed with swords, arquebuses, and cross-bows. They took him back to Palma, the town of Majorca, whence he had come, and delivered him to the Inquisitor, who loaded him with chains and fetters. After two days had passed, the jailers conducted him to an underground vault. The Inquisitor was there, and another official, and a Dutch woman, who it soon became plain was there to act as interpreter, for Hasleton spoke Dutch. Another grim figure stood silent by a hideous-looking iron bed, fitted with seven new pieces of rope. Recognizing the rack, a spasm of terror shook the prisoner for a moment. He quickly conquered it, and fell upon his knees in prayer, beseeching the Lord to forgive him his sins and grant him patience to endure to the end. They made him lie upon the rack, bound the ropes round his limbs and to the rack, and twisted pieces of wood into the ropes to draw them tight. The Dutch woman begged him to profess the Catholic faith. He refused. The Torturer twisted the rope until Hasleton felt his limbs would be torn off. As if this agony were not enough, a hollow cane was put into his mouth, and water was poured in till he could hold no more. Then the Inquisitor ordered the Torturer to increase the tension on Hasleton's left arm. He did. The rope broke. Hasleton still steadfastly refused to yield. The Torturer put a final strain upon the rack. In intolerable anguish Hasleton cried out, "Now farewell wife and children, and farewell, England!" and lost consciousness. They unbound him, and when he came to himself, he lay in prison for five days vomiting blood and water. Long before he recovered his strength he was whipped through the streets of the town till he was dripping blood.

He was no longer in the deep dungeon, but in an upper room. His body had been racked and twisted, but his spirit was unbroken. He searched about and found a rusty iron bar. With this he made a hole in the wall, and crept through into another room, where in further rummaging he discovered some towels, table-napkins and some knives. Knotting together the linen, and digging out the bar of the window, he crept through, and let himself down. Making for the moat, he again swam through the water-gate, and got away to the woods once more.

Travelling by night he reached the coast, and in a garden under a pomegranate-tree, half a bowshot from the sea, he found a little boat, and in the boat a hatchet. With this he cut some rollers in order to get the boat down to the shore. With an olive branch for a mast and his breeches for a sail, he set out on a desperate voyage. There was a calm sea and a favouring breeze, which on the second day bore him to the Barbary coast, near Jijelli, in the Kabyle country. He had to hide from the Moors. The Spaniards had the habit of raiding the coast of Morocco and Algiers, and kidnapping men as galley-slaves. The Moors also treated in like manner any Christians they could catch. After dodging pursuit Hasleton was so weak from want of food that he came out into the open, and addressing in the lingua franca of the Mediterranean an old man who was weeding a field of wheat, he threw himself on his mercy. The old man took pity on him and gave him food, and he set out for Algiers, where he had some faint hope of freedom. The chief of the local tribe of Kabyles intercepted him in his march, and thinking he might be useful, offered him freedom and honour if he would turn Moor. Hasleton had no more intention of becoming a Moslem than he had of turning Catholic, and he again found himself in captivity. When they found he knew how to fire a cannon, and could teach the Moorish carpenters how to build a house in the English fashion, he was given a certain amount of liberty, and offered full freedom and a wife if he would only turn and serve the chief. Hasleton's resolution was proof against this temptation. He replied that he had a wife in England, which the chief thought an insufficient reason for refusal. After one unsuccessful attempt at escape, he finally got clear away in Moorish disguise out of the Kabyle country to the territory of the Dey of Algiers. He hoped to board an English ship in Algiers, for despite the piratical doings of the Algerines, a trade was carried on, and there was an English consul in the port. With the ill-luck that had so often befallen him, he was recognized by his old master. Although he appealed to the English consul, who was evidently corrupt and did not do his duty, Hasleton was again dragged off to the galleys, and to his despair, the whole terrible cycle began again. He made eight voyages in three years, with a bread and water diet when on shore. Somehow he got into touch with an English merchant, who appears to have bought him. Once he was on board the *Cherubim*, on English ground at last, his luck held. With a happy gale behind her, the good ship reached London in February 1593, and seldom has an exile suffered so much and trodden those narrow streets with greater joy.

It must not be supposed that all Englishmen were such steadfast Protestants as Hasleton. There were many English merchants resident in Spain or the Barbary coast who conformed to the religion and customs of the country. Yet Hasleton's case was by no means unusual. His tale was printed in London in 1595, and was one of many such pamphlets. They were widely read and discussed, and the stories went from lip to lip all over the country, doubtless losing nothing in the re-telling. During the latter part of the reign of Elizabeth a bitter feeling was aroused against the Catholics by the experiences of such men as Hasleton, and also by the plots to assassinate the Queen. The hatred and alarm that ensued led to many Catholic priests and laymen being put to death.

Sir Edward Osborne, during his year as Lord Mayor of London in 1584, wrote to the Dey of Algiers on behalf of Hasleton and his companions. He reminded the Dey that his overlord the Sultan of Turkey had signed a treaty with the Queen of England giving her subjects the right of unhindered trade within his dominions. He wrote: "One of our ships which came from Patras which is in Morea, laden with currants and other merchandises which were bought in those parts, was sunk by two galleys of your city of Algiers, and the greatest number of the men thereof were slain and drowned in the sea, the residue being detained as slaves: an act very contrary to the meaning of the aforesaid articles and privileges. . . ." He asked that "these

248

poor men so detained in captivity be set at liberty," and that the right of English ships to trade be respected. The identity of the "poor men" had long since been lost in the galleys.

Not only had Spain arrested all English ships and crews in her own territories in 1585, as has been related, but also news reached the merchants of London that orders had been sent to the captains of the King's galleys in the Mediterranean Sea that they should seize all English ships passing to and fro on their lawful occasions. The traders therefore went prepared for trouble. In November 1585 five tall stout ships, well armed, laden with merchandise and sailing in convoy, left the Thames for Palermo in Sicily. They were the *Merchant Royal*, already a famous ship, the *Toby*, *Edward Bonaventure*, *William and John*,[1] and *Susan*. At Palermo they separated for their several destinations, Tripoli, Constantinople, and other ports. The rendezvous for the homeward journey, to be made in company, was the island of Zante, off the west coast of Morea in Greece. It was agreed that the first comer should wait twenty days for the rest, and then proceed. The *Toby* arrived first, having been to Constantinople, and having had fair weather. The *Merchant Royal* and the *William and John* came in next from Tripoli in Syria. The three ships' companies expressed their pleasure at this happy meeting by hoisting their colours, by firing salutes, by the beating of drums and by the sounding of trumpets. Then arrived the *Edward Bonaventure* and the *Susan* laden from Venice. They too were saluted "according to the manner of the seas."

The port of Zante hummed with rumours and

[1] Almost certainly William and John Hawkins.

news of Spanish galleys. No less than thirty were supposed to be lying in wait somewhere near the Straits of Gibraltar. They were said to be under the command of Juan Andrea Doria, a famous captain of Spain. Twenty more were based on Sicily and Malta. The longshoremen of Zante shook their ear-rings and were positive that the Englishmen had no chance at all of getting through. The Englishmen swore that they would have a good try. The *Merchant Royal* was chosen as admiral, and the fleet set sail. They sighted Pantellaria, an island between Sicily and Tunis, at dawn on 13th July, 1586. At seven o'clock thirteen galleys came into view. The English cleared for action, ran out their guns, scoured, charged and primed them, hoisted their colours, and stood to arms. The galleys came foaming up, and it was seen by their ensigns that they were in two squadrons, Sicilian and Maltese. The Sicilian squadron first sent forward a vessel, which hailed the *Merchant Royal*: "Where are you from?" "England," was the reply, "don't you see our colours?" The Sicilian demanded to know why their captains and pursers had not come to his admiral to render obedience and pay dues in the name of the King of Spain, Lord of the Seas. "We owe no obedience," replied the English, "nor dues either. Take yourself off with that answer and if you stay there babbling, you'll do it at your peril." So away he went, and a Maltese ship came along. He, too, hailed the *Merchant Royal*, with the same foolish question. The English said they were merchants of London, homeward bound from Turkey, and who were they? The reply was that the galleys were in the service and pay of the King of Spain, Don Pedro de Leiva in command. "We are here to intercept you. You will do well to go aboard him and learn his pleasure. He is a noble-man of good courtesy, and means you no ill." Captain Edward Wilkinson, of the *Merchant Royal*, made reply: "We do not propose to make trial of Don Pedro his courtesy. We are suspicious of it, and not without good cause. Come aboard yourself, we will treat you well." So the Spaniard did. A cup of wine was drawn for him. He drank to the health of the Queen of England, and was profuse with his compliments, especially about the *Merchant Royal*, which he remarked he had seen before in the Thames. "For I myself have been in London," he said, "with the Duc d'Alençon."[1] He took his leave, but was quickly back again with a peremptory message from Don Pedro. Either their captains, masters, and pursers must come to him immediately, or he would take or sink them. Wilkinson retorted: "Not a man shall go to him. As for his threats, we are ready to resist them." The Spaniard begged that the supercargo should go with him to Don Pedro, swearing that as he was a true knight and a soldier he would bring him back safe. Wilkinson had no use for Spanish oaths, but the merchant concerned, a Mr. Rowett, asked to be allowed to go, as he thought he could make Don Pedro see reason.

Mr. Rowett therefore went. He was received by Don Pedro in his armour in the midst of an armed guard. The Spaniard addressed him haughtily: "Do you not know your duty to His Catholic Majesty, whose person I here represent? Think you I am in these seas in vain? Let my commands be obeyed

[1] Brother of the French King, at one time a suitor for Queen Elizabeth's hand in marriage.

out of hand, upon pain of the spoil of you all." Mr. Rowett answered mildly but firmly that they were all honest merchantmen, seeking to pass quietly, but that there was no duty owing, and none would be paid. Don Pedro replied: "If they will not obey, I will either sink them or bring them to harbour. Tell them that from me." Rowett was brought back according to promise, and as he clambered aboard the *Merchant Royal*, the trumpets sounded to arms. The Spaniards hacked off the beaks of the galleys, in order to get an uninterrupted field of fire. The English ran to action stations. The fight was opened by a cannon shot from Don Pedro's flagship, which was answered by a culverin in the *Merchant Royal*. The fight "grew hot and terrible," but in spite of the disparity in numbers, the English seem to have had matters all their own way. The Spaniards made no attempt to board, and the superiority of the English gunnery was evident from the start. At length the admiral of the Sicilian galleys began to draw out of the fight, followed by two others. All three were badly holed under water, and likely to sink. After five hours' fighting, the galleys withdrew, leaving the English free to proceed upon their voyage. The English claimed that they had only two killed and one wounded, so ineffectual was the Spanish fire.

After watering and re-victualling at Algiers, where the news of their victory over the Spanish galleys much pleased the Dey, they sailed for the Straits of Gibraltar, wondering if they would meet with the other fleet of galleys. As they neared the Straits "it pleased God to raise at that instant a very dark and misty fog, so that one ship could not discover another if it were 40 paces off." When this

lifted, the galleys were far behind. The Spaniards
fired off their bow-chasers, but had no hope of
catching the swift English ships, with the Levanter,
or strong easterly wind, blowing hard.

The *Merchant Royal* won fresh glory in the following year. Drake took her into the inner harbour at
Cadiz to burn and plunder. In 1591, with the
Edward Bonaventure, she sailed for the East Indies
with Raymond and Lancaster. The *Toby* came to
a tragic end through bad seamanship. She was a
vessel of 250 tons, with a crew of fifty, and cleared
from Blackwall over against Greenwich in the
Thames in August 1593, bound for Leghorn,
Zante, and Patras, with a valuable cargo. She took
in a heavy load of wheat at Portsmouth, and left
Stokes Bay early in October. The master, George
Goodley, was a young man who had not made this
voyage before. Full of self-confidence and ignorant
of the coast, he sailed all night for the entrance to
the Straits of Gibraltar. About an hour and a half
before dawn he ran the *Toby* aground on the
African shore near Cape Spartel hard by Tangier.
The master weakly said: "Forgive me, it was all
my fault." A man ran up: "The ship is full of
water, sir." "Cast away the mainmast," ordered
the master. It was done. The after part of the ship
broke off. The men clung to the foremast shrouds.
"We committed ourselves unto the Lord and began
with doleful tune and heavy hearts to sing the
12th psalm 'Help Lord for good and godly men,
etc.' Howbeit before we had finished four verses
the waves of the sea had stopped the breaths of
most. For the foremast with the weight of our men
and the force of the sea fell down into the water,
and upon the fall thereof there were 38 drowned,

and only twelve by God's providence partly by swimming and (by) means of chests got on shore, which was about a quarter of a mile from the wreck." The master and the mate were both drowned, as was also Mr. Caesar, captain and part owner. The twelve survivors were taken by the Moors, and brought captive to Morocco, where after suffering many hardships from which two died, they were ransomed by some English traders and sent home.

It is evident that there was a regular patrol of galleys near the Straits of Gibraltar. It is also clear that these galleys, which were useless outside the Mediterranean Sea, were quite useless even there against the numerous, heavy, and well served guns of the English ships. Encounters were frequent, but the galleys appear to have been worsted every time. A convoy of ten London merchantmen homeward bound in April 1590 from Constantinople and other Levantine ports, met twelve of Doria's galleys near the Straits. This was the same patrol that the *Merchant Royal* and her consorts escaped in the fog. The galleys were sighted before dark on 23rd April, and all night the Londoners made preparation for defence, and awaited the onslaught of the Spaniards. There was but little wind, and as day broke they could hear the thresh of twenty-four banks of oars, and saw the galleys crowded with troops approaching. Prayers said, the English stood by their guns.

The four biggest ships, *Solomon, Margaret and John, Minion,* and *Ascension,* were in rear of the convoy. The *Solomon* opened the battle by a broadside which swept away scores of soldiers from the deck of her antagonist, and hulled her through and through.

The engagement lasted for six hours, when the galleys drew off. The Londoners had not lost a single man killed, and had sustained only trifling damage. The smoke clouds hanging in the windless air prevented them from seeing what punishment they had inflicted, but subsequent reports from Tetuan made it clear that it was severe.

The following year the galleys were again active. Five of them attacked the *Centurion* of London, and but for a desperate defence would have taken her. She had won through on her outward journey to Marseilles. With a few small ships she had picked up there she was actually in the Straits when she was becalmed. The hungry galleys thought their chance had come. They were a brave sight as they came swiftly up. There were about two hundred soldiers in each. The officers were "apparelled in silk coats, with their silver whistles about their necks, and great plumes of feathers in their hats." The *Centurion* opened fire with her guns, but was not able to prevent two galleys frothing up on each side and grappling her, while the fifth lay at her stern. She was soon rather badly shot up, her main-mast being greatly weakened, her mizzen-mast and rudder almost unserviceable, and great rents in her sails. The *Centurion*'s trumpeter played to encourage her men—there were only forty-eight men and boys. The Spaniards swarmed up her sides, to be repulsed with pikes. The *Centurion* lost her mate and three men killed, and ten wounded by flying splinters, but her gallant resistance by cannon and pike thrust was too much for the Spani-ards, who backed away.

The narratives of these sea-fights are one-sided. The Spanish accounts would no doubt be different.

There is, however, no reason to suppose that they are generally untrue. The English had a great superiority in *moral* over the Spanish, especially after the battles against the Great Armada. Of the very numerous encounters detailed by the chroniclers of the time, English or Spanish, only three describe the taking of English ships. They were John Hawkins' *Jesus of Lübeck*, Richard Hawkins' *Dainty*, and Grenville's *Revenge*. In the Armada fight the English did not lose one cockboat, and only lost one officer killed.

At this time London had a very considerable trade with the ports in the Eastern Mediterranean, and it was during the reign of Queen Elizabeth that the Levant Company, or as one might say, the Orient Company, was founded. Trade had been carried on early in the century between London and Syria, and to a lesser extent between Southampton and Bristol and the Near East. The exports were chiefly woollen cloth, and the imports silks, spices, carpets and wines. However, the hopes raised by the Muscovy Company and the Cathay Company caused the commerce to be abandoned. In 1575 a revival was attempted. Sir Edward Osborne and Mr. Richard Staper, leading merchants of London, sent representatives to Constantinople to prepare the ground. Three years later Mr. William Harborne, a colleague of Osborne and Staper, left London to negotiate a treaty with Sultan Murad the Third. He went by sea to Hamburg and thence overland through Poland. Poland's frontier then marched with the Sultan's dominions. Before crossing the frontier he, his guide, and his servant changed into Turkish dress. He passed through Moldavia, Wallachia, Bulgaria and Rumania, and reached Constantinople in October 1578. He obtained an encouraging letter from the Sultan to the Queen. In his preamble the Sultan addressed her among other titles as "cloud of most pleasant rain and sweetest fountain of nobility and virtue." He announced that he had given orders to all his vassals and officials to facilitate the entry of two English merchants into his territories. The reply written by the Queen or one of her ministers was skilful. It was sent on 25th October, 1579, in the *Prudence* of London by a Mr. Richard Stanley. In it the Queen asks that the permission for two merchants to trade be "enlarged to all our subjects in general." She argues that as the Turkish Empire must need English goods, it will benefit by buying direct rather than at second-hand from England's rivals. She also slips in a request that "certain of our subjects, who are detained as slaves and captives in your galleys, may be delivered from their bondage."

The result of these negotiations was a Charter signed by the Sultan in 1580. The safety of English merchants was guaranteed, trade was freely permitted throughout the Ottoman Empire on payment of customs dues, and English consuls were to be established in the ports for the protection of the merchants' interest and persons. In 1581 therefore a Company was formed under Royal letters patent. A renewable monopoly was granted for seven years to fifteen London merchants and two Government nominees. Osborne was Governor for the period, and Harborne was appointed ambassador at Constantinople by the Queen in 1582.

On 14th November in that year the tall ship *Susan* of London, master Richard Parsons, left

Blackwall in the Thames for the Isle of Wight, where she was to pick up Harborne and convey him to Constantinople. Owing to contrary winds it was actually two months before the *Susan* arrived at Cowes, and Harborne did not leave the little port of Yarmouth (I.W.) till 19th January. On 1st February the *Susan* put in at a harbour in the island of Majorca, which belonged to Spain. Almost simultaneously there arrived a French ship of Marseilles from Algiers, the master of which happened to know Harborne the ambassador very well. On 6th February the purser, one of the merchants, and three others went ashore to purchase supplies. They were suddenly and without warning or reason arrested, and placed under a strong guard. The purser was sent for by the Governor, and questioned as to the purpose of their voyage. He gave nothing away. Meanwhile a priest had examined the others, who, seeing that the voyage was in no way directed against Spain, thought it no harm to declare its destination. A day or two after the arrest, two mounted officers appeared on shore by the ship and asked to speak to the captain. The ambassador's presence had not been revealed. The ambassador himself went ashore as if he were the captain, with an escort of a dozen lusty fellows, each armed with a boar-spear or a caliver. Captain John Gray was one of them. The boat's crew was kept alert and ready. When questioned as to the meaning of this display of force, answer was made that it was the custom of English captains to have a guard with them in strange places. The two officers spoke fair words, promising them supplies and the return of their men the next day. Harborne and Gray did not believe them. They noticed men on

horseback and on foot among the trees, and it was
clear an ambush had been intended had they not
come prepared for trouble. Harborne wrote twice
to the Governor in the captain's name, demanding
the return of the prisoners, but got no answer.
Another day passed, and that night the watch on
the ship saw lights moving among the trees. When
day broke a gun-carriage was observed on shore.
A man was ordered into the foretop, from which a
better view could be obtained, and from there he
saw three guns mounted. As he looked, three or
four brass cannon were placed on either side of the
harbour to command the exit, and camouflaged
with stones and bushes. The meaning of this was
plain enough. The *Susan* would have to take up her
anchor and go. The anchor weighed, and there
being little or no wind, the boats were ordered out
and took the *Susan* in tow.

The Governor himself was at the water's edge,
with several hundred men on either side. Harborne
and the captain were in their armour, officers and
men at their stations. There was a gun mounted
openly on the north side, and a gunner standing by
with a long lighted linstock in his hand, ready to
fire. As the ship passed slowly by, the Spaniards
traversed that gun right from the mainmast to the
stern of the ship. The English gunners traversed
their guns mouth to mouth with those on shore,
ready to answer if the Spaniards fired. Meantime
the ship's drum, flute and trumpets were sounding
merrily. The master, standing on the poop, shouted
to the Governor, "Have you wars with us? If you
have, shoot, in God's name!" But they did not.
Then the Governor held up his hand, and called on
them to wait, as he had a letter for the captain.

"Send it by the French ship's boat, and our men also," was the reply. "All this while our trumpets, drum and flute sounded, and so we passed out in the face of them all." In less than three hours the missing men were on board, with a polite letter and apologies from the Governor. The *Susan* fired a salute, and went on her way.

On arrival at Constantinople there was a great giving of presents, and rather tedious ceremonies. The ambassador and his retinue paid an interesting visit to the Pasha who was Admiral of the Seas, and went aboard his galley. The poop was gilded within and without. There were seven brass guns in the prow, and thirty oars on either side, with seven men pulling at each. Three days later they watched the admiral put to sea with six and thirty galleys, all lavishly painted and gilded, and dressed with flags and streamers. They visited Saint Sophia, and were entertained at a colossal banquet. The ambassador was received by the Sultan in state, a scene of great splendour. Harborne brought rich and various presents, cloth (for advertisement, no doubt), gold and silver plate, dogs of different breeds and sizes, and above all a jewelled silver clock, designed to impress by its curious features rather than by its taste. It was valued at £500 sterling then, and among other incidents, it had a hunting scene done all in silver. It was a most ornate production, and pleased the Sultan very much. It quite took the wind out of the sails of the French and Venetian ambassadors who were striving to defeat the concession.

English consuls were appointed throughout the Empire. The consuls and the ambassador were most useful in curbing the rapacity of the local pashas, and keeping customs duties within bounds. Factories were started at such ports as Cairo, Alexandria, Aleppo. The sale of woollen cloth was pushed forward, especially kerseys, stockings, and caps. As Richard Hakluyt himself wrote: "This realm yieldeth the most fine wool, the most soft, the most strong wool, the most durable in cloth, and most apt to receive dye, and that no island or any one kingdom so small doth yield such great abundance of the same: and that no wool is less subject to moths, or to fretting in press, than this. . . . There is no commodity of this realm that may set so many poor subjects on work as this doth, that doth bring in so much treasure, and so much enrich the merchant, and so much employ the navy of this realm as this commodity of our wool doth." Homeward bound ships were laden with very valuable cargoes of pepper, cloves, ginger, cinnamon, cassia,[1] mace,[2] nutmegs, indigo, silk, and cotton.

On 7th January, 1592, a Royal Charter was granted to the "Right Worshipful Company of English Merchants for the Levant." It was generally known as the Levant Company. There were fifty-three original members, and Sir Edward Osborne was the first Governor. It must be noted that like other similar Companies it was an association of individual traders, who made their own individual contracts, and to whom alone was reserved the right of trading to the Levant. The Sultan Murad died in 1595, and a new treaty became necessary. This meant much expenditure in new presents and bribery. The Levant merchants

[1] A coarse kind of cinnamon.
[2] The dried pithy husk of a nutmeg.

found it wise to dress in the costume of the country to avoid molestation by the curious Oriental crowds. Before long the possibilities of the Cape of Good Hope route, giving direct access to the spices of the East Indies, were becoming clear. The Levant Company's charter was renewed in 1600, when its offshoot, the Honourable East India Company, caused a change in the character of its trading. The success of the latter company caused the Levant Company to be wound up in 1825. It had done useful work while it lasted, especially in the seventeenth century.

By its vigorous enterprise London was fast outstripping Venice in the race for commerical supremacy in the East. Up till the latter end of the fifteenth century, Venice was not only the greatest maritime power in Italy, but one of the most powerful in the world. She had a very important overland trade with the Far East, and factories in the Morea, Constantinople, and in the Syrian coast towns. Her slow decline began with the capture of Constantinople by the Turks, which cut off her Far Eastern commerce. It was accelerated by London's competition in the Levant. When England went to India by way of the Cape, London began to take the place of Venice as the principal market for the products of the East.

CHAPTER VIII

THE BIRTH OF THE EMPIRE AND THE AMERICAN NATION

THE intellectual ferment that was seething in Europe during the Renaissance made attempts at colonial expansion inevitable. The urge first came to Spain and Portugal. The Dutch, French, and English followed later. The same causes operated at the time when the intellectual activity of Greece was at its height, and it was then that the greatest era of Hellenic colonisation began. Behind it all was the curiosity that tempted men beyond the skyline "where the strange roads go down," to know, to possess, to do and dare. The old lodestones were present, the desire for honour and the thirst for gold. The ideal and the material were inextricably mingled. Honour was to be won by pioneering adventure, but without the stimulus of gain ordinary men could not be expected to leave comfortable homes, and exchange them for the wilderness, to leave their friends for the dangerous company of painted savages, to forsake the ordered settled life of an English village for the privations inseparable from the taming of a primeval forest. The only other incentive besides gain that would make men and women in any numbers endure these hardships was the desire for religious or political freedom, such as drove the pilgrims in the *Mayflower* to the shores of New England. This state of mind had not yet begun to exist in Elizabethan days.

That is not to say that there was no idealistic motive, besides the honour of being first in the field, animating the minds of these early would-be settlers. There was undoubtedly a confused feeling among some of them that they would be able to start afresh, to build a new society free from the trammels of the old. Perhaps somewhere on those far shores a Utopia, such as Sir Thomas More had described, might be founded.

If idealists and hard workers had formed the sole personnel of the colonising expeditions the results might have been very different. Too often the adventurers were ill-chosen. They were frequently composed of eager greedy spirits who looked for easy wealth to be won with little toil. Then also, as sometimes in later days, colonisation was looked upon as a means to solve the unemployment problem at home. Disbanded soldiers, men who had never learnt a trade, or through long unemployment had forgotten how to work at the trade they knew, even men frankly unemployable, were sent abroad. Whereas if the enterprises were to succeed, it should have been understood that the men would have to be even more carefully selected than the equipment. This lesson was painfully learnt in due time.

Relations with the natives were not always happy, though had the advice of an early would-be planter been more generally observed, much loss and embitterment might have been avoided. He wrote: "Yet must there hereof be heedful care had, that whereas the savages be fearful by nature and fond (foolish) otherwise, the Christians should do their best endeavour to take away such fear as may grow unto them by reason of their strange apparel, armour, weapon or such like, by quiet and peaceable conversation, and letting them live in security and keeping a measure of blameless defence, with as little discommodity to the savages as may be."

The first real colonising venture on the North American Continent was that of Sir Humphrey Gilbert in 1583. He was a handsome man of forty-four at that date, with an eager, youthful, and inquiring mind. The motto on his coat of arms was *Quid Non?* Why Not? He lived up to it. In 1563, in his early twenties, he joined the Muscovy Company, which at that time, under pressure from the Privy Council, was interesting itself in the North-West Passage. Gilbert to the end of his life passionately believed in this route to Cathay. In 1576 he wrote and published a long treatise on the subject. The Emperor Charles V, so the story went, had heard from a voyager in 1527 that a North-West Passage had been found. The King of Portugal had paid him the immense sum of 350,000 crowns to keep quiet about it, to bury the secret. Gilbert believed this tale and used it as a strong argument for the existence of the Passage, for, said he, the King of Portugal would not have parted with so much money for "eggs in moonshine."[1] Gilbert set out to prove in his "Discourse" that there was a North-West Passage, that it had been sailed throughout, and that there was no other way by the North-East round Asia. Some of the argument is sound enough, though much is irrelevant, based on fable, and not evidence. He cannot be said to have proved anything, though he satisfied himself at least.

For a long time Gilbert did not go a-voyaging. Like many another Elizabethan, he went to the wars in Ireland. Like them, in the spirit of the age, he

[1] Poached eggs in sauce.

did not shrink from the scenes of massacre and terrorism enacted in that unhappy island, and like most of them, he hated the place. His personal courage was rewarded in 1570 by a knighthood. In the following year he left Ireland, was Surveyor-General of Munitions, and a member of Parliament for Plymouth. His curiosity was insatiable. It was about this time that he was associated with Leicester, Burghley, and Sir Thomas Smythe in a syndicate to back an alchemist, in a project to treat iron with vitriol, and so make copper. He is next found, like so many of Elizabeth's young men, in the Low Countries, helping the Dutch rebels against Spain.

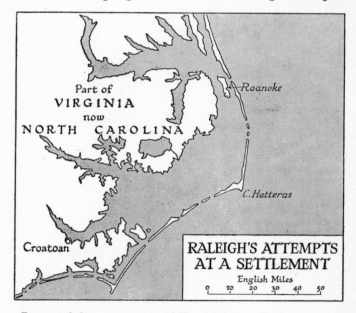

Part of
VIRGINIA
now
NORTH CAROLINA
Roanoke
C. Hatteras
Croatoan

RALEIGH'S ATTEMPTS
AT A SETTLEMENT
English Miles
0   10   20   30   40   50

In 1576 he was one of Frobisher's backers in the latter's first voyage to discover the North-West Passage, and two years later he began to take a hand himself in the sea adventure. He was granted

Royal Letters Patent to equip a fleet and found a colony in America or elsewhere, with a six-years' monopoly of trade. Gilbert himself was to be the first Governor. "We . . . do give and grant to our trusty and well-beloved Sir Humphrey Gilbert of Compton, in our County of Devonshire, knight, and to his heirs and assigns for ever, free liberty and licence from time to time and at all times for ever hereafter, to discover, find, search out and view such remote heathen and barbarous lands, countries and territories not actually possessed of any Christian prince or people." He collected eleven ships, reduced to seven by a quarrel with Knollys, his vice-admiral, who left him. The seven ships set sail from Dartmouth on 26th September, 1578. For various reasons nothing was accomplished. The expedition returned home, with the loss of a tall ship, a complete failure.

With the shadow of this fiasco upon him, Gilbert had some difficulty in making a fresh start. In addition there was the problem of the alleged rights of Spain and Portugal to be considered, particularly to the southward, while to the northward the claims of the Muscovy Company had to be met. However, his half-brother Raleigh's influence at Court smoothed away most of the troubles, and the financial question was partly answered by the dubious expedient of promising territory in advance to the backers of the enterprise. Gilbert and his fellow-adventurers determined to take Newfoundland on their way southwards to a more sunny clime. The expedition consisted of five ships, the two largest being the *Delight*, 120 tons, as "admiral," in which sailed the "general," and the *Bark Raleigh*, equipped by Sir Walter Raleigh, 200 tons. The three small vessels were the *Golden Hind*, 40 tons, with Edward Hayes as captain and owner and the narrator of the voyage, the *Swallow*, 40 tons, and the *Squirrel*, of only 10 tons. Even in those days it was foolhardy to take such a small vessel as the *Squirrel* across the stormy North Atlantic, and besides this folly, the crews seem to have been recruited haphazard. Many of the seamen proved most unsatisfactory and undisciplined. One ship, the *Swallow*, was actually a pirate caught red-handed robbing some Frenchmen in the Channel. Maurice Browne, the luckless captain, found himself placed in charge of a crew of pirates.

They weighed anchor in Cawsand Bay, near Plymouth, with a soft gale of wind filling their sails, on Tuesday, 11th June, 1583. Two days out, the *Bark Raleigh*, the biggest ship of all, sent word that her captain and very many of her crew were down with sickness. Thus early in the proceedings she forsook the fleet and made her way back to Plymouth. Raleigh, who was invariably unlucky with his seafaring speculations, was perhaps fortunate on this occasion to get his ship and stores safe home, though at the time he must have been annoyed. Off Newfoundland the fleet crossed the Grand Banks, the famous fishing grounds. The French, Portuguese, Spanish, and English all had fishing fleets on the Banks. There were often as many as a hundred sail at a time. The voyagers knew without sounding that they were over the Banks "by the incredible number of sea fowl hovering over the same, to prey upon the offals and garbage of fish thrown out by fishermen and floating upon the sea."

The *Delight* and the *Golden Hind* had lost the *Swallow* and the *Squirrel* in the foggy weather usual off that coast. They sighted the *Swallow* when they were close in shore at Newfoundland on 3rd August. There seemed something strange about the appearance of the crew. They were all wearing unusual clothes, and they seemed careless of them, for on seeing the *Delight* they tossed their hats and caps in the air and overboard in salutation. It transpired that the *Swallow* had fallen in with a fishing boat returning to Europe with its catch, and the men, being short of victuals and apparel, asked permission from their captain to go on board the fisherman and do a deal with him. Browne, the captain, who seems to have had little control over his gang of ruffians, consented. Whereupon they boarded the unfortunate fishing boat, and gutted her of victuals, tackle, cables, and robbed the crew of their clothes. In true pirate fashion they resorted to torture by winding cords round their victims' heads, to drag out more information of what was worth stealing. How the poor fishing vessel, cleaned out like this, faced a voyage of several weeks across the Atlantic, "God alone knoweth."

On the same day they approached the mouth of the harbour of St. John's, outside which they saw the *Squirrel* lying at anchor. The English owners of the fishing fleets would not allow the newcomers inside until they learnt that Gilbert had the Queen's commission. The entry into the harbour was marred by a shocking example of bad seamanship. In the very entrance the *Delight* ran upon a rock. It shocked Captain Hayes. He says that the weather was fair, the rock was well above water, and there was hardly any current. A number of boats dashed out to pull her off. No damage was done, but there was slackness everywhere on that voyage.

The owners and masters of the fishing fleet all came aboard to see Gilbert's commission. After satisfying themselves that everything was in order, they revictualled the little squadron. On Monday, 5th August, Gilbert pitched his tent on shore, and summoned all the English and foreign population of the port to take part in the ceremony of proclaiming Queen Elizabeth sovereign of Newfoundland. The commission was read in the various languages. Gilbert was seized of the soil by being handed a wand and a sod of turf. He announced that a code of laws would be established in due course, and meanwhile here were three to be in force immediately. First, the official religion was to be according to the Church of England. Second, if anything were done prejudicial to the Queen's sovereignty the offender would be subject to the treason laws of England, and might lose his head. Third, if anyone spoke against the Queen's Majesty, he would certainly lose, not only his ship or goods, but also his ears. When the ceremonial was done, the Arms of England, cast in lead, were set upon a wooden pillar.

Gilbert and his officers were well entertained by the Englishmen they found there. They were shown with no little pride the wild gardens, in which were roses growing profusely, and whortleberries, well known in the rural districts of England as "hurts." An admiral of the fishing fleet was elected each week, and Gilbert and his officers were invited to the weekly dinner held in celebration. But all this time discipline in the squadron was going from bad to worse. Many of the men stole into the woods to hide until they could get an opportunity to leave for home in one of the ships that at this season almost daily left for Europe. Many were sick and a good number died, and so weakened was the company that Gilbert decided to leave the *Swallow* to bring home the sick, and to go on without her. The captain of the *Delight* returned to England in a fishing vessel, and Browne of the *Swallow* was appointed to *Delight*. Gilbert chose to go in the *Squirrel*, the better to explore the creeks, and in this tiny overloaded craft he remained to the end. The *Delight*, *Golden Hind*, and *Squirrel*, thoroughly well supplied, were ready to start for the southward on 20th August. A consignment of ore was put on board the *Delight*. The assayer that they had with them swore that it contained silver, though in all probability it did not. Gilbert's expectation of wealth from this ore was unbounded, but he did not allow himself to be deflected from his main objective.

The adventurers sailed more or less in a south-westerly direction. After nine days at sea, for some reason the *Delight*, which was leading, altered course to west-north-west. The wind arose, and blew violently south and by east, bringing rain and fog. They could barely see a cable's length in front of them. Suddenly, as the misty curtain shifted in shreds and tatters of fog, Cox, master of the *Golden Hind*, spied white cliffs ahead. "Land!" he cried, and the men of the *Golden Hind* and the *Squirrel* put about for their lives. The *Delight* was too near and too late. With a shuddering crash she struck. In half an hour the after part of the ship was dashed to pieces. Nearly a hundred men were drowned. The *Golden Hind* and *Squirrel* beat up and down all that day and night as near to the wreck as possible, in the hope of picking up some survivors, but not a man was seen. The *Delight* had only one boat available. When it became clear that each man must shift for himself, Maurice Browne, the captain, was urged to take a place in the boat. He said he would rather die than be the first to leave his ship. He stood on the upper deck and calmly awaited death there, perhaps the first to inaugurate a great tradition. Fourteen men leapt into the boat and, after six days adrift without water or food, twelve of them reached land.

With the loss of the *Delight* all the provisions, spare clothing, and colonial equipment had gone, and the precious ore also. Faced with this disaster, but buoyed up by hope of great wealth if he returned next year, Gilbert decided to go home. On Saturday, 31st August, the two little ships altered course for England. In the very act of turning "there passed along between us and the land a very lion to our seeming, in shape, hair, and colour . . . turning his head to and fro, yawning and gaping wide, with ugly demonstration of long teeth and glaring eyes, and to bid us farewell (coming right against the *Hind*) he sent forth a horrible voice, roaring or bellowing as doth a lion . . . a wonder to see a lion in the Ocean Sea." Most of the men had an uncomfortable feeling that the sea-lion might be the devil.

The wind was large for England, but very high and the sea was rough. Time after time the little *Squirrel* disappeared from sight in the troughs of the waves, but Gilbert would not leave her. When the wind abated Gilbert came over and said to Hayes: "I will not forsake my little company going homeward, with whom I have passed so many storms and perils." Early in September there was foul weather again, terrible seas breaking short and high. On Monday, the 9th, the watch in the *Golden Hind* saw an immense sea sweep over the *Squirrel*. She shook herself free. "The General sitting abaft with a book in his hand, cried out to us in the *Hind* (so oft as we did approach within hearing), 'We are as near to heaven by sea as by land.'" That night, about twelve o'clock, suddenly the *Squirrel's* lights went out. When morning broke the crew of the *Golden Hind* gazed with sad solemn faces over the wide waste of sea and found it empty.

The quest went on. The Queen at once transferred to Sir Walter Raleigh the powers given to his lost half-brother, and granted him new Letters Patent. Walter Raleigh, the most versatile of men, might have been really great in four or five different ways. His activities were too diffuse. Not only did he seek fame, honour, wealth and new knowledge by adventure overseas, but he dared new paths in literature, poetry, philosophy and religion. His intellectual equipment was such that when his eager active spirit was caged in prison, he could set his old life aside, and though he pined for freedom, could sit quietly down and write that immense, somewhat dreary work lit by many flashes of sublime prose, the *History of the World*.

He was a man of action with imagination. There is always a large section of public opinion that takes fright at such an explosive combination, and there were times when he was the most unpopular man in England. Aubrey, a gossiping and rather untrustworthy antiquary, who was born a few years after Raleigh's death, sums up his presence neatly enough in the words: "He was a tall, handsome, and bold man, but damnable proud." Aubrey also says that he spoke broad Devonshire to his dying day, even at Court.

Raleigh promptly fitted out an expedition to carry on the work begun by Gilbert, and fully intended to take it out himself. It would not have been his first seafaring enterprise. He had already been to the West Indies, but it was many years before he was to go to sea again. He had been too successful as a courtier. He had exerted to the fullest extent his personal charm, and by his skill in the extravagant flattery which was the fashion of the day, had made himself so much the favourite of the Queen that she would not let him go. Elizabeth would not have so treated her professional, deep-sea, salt-water sailors. Her relations with them were cordial, but not on the lover-like plane. Drake was always successful with her. His downright earnestness and patriotism pleased her. For some reason she did not seem to care for Hawkins so much, though she greatly appreciated his work as Treasurer of the Navy. Frobisher, that long-legged Yorkshireman, and the elder Winter, she always liked. Her relations with men like Raleigh depended more on their success as courtiers than on their amateur doings at sea. With reluctance Raleigh had to see his expedition sail without him.

He had two trusty captains, Philip Amadas and Arthur Barlow, in command of two well-appointed ships. These men seem to have been altogether of the right type of pioneers, courageous, cautious, energetic, conciliatory. They sailed out of the Thames, and left Plymouth behind on 27th April, 1584. On 2nd July a change in the colour of the sea caused them to take soundings. They found shallow water, and a sweet smell as of flowers,

SIR WALTER RALEIGH

apparently blowing off the land. Two days later they put in to a natural harbour on an island, which was twenty miles long and six broad. It is certain that they were off the coast of what is now North Carolina. They stood upon a hill, and surveyed the valleys below, thickly wooded with immensely tall cedars. "Having discharged our arquebus shot, a flock of cranes (the most part white) arose under us, with such a cry redoubled by many echoes, as if an army of men had shouted all together."

It was not until the third day that the adventurers saw any signs of human life. From their ships they spied a canoe with three men landing on the island. Amadas and Barlow, with a few others, rowed to the island. One of the Indians fearlessly awaited their coming. They invited him on board, gave him a shirt and a hat, and what was of more use, some wine and food. After he had been shown over both ships, he departed and fell to fishing. In less than half an hour he had filled his canoe with fish, which he presented to the English. The next day several more canoes arrived with forty or fifty men, "very handsome and good people, in their behaviour as mannerly and civil as any in Europe." They made signs of friendship and amity, and accepted presents. A day or two later, trading began. Of all the things the Indian chief saw, that which pleased him best was a bright tin dish. He took it up and clapped it to his breast. Then he made a hole in the brim and hung it round his neck. The English exchanged their tin dish for twenty skins, and copper pot for fifty more. The Indians would have given anything for swords, but the English would not part with them. In due course the chief brought his wife and daughter in a canoe to the ships to see all the marvels. The white men marvelled at the Indian canoes. They were made of hollowed-out trees. The Indians had no edged tools, so they used to take a fallen tree or fell one by fire. Then they applied gum and rosin to the trunk, set fire to it, and chipped away the charcoal with their primitive implements made of shells. The result was a fine dug-out canoe capable of holding twenty men. Their principal weapons were bows and arrows, the latter tipped with a sharp shell or bone, which could kill a naked man.

Captain Barlow, with a party of seven, went exploring. He came upon a village in the adjacent island of Roanoke, where he found the wife of the chief he had already met. She made them very welcome, dried their wet clothes, and fed them well. When they took their leave in the evening and refused an invitation to stay the night, she seemed very sorry. She sent to their boat their supper, which was half cooked, and provided awnings to shield them from the rain. The English lay in their boat a little off shore, to the dismay of the hospitable Indians. However, the white men were few in number, and it might have prejudiced the success of the voyage if anything had happened to the exploring party. They therefore thought it better to be cautious, though they had no reason to fear any harm. They went on to explore the chain of islands, the great sea lagoon, and a little of the coast of the mainland.

Amadas and Barlow came home in September. They reported to Raleigh the good news that a settlement was possible in fertile fruitful country. Raleigh was struck by a brilliant idea. He would ask the Queen's permission to name the newly discovered territory VIRGINIA, in honour of herself, the Virgin Queen. Permission was graciously given. The Queen was immensely flattered. For many a year the whole seaboard from Newfoundland to Florida was called Virginia, and part of it remains so called to this day as a reminder of Raleigh's enterprise and the great Queen's interest.

Raleigh, still tied to the Court, enlisted the help of his cousin, Sir Richard Grenville, as commander of the colonising expedition which followed. Grenville had been leading an active life as a public-spirited country gentleman since his disappointment at the cancellation of his South Sea project, an ambitious proposal in which he was associated with nine other West Countrymen, including Edward Tremayne and William Hawkins. It was really the same scheme that a few years later Drake put forward and carried out in his circumnavigation voyage. The adventurers proposed to discover, occupy, and trade with any lands south of the Equator not possessed by any other Power, to pass through the Strait of Magellan, sail up the west coast of the American Continent, and either return home by the route round the north of North America or make for Cathay. By so doing they hoped, so they said, to spread the true reformed faith, to bring home treasure, to set the unemployed to work at making cloth for export, and to lower the price of spices by direct trade, all the familiar arguments and hopes. A licence to undertake the voyage was actually granted, and Grenville had gone so far as to provide ships, including the famous *Castle of Comfort*, when the Queen revoked the licence. The revocation was due to Burghley, who did not trust the adventurers. He feared they would do as Drake did later, attack the Spanish ships and towns. It is easy to see why Drake's expedition had to be kept a secret from Burghley.

After this fiasco Grenville sold the ships, and busied himself with work at home. He was a commissioner for the repression of piracy, and had some Cornish pirates hanged and imprisoned. He was also concerned with harbour works at Dover. As Sheriff of Cornwall in 1577 he was knighted for no very glorious deed, the apprehension of a Romish priest who was subsequently hanged. In 1585 Grenville, "for the love he bore unto Sir Walter Raleigh, together with a disposition that he had to attempt honourable actions," undertook to command the new colonising venture.

Grenville with seven ships left Plymouth on 9th April. Under him were numerous gentlemen adventurers, including Ralph Lane, the Governor-designate, and Thomas Cavendish, with about a hundred colonists, besides crews. They had an uneventful crossing of the Atlantic, and landed on an island near Dominica, one of the Antilles in the West Indies. They built a fort there, and because of their strength they were unmolested by the Spanish. At the end of May they left. They could not resist the temptation to take two small Spanish ships as prizes. Then they made for Hispaniola. Here the Governor, accompanied by a "lusty friar," twenty other Spaniards, with servants and negroes, came down to the shore. Grenville landed, and mutual compliments were exchanged. The English built two large huts, thatching them with green boughs, one for the gentlemen and one for the servants, and entertained the Spaniards to dinner, served on silver, with trumpets to summon them, and music playing while they ate. After dinner the Spaniards staged a bull fight, three bulls being killed. The English departed with much goodwill expressed on both sides, but the Spanish knew that their shipping was not safe with these English about, and the English knew that if they had not been in force they would have been served by the Spanish as John Hawkins was at San Juan d'Ulua.

On 20th June Florida was sighted, and a week later they anchored off the coast of North Carolina. Some exploratory work was done, but the good relations with the Indians established by Amadas and Barlow were interrupted. Grenville and his men were of a different temper. In savage reprisal for the theft of a silver cup, a village and its fields were burnt. Actions like this roused the Red Indian braves, and Lane, who remained for a year with five score men at Roanoke had much trouble with the natives. Grenville left for England at the end of August. Four days out he chased and boarded a Spanish vessel, the vice-admiral of that year's fleet from San Domingo due to sail for Spain. He boarded her with a boat made of old sea-chests, which fell to pieces as the men scrambled out of it. The most valuable part of the treasure consisted of a box of pearls. Raleigh got very few, for the Queen took a fancy to them.

The colonising effort was a failure. Lane quarrelled with Grenville, accusing him of "intolerable pride, insatiable ambition and proceedings towards them all." It may well have been that Grenville was an impossible person with whom to work. On the other hand, it is not improbable that the colonists needed discipline, and resented it when applied. Through mismanagement and by reason of the hostility of the Indians food became scarce. When Drake, on his way home in 1586 from the sacking of San Domingo and Cartagena, called to visit the settlement, Lane asked for supplies. Drake furnished him with what he needed, but the provision was lost during transhipment in stormy weather. Drake therefore embarked all the colonists and brought them home. For the most part they were a useless lot for the purpose, townsmen and hasty treasure-seekers.

Raleigh received from Lane and others very full reports of the prospects and conditions in Virginia. As an example one quotation will suffice:

"There is a herb which is sowed apart by itself and is called by the inhabitants Uppowoc: in the West Indies it hath divers names according to the several places and countries where it groweth and is used: the Spaniards generally call it Tabaco. The leaves thereof being dried and brought unto powder, they use to take the fume or smoke thereof, by sucking it through pipes made of clay, into their stomach or head; from whence it purgeth superfluous phlegm and other gross humours, and openeth all the pores and passages of the body: by which means the use thereof not only preserveth the body from obstructions, but also (if any be, so that they have not been of too long continuance) in short time breaketh them: whereby their bodies are notably preserved in health, and know not many grievous diseases wherewithal we in England are often times afflicted."

In the same year (1586) Grenville took out another fleet laden with victuals, munitions, and clothing for the relief of the colonists, but found them gone. Not wishing to see undone all the work thus far begun, he left behind fifteen men at Roanoke with provisions for two years. Undefeated, Raleigh in 1587 equipped yet another expedition with more than a hundred colonists, including a few women and children, under the charge of a Mr. John White, whom he appointed Governor. As usual, the route was by way of the West Indies and Florida. They reached "Virginia" safely on 22nd July, and the Governor landed at Roanoke to look for Grenville's fifteen men. On reaching the settlement they found no trace of the missing colonists, save the bones of one. The fort had been razed to the ground, but the houses still stood. "They were overgrown with Melons of divers sorts, and Deer within feeding on those Melons."

A great effort was made by White and his assistants to resume friendly dealings with the Indians. This was not too easy, as the various tribes were at enmity with each other, and to be friends with one meant that some other was their foe. Hence the success of this effort was only very partial. On 18th August a great event took place, the birth of the first English child in the New World. Eleanor, daughter of the Governor, and wife of Ananias Dare, one of his assistants, was delivered of a daughter, who was christened Virginia. The question arose as to who should return to England to report and obtain fresh supplies. White was for sending two of the assistants, but the whole colony begged him to go himself, as being the one man with enough knowledge and influence to get things done. Greatly against his will, he agreed. After an adventurous voyage, in which many seamen were lost by accident and sickness, he arrived safely home. There were 91 men left behind, 17 women, 9 young boys, and the girl-child lately born.

As soon as White arrived, Raleigh at once set about equipping some ships, and by 9th April, 1588, Sir Richard Grenville was ready to sail from Bideford in command of the relief expedition. Unfortunately just at this time the hour of England's greatest danger was drawing near. The Spanish Armada was about to sail. Orders were sent to Grenville to hand over his ships to Sir Francis Drake at Plymouth for war purposes. It was, therefore, not until early in 1590 that Raleigh's last expedition to Virginia sailed under White's command, and it was August before it reached its destination. Boats put out from the ships to make a landing at Roanoke, but the sea was very rough. One boat capsized. Captain Spicer and Ralph Skinner, his master's mate, were drowned with five others, but four men struggling in the water were saved by Captain Cooke and some other strong swimmers. It was dark before all the party was ashore. A trumpet call was sounded, and the men sang familiar English songs, but there was no answer from the silent trees. At daybreak they discovered a deserted stockade, all overgrown with weeds. On a post by the entrance was carved the word CROATOAN, the Indian name of another island. The inference was that the colonists had gone there.

Next morning it was agreed to make for Croatoan, and the crew attempted to weigh anchor. The weather was foul. They lost three out of their four cables and anchors. Fierce westerly and north-westerly winds blew them to the Azores, where at Flores they fell in with Sir John Hawkins's expedition. Eventually they came on to England, having accomplished nothing. What became of the colonists no one ever knew. No trace of them was ever found. They were either all slain or completely absorbed into the native population. Years afterwards, when the next colonists came on the scene, it was reported that there were alive among the Indians four men, two boys, and a young girl. It was not until the next reign, in 1606, that Captain John Smith took out 105 emigrants to the James River in Virginia, and made a permanent settlement. Before Raleigh died, he had the gratification of knowing that the seed he had sown and tended with so much determination and expense had borne fruit. Smith was a man of sturdy common sense. He understood that settlers in a new country must be picked men and not a sweeping of unemployables, that time and energy should not be wasted in mining for gold, and that above all the natives must be conciliated. He carried out in practice what Bacon wrote in his *Essay on Plantations*: "Do not entertain savages with trifles and jingles, but show them grace and justice, taking reasonable precautions against their attacks, but not seeking the favour of any one tribe amongst them by inciting it to attack another tribe."

Raleigh's attempts were one and all unsuccessful, but he had nevertheless a vision, a goal and an ideal. His expenditure had been colossal, rich man though he was. He was Lord Warden of the Stannaries. The Stannary towns of Devon and Cornwall were the towns where the ingots of tin from the mines were stamped with the Government mark, and considerable wealth in dues accrued to the Lord Warden. Raleigh had also been granted by the Queen exclusive licences for the export of cloth and the selling of wines. These monopolies made him rich, but they also made him hated. In spite of his wealth, the expenditure incurred in voyages of exploration and privateering was a great drain upon his resources, and he began to cast about for a more profitable investment. Here comes in the gold motive. Gold was the source of all power, and gold he would have. He would seek the Golden City of El Dorado, which report said lay in the hinterland of Guiana, somewhere up the Orinoco where the State of Venezuela is now. Many and persistent rumours set Raleigh's eager spirit on fire for the adventure. Not only did he gain the support of the Privy Council, but he won the Queen's permission to go himself. He had a wide commission. It allowed him to engage in hostilities, in case of need, against Spaniards or native Indians. On 6th February, 1595, he set out for "the discovery of the large, rich, and beautiful empire of Guiana, the great and golden city of Manoa, which the Spaniards call El Dorado."

In six weeks he reached Port of Spain in the island of Trinidad. While he was there some Spaniards came aboard to buy linen and other requirements. Raleigh gave them as much wine as they could drink to get them into a happy and talkative state, so that they might tell all they knew about the riches of Guiana. He himself gave out at first that he was bound for Virginia to relieve the colonists. Don Antonio de Berreo, the Governor of Trinidad, was a man of good family and education, who had served his country in Italy and the Netherlands, but who had made himself hated by the natives for his cruelty. He had, as Raleigh knew, already essayed to go up the Orinoco on the same quest. Raleigh did not dare to go hundreds of miles from his ships and leave a Spanish garrison at his base. He therefore made friends with the Indian chiefs, telling them that he was the servant of a great Queen who was an enemy to the Spanish, and who, having freed all the peoples of the northern world, had sent him to free them also. Under his leadership, stiffened by a hundred armed Englishmen, the Indians revolted. The Governor's bodyguard was put to the sword, and the new town of San Josef was taken and burnt. Raleigh took Don Antonio de Berreo prisoner. He proved to be friendly and communicative, and Raleigh soon got from him all he knew.

Raleigh had fitted out one of the small ships of his squadron as a galley with a bank of oars on each side. Into this and four ships' boats he crowded one hundred men, and provisions for a month. He wrote that they were "all driven to lie in the rain and weather, in the open air, in the burning sun, and upon the hard boards, and to dress our meat, and to carry all manner of furniture[1] in them, wherewith they were so pestered[2] and unsavoury, that what with victuals being mostly fish, with wet clothes of so many men thrust together, and the heat of the sun, I will undertake there was never any prison in England that could be found more unsavoury and loathsome, especially to myself, who had for many years before been dieted and cared for in a sort far more differing." They suffered terrible privations in this voyage up the great river, but the thought of the Golden City kept up their hearts. They had never any doubt that it existed. Although there certainly were gold deposits up country, the Imperial City of Gold was a legend. Yet tales as strange had proved true. The city of

[1] arms.   [2] crowded.

the Incas in Peru had been as wonderful as Manoa was reported to be. If Pizarro had found an El Dorado, why should not Raleigh? The evidence was substantial, was indeed in writing. Berreo had a copy of a statement by one Martinez, who said he had actually been to Manoa, and spent seven months there. Berreo himself had tried to reach it and had failed, but had picked up a store of confirmatory legend and hearsay. Raleigh's hopes were boundless, his resolution strong.

The Orinoco at its delta splits up into several mouths. John Douglas, one of the ships' masters, was sent in a boat to explore, and returned with the news that there were four main mouths, the least of which was as big as the Thames at Woolwich. Silt had made the sea entrances shallow, so that there was a long dangerous journey in the boats ere they could reach the stream. When they had entered, they quickly lost themselves. But for a fortunate chance, they might have wandered for ever in a labyrinth of rivers. There were so many streams and all alike. The thick green dark forest came down to the water's edge, and obscured their view. They were lucky enough to come across an Indian canoe, from which they took an old man to serve as guide. Of these Indians of the Orinoco Raleigh says that never in all his life did he behold "a more goodly or better favoured people or a more manly." With this new pilot the adventurers passed up the river with the flood and anchored with the ebb. The third day the galley ran aground, and much tugging and hauling was necessary before they got her off. The next day they passed above the tidal water, and had to row hard against a violent current. Raleigh and his officers told the men that Manoa was only a few days' journey away, and that they must put their backs into it. The officers took their turn at the oars, in hourly shifts. After three days more, the men's spirits began to droop. The heat was insufferable. The tall trees at the waterside prevented any breeze there might be from reaching them. Each day the current seemed stronger to the weary rowers. As day succeeded day, it grew hotter and hotter, rations grew smaller, and water scarce. Hour by hour they became weaker, and the current raced yet more madly. Their food was all gone, and there was only the turbid muddy water of the river. They caught fish, and shot a few birds, and there were fruits. They rowed on and on through the teeming forest, aglow with many-coloured flowers and birds of every hue, carnation, crimson, orange-tawny, purple and blue.

The old Indian guide told Raleigh that if he were to leave the galley at anchor in the river, and go up a certain tributary with the small boats, he would bring them to a native village, where food could be obtained. Raleigh rejoiced to hear it. He took three boats, with two officers and sixteen men. The guide said it was quite close, so they took no food with them. They set off in the morning and rowed for three hours. The guide said it was just a little way further. All day they pulled at their oars, it began to grow dark. "Four reaches more," said the guide. The men began to growl. "Hang that pilot," said one. If they hanged him, how were they to get back? It was now as dark as pitch. The stream began to narrow, and branches barred the way. They had to use their swords to cut a passage. They had made only a scanty breakfast aboard the galley, and were very hungry. At last about one o'clock in the morning they saw a light, and as they approached heard the village dogs barking. They feasted well that night, and next day returned to the expectant galley with a store of bread, fish, and chickens.

Up the main tributary the Englishmen continued, past park-like grassy country where the deer were feeding by the water's edge, on and on till their food had given out again. Fortune favoured them once more, for they came upon four canoes laden with bread, which were at once abandoned by their occupants. Nothing could have been more welcome. The men shouted: "Let us go on, we care not how far it is." They captured one of the Indians, treated him well to his great surprise, and pressed him as a guide. They sent the old Indian home in a canoe. Raleigh was very careful to have the Indians on his side. He promptly punished any thieving of their property on the part of his men, and saw to it that none of their women were molested.

At length far away they saw the high mountains wherein lay hidden their goal, and came on to the great river Orinoco. The local chief, a man named Toparimaca, came down to meet them with a good supply of food. "Some of our captains caroused of his wine till they were reasonable pleasant, for it is very strong." Toparimaca gave Raleigh a new guide. A guide or pilot was very necessary, considering the great width of the mighty river, its racing currents, snags, whirlpools, rocks, and shoals. Mile after mile they journeyed on, and now the river began to rise. The rainy season was at hand. The river rose four or five feet, and the current was so tremendous that no boat could make head against it. Raleigh sent a large party to go on overland, while he and a few others marched off to see the great waterfalls on the Caroni, the roar of which had for long been in their ears. As they topped a hill, they saw, twenty miles away, the immense sweep and rush of the waters over the falls, with clouds of spray like the smoke of a burning town. Raleigh becomes lyrical in his description of the view spread out before him. "I never saw a more beautiful country, nor more lively prospects, hills so raised here and there over the valleys, the river winding into divers branches, the plains adjoining without bush or stubble, all fair green grass, the ground of hard sand easy to march on, either for horse or foot; the deer crossing in every path, the birds towards the evening singing on every tree with a thousand several tunes, cranes and herons of white, crimson, or carnation perching in the river's side, the air fresh with a gentle easterly wind, and every stone that we stooped to take up promised either gold or silver by his complexion."

They could not linger in that paradise. Orinoco increased his fury, began to spill over his banks. The tropical rain, against which the men had no shelter, wetted them through and through. They turned east, and sped downstream. It seemed clear, after consultation with native chiefs, that Raleigh's numbers were too few to advance further unaided, and that in any case the rains made transport impossible. So back to the ships, was the cry: come again next year. They had difficulty in getting the galley over the bar, and the sea was very rough for small boats. However, they safely made the island of Trinidad, after an absence of a month.

Raleigh, like the other explorers, hopefully

brought home some ore, alleged to contain gold. Scoffers said it was marcasite, or iron pyrites, enemies avowed that he had bought the ore on the Barbary coast, and taken it out to Guiana. "For mine own part," said Raleigh, "I am not so much in love with these long voyages, as to devise, thereby to cozen myself, to lie hard, to fare worse, to be subjected to perils, to diseases, to ill savours, to be parched and withered, and withal to sustain the care and labour of such an enterprise, except the same had more comfort than the fetching of marcasite in Guiana, or buying of gold ore in Barbary." Many a year afterwards, gold mines were worked up the Orinoco, but the city of El Dorado became the symbol of an unsubstantial dream.

Raleigh preserved entire his belief in the dream, though the war with Spain absorbed his energies until the death of Queen Elizabeth. With her passing the last fragments of Raleigh's good fortune also passed away. In 1603, the year of King James's accession, the false accusations of his enemies brought him low. After a trial, which was a scandalous travesty of justice, he was condemned to the axe as a traitor. Raleigh in prison is a more attractive character than Raleigh at liberty. The farewell letter to his wife is a moving document:

"I cannot write much. God knows how hardly I stole this time, when all sleep, and it is time to separate my thoughts from the world. Beg my dead body, which living was denied you; and either lay it at Sherborne if the land continue or in Exeter church by my father and mother. I can write no more. Time and Death call me away."

At the last moment King James refused to sign

the death-warrant. Raleigh was not pardoned, but was imprisoned for years in the Tower of London. Here he wrote his *History of the World*. In spite of the intellectual activities which were his solace, he yearned for freedom, and longed to pursue his golden dream. After the King and the Privy Council had been bombarded with petitions from Raleigh during the last five of his thirteen years' imprisonment, he was released to go treasure-hunting up the Orinoco. Peace had long ago been made with Spain, and the Spanish ambassador protested. The English Government gave an assurance that the rights of Spanish settlers would not be infringed. Raleigh cared nothing for this. He attacked the new settlement of San Thomé at the river's mouth, and though he fired it, he was prevented from going up the river. Thereafter his enterprise crumbled into ruin. He had to come home, irretrievably compromised, convicted of an act of piracy, his head already loose upon his shoulders. He was at once sent to the Tower, and made to suffer, not for the new offence, but under the old sentence. In the last reign men had been honoured for what he had done, but now the circumstances were different. The long war had strained England's resources to the uttermost. People had come to see that peace with Spain was a necessity.

Raleigh dressed for his last ceremony with care, and put on his richest clothes. He received Communion, and smoked his last pipe. He jested with the executioner, and laid his head upon the block. The grim official hesitated. "What dost thou fear?" said Raleigh. "Strike, man, strike!"

So died the last of the great Elizabethans.

CHAPTER IX

THE INFLUENCE OF THE SEAMEN ON THE LIFE OF THE REALM

IN two or three generations the whole life of the western world had been transformed. It was is if a man lived in one room, spacious indeed and well if rudely furnished according to his needs. A top light gave on to the heavens above, a window at the side looked out at a blank wall and a courtyard below, dark, narrow, and forbidding. One day the man discovered at one end of the chamber another window, blocked up, the existence of which he had never suspected. It opened towards the sunrise, and new light came flooding in.

The discoveries of the seamen of the world, coming at a time when the learning of Greece and Rome had been released, gave a new orientation to the life of man, and affected most profoundly his mode of life, his religion, his social habits. The Church had been the sole repository of knowledge. It had held the keys of heaven and hell. The problems of life were material only. There was no intellectual unrest, for everything was certain and settled for ever. Into this dark room came pouring in a strange light. The new light came to England a little later than elsewhere by reason of her geographical position, but nowhere did it have a more striking effect. At this time England was breeding a hardy daring race of seamen, who in their enterprise, audacity, and curiosity were second to none.

The call of the sea to Elizabeth's young men was at least as compelling as the call of the air to the youth of to-day.

The Tudor seamen, questing, roving, trading, fighting, brought an exciting change in the geographical outlook. Every year some new landfall was made. They went ranging up and down the seas like the tides themselves, to Greenland, Labrador, Newfoundland, Virginia; Vardö and North Russia; the Pacific coasts; Africa and India. Every year the maps became more accurate and more complete, more like charts and less like fantastic picturesque guesses. With the increased knowledge came the expansion of trade. Baulked in the Spanish West Indies, the English voyagers tried to open up North America. They succeeded in beginning trade with Russia and the Levant, with India and the Eastern islands, and it grew steadily as the years went by. Early in the sixteenth century, as the result of the increase in the maritime affairs of the City merchants, marine insurance began to be effected in England. Edward Lloyd's coffee house in Great Tower Street, London, was the first rendezvous of underwriters, and from this small beginning grew the vast organization still known as Lloyds to-day.

The activities of England's seafaring men brought about a change in the social habits of the people. Tea drinking as a social custom in England is so universal that it is hard to imagine the time when tea was a rare Chinese herb. It was first used in Venice in 1550, in Portugal in 1558, and in England in 1598, but for fifty years it remained a rarity, and even then was so expensive that it was for long a luxury of the rich. It was not until after 1836, when

Indian tea was first shipped from Assam, that tea drinking became really universal in the sense that it is to-day. Tobacco, however, jumped into popular favour at once. Tobacco smoking became with extraordinary rapidity an almost universal habit among men. Raleigh's agents from Virginia brought home the herb and its use. A few years after their return Camden the historian wrote:

"That Indian plant called Tobacco is grown so frequent in use, and of such price, that many, nay the most part, with an unsatiable desire do take of it, drawing into their mouth the smoke thereof, which is of a strong scent, through a pipe made of earth, and venting of it again through their nose; some for wantonness, or rather fashion sake, or other for health sake. Insomuch that Tobacco shops are set up in greater number than either Alehouses or Taverns."[1]

Though Sir Walter Raleigh and Sir Francis Drake did a great deal to popularise the habit, they were not the first to introduce tobacco into this country. As early as 1565 Sir John Hawkins brought it to England, and a considerable amount of smoking was practised by about 1573. The tobacco was not the Virginian variety which was to become so popular, but West Indian. Virginian leaf was grown in England during the seventeenth century.

The introduction of the potato was an event of considerable economic significance, and was also due to the voyagers. At first the potato was known as the potato of Virginia to distinguish it from the sweet potato (batatas) which was already known. The Virginia potato, the variety cultivated in England, was brought home by Raleigh's explorers.

[1] *Annales*, 1625, Book III, p. 107.

It was nearly two centuries before it became universally used. Raleigh introduced it on his estate in Ireland, and in due time it became the staple food of the peasantry in that country. Flowers as well as vegetables were sent home from America. Nasturtiums, or Indian cress, as they were called, passion flowers, bergamot were among the transatlantic flowers and fruits which are seen to-day in the gardens of England. Flowers and fruits arrived from the East also, lilacs, tulips, syringa, laburnum, and the apricot.

The beginnings of the Royal Navy under Henry VIII, and its gradual growth in the hands of seamen like Hawkins and Drake have been traced, but the results of the long war which it had waged with Spain and which ended with the death of Queen Elizabeth must briefly be considered. The religious results of the war were far-reaching. The Counter-Reformation had been checked. Spain and the Pope had failed to impose Roman Catholicism on the northern races of Europe, and Protestantism became a great force which to this day has enormous power and weight. Holland had asserted her political independence, France was a nation, Great Britain, united, was sure of herself. Spain was still a mighty Power, but had begun her slow decline, and the menace with which she had overshadowed the world had passed away. The English Queen had kept her throne against all that threatened her. England's soil was still untrodden by an invader. From the defensive aspect England had won the war. She had inflicted defeat after defeat on the Spanish fleets, but a navy alone could not bring down with a sudden crash the empire of Spain. A great and powerful standing army to work in co-operation with the navy was the only force which could have done that, a force strong enough to hold and occupy what had been seized from the sea. England had no such army. If a base had been taken and held, at Lisbon, Sagres, or Cadiz, the fleet could have effectively blockaded Spain. As it was, the lack of victual and water, the constant outbreaks of disease, and the fact that the ships were not as staunch as they became in Nelson's day, made an extended blockade impossible. Ships could not keep the sea for long enough to undertake such an operation. Therefore time and money and lives were wasted in attempts to capture the Spanish treasure ships. In spite of individual successes, the plan was on the whole a failure. The regular convoys still arrived in Spain and Portugal out of the West and the East.

The heritage left by Elizabeth's navy to the Royal Navy of to-day is chiefly one of *moral*. Naval strategy and tactics were in their infancy in the days of the Armada, and the principles of naval warfare were only just beginning to be grasped. In the Elizabethan era the prestige of the Royal Navy continually grew. The Navy became an independent service. Its ships were more than mere floating castles ferrying troops. They began to be parts of a fighting machine. Until this period a sea-fight was really a land-fight at sea, with ships grappled together, and men fighting hand-to-hand. When heavy guns were mounted, battle at a distance began, and the importance of gunnery was quickly realised. The modern destroyer and submarine were foreshadowed by the fireship, which embodied in one the ship and the torpedo. It is interesting evidence of the continuity of the Royal Navy from

Tudor days to note how the names of the Elizabethan ships persist in the Navy Lists of to-day. Besides H.M.S. *Queen Elizabeth*, H.M.S. *Drake*, and H.M.S. *Hawkins* and *Frobisher*, which recall the great actors in the drama, there are *Vanguard*, *Victory*, *Revenge*, *Dreadnought*, *Swiftsure*, *Tiger*, and others, all Elizabethan ships.

Service in the Royal Navy was only a small part of the activities of the seamen whose exploits have been recorded here. It is necessary to speak of their failures and successes in other directions, particularly in that of colonisation. At first sight the results seem insignificant. They failed to discover the North-East and North-West Passages. Not a single colony in America had been successfully established. Spanish sea-power was actually stronger at the close of the reign than it had been at the beginning. They had not even discovered a real gold mine. The explorers and fighting men were too thrilled with the excitement of discovery and war seriously to attempt the hard and strenuous work of founding settlements. Those, like Raleigh, who did make an endeavour to do so, lacked any clear idea of what they were about or what the ultimate organization of the colony should be. To set up trading posts seems to have been their main object, an object that somehow became confused with the notion of shipping the unemployed and unemployable out to the new lands instead of picked men. The colonists also had no knowledge of how to deal with the natives. In years to come the English learnt the knack of colonizing, but it was a slow process. The Elizabethan era only saw the first fumbling experiments. But in retrospect the results are seen to have been stupendous, the beginnings of the

British Empire and the United States of America. Raleigh's pioneers perished, but they blazed a trail for those who followed after.

The influence of the seamen on the poetry and general literature of the time was profound. The wonderful flowering of the imagination in Elizabethan days, the work of the poets and dramatists, was nourished by the deeds and discoveries of the seamen. The sea victory of 1588 liberated a fresh store of intellectual energy. The confidence that was engendered by deliverance from an immediate and pressing danger gave new life to the literary activity of the time. Literature displayed the same fullness, vitality, and audacity as the seamen themselves. The reign of Elizabeth was one of the great ages of English history. A curtain was rung up on a new drama. A nation of farmers and traders gradually realised that they had become a seafaring race sharing in the sovereignty of the seas. The result was an exaltation of spirit which fired men's hearts and caused the literature of the island to blossom out in splendid colour. England found herself.

> "This fortress built by Nature for herself
> Against infection and the hand of war,
> This happy breed of men, this little world,
> This precious stone set in a silver sea. . . .
> This blessed plot, this earth, this realm, this
>   England. . . .
> This land of such dear souls, this dear, dear
>   land. . . .
> England, bound in with the triumphant sea,
> Whose rocky shore beats back the envious siege
> Of watery Neptune. . . ."

Such lines could hardly have been written before the days of the Elizabethan seafarers. The minds of

the poets went exploring with the explorers, vision-
aries all, looking forward to a far horizon. Here is
Marlowe's prophetic vision:

> "Here, not far from Alexandria,
> Whereas the Terrene and the Red Sea meet,
> Being distant less than full a hundred leagues,
> I meant to cut a channel to them both
> That men might quickly sail to India."

"Give me a map!" cries the dying Tamburlaine in
Marlowe's play. Maps and the quickly unfolding
wonders of geographical science were the preoccu-
pation of men of letters as well as the men of action.
Though as far as is known Shakespeare never went
to sea, his mind and imagination were captivated
by it. His plays are full of graphic allusions to the
sea. *The Tempest* is a fantasy of the stormy ocean
and of the colonisers in the Americas. In the
sailors' taverns of Greenwich or Deptford Shakespeare may have heard a sea shanty like the one he
puts into the mouth of Stephano, and in imagination
he must have followed the ships out to share their
battle with the elements:

> "May the winds blow till they have waken'd
>   death,
> And let the labouring bark climb hills of seas."

To cross the harbour bar was to open the road
to wealth by trading, to gold to be won by fighting.
The sea was the pathway to discovery, to adventure,
to honour, to the land of El Dorado. Along this
pathway went the Elizabethan seamen, sick, thirsty,
hungry, always at peril of the winds and the waves,
yet caring little, for their hearts were steadfast to
the cruel, mysterious, and magical sea.

CHAPTER X

ELIZABETH: HER MEN AND HER SHIPS

THE English rally round a Queen. Elizabeth evoked a passionate personal loyalty in the mass of her subjects. In spite of a certain coarseness and meanness and a quite extraordinary vanity, she had dignity, courage, and charm, she had wit, she was an accomplished linguist and a brilliant classicist, she exploited her femininity, but was wise, cool, calculating, and far-seeing. Above all she kept her finger on the nation's pulse, her heart beat with its heart. Was she not, on her mother's side, the great-great-grand-daughter of a Lord Mayor of London? Her young men hailed her as Gloriana, as Belphoebe, as the Phoenix Maid. Flattery maybe, but she was a very real inspiration to the fiery, quick-tempered, daring, arrogant men of her day. For years she sent them out to fight and die for her and their country, well knowing as they did, for they joyfully accepted her terms, that success did not necessarily mean recognition, and failure might bring upon them the rack and fire of the Inquisition, with no help from her. And, as if in response to her call, a host sprang up to glorify her reign, a company of poets, statesmen, sailors, soldiers, musicians, ecclesiastics as had never before been seen in that little England and hardly since in this much greater one. They "were like a suit of clothes made for her and worn out with her," for she outlived most of her paladins, and Raleigh, the last of them, met his death soon after her.

Behind all Elizabeth's caprice and play-acting a wise brain glowed. She was a Tudor, and the Tudors were autocrats, but she loved her England, and knew exactly how far she could go with her Englishmen. Of all her Englishmen the sea captains were the most typical of the age. They had the large vision that urged them on through every danger and disappointment, most of them were practical seamen, and many were possessed of a wide culture, they were hot-tempered, full of energy and daring, sometimes barbarous, sometimes chivalrous. In the earlier part of Elizabeth's reign, before a state of war existed, most of the voyages were primarily for trading purposes. Even the Queen's ships, in times of peace, had to be made to pay, and were lent to private merchant adventurers. The Government of the country was financed out of the Crown's private estates and funds. Special needs were met by special taxation voted by Parliament, but taxes were unpopular and difficult to raise. Elizabeth's habits of economy helped to avoid the excessive taxation that caused the downfall of Charles the First. She was not responsible for all the details, but she kept a firm grasp on general incomings and outgoings, which was as well, for corruption and peculation were common. She and her ministers have been accused of parsimony with regard to the Navy. It was not so much economy that starved the Navy, as the difficulty of providing abnormal quantities of victuals and munitions. It is indubitable that if the Government had not been extremely cautious and economical, England would have been bankrupt as the result of the long struggle with Spain. England was not a rich country in those days.

For ten years before her accession Elizabeth was constantly in peril of her life. In those years she learnt much, how to be crafty, wise, and tactful. She had the feminine gift of managing men, and her people believed in her and loved her proud, high-spirited ways. She had a high personal courage. When she told her troops at Tilbury in 1588 that she had the heart of a king, and would lead them herself against an invader, she was not speaking for effect. In her last speech to the House of Commons she also spoke from her heart:

"For above all earthly treasure I do esteem my people's love . . . though you have had and may have many princes more mighty and wise sitting in this seat, yet you never had or shall have any that will be more careful and loving."

She was superbly served by her seamen. To be a successful merchant captain needed exceptional qualities of heart and hand. The Elizabethan merchant captain was often like the captain of a tramp steamer to-day, except that he was either the owner or part owner of his craft, and carried on the trading himself. He had his merchandise on board, knives and beads for the savages, woollen cloth perhaps for civilized buyers. He set out from port to port, according to wind and tide, keeping a wary watch, for at any moment he might have to fight for his goods and his life against the pirates that infested the seas, and perhaps in times of political unrest against privateers as well. It will be seen that the nature of his trading was haphazard and adventurous, and that armament was essential. This being so, the warship could be a trader and the trader a warship on occasion, and though the royal ships came to be designed primarily for fighting it was not until the end of Blake's career in the next century that merchant ships ceased to be impressed into service with the battle fleet.

The seamen were a tough and hardy breed, recruited mostly from the sea-coast ports along the Channel, from the City of London round Devon and Cornwall to the City of Bristol at the head of the Severn Sea. Adventure, pay, prize-money, and loot were the attractions that made the work of the press-gangs more or less unnecessary in Queen Elizabeth's reign. Enrolment in the merchant ships was voluntary. There was no lack of crews for them, and when a great captain like Drake was about to sail in the Queen's ships, volunteers flocked to his standard. The men wore no uniform, but were dressed in picturesque and colourful breeches, shirts, coats, sashes, caps. Making allowance for the fact that to-day's equivalent in money would be eight or ten times as much, the pay in the Queen's ships was fairly good, especially after 1585. Before that date it was 2¼ a day, after that 4d., with rations,[1] prize-money, and loot. The rise in the cost of living absorbed some of this increase. Conditions and opportunities, and very often pay as well, were much better in the privateers and merchantmen. Such service, therefore, was more popular than the regular Navy.

The officers, and what would now be called warrant officers, such as the gunner and the boat-

---

[1] Rations per man per day, 1588:
Meat day: Biscuit 1 lb., 1d.; Beer 1 gallon, 1¾d.; Beef 2 lb., 5½d.: 8¼d.
Fish day: Biscuit 1 lb., 1d.; Beer 1 gallon, 1¾d.; Butter ¼ lb., ½d.;
Cheese ¼ lb., ½d.; Stockfish, ¼ fish, 1d.: 4¾d.

swain, wore steel helmets and body-armour. The men's personal weapons were swords and cutlasses, pikes (long heavy thrusting weapons), bows and arrows, and matchlock arquebuses or muskets. Their spirit was something at which to marvel. The ships were dark, stuffy, wet, and abominably overcrowded. They knew they would be obliged to eat little else but bad salt meat, weevily biscuit, and mouldy bread. Drake's men on the voyage of circumnavigation lived on salted penguin for weeks. The beer was generally bad, and there was no means of keeping drinking water fresh, it always stank after a few days. They had to land as often as possible to get fresh water, and if they were off hostile coasts, or shores populated by savages, they would probably have to fight for it. They were doomed to suffer from scurvy, their gums would become soft and spongy, and their teeth be loosened, so that they could not eat, and unless they could get some "scurvy-grass" or fruit they would die. If they did not die of scurvy, there were malaria, yellow fever, and other deadly plagues. Nor was death by disease or battle their only risk. Capture by the Spaniards might mean a worse fate, to perish miserably and in agony in the clutches of the Inquisition unless they renounced their stern Protestant faith. If taken prisoner by a Sallee rover or Turkish pirate, they would be compelled to toil and sweat and shiver at a galley oar with the lash playing about their backs.

So much for the men. Something must now be said about the ships in which these high adventures were pursued. What strikes a modern most forcibly about them is their extremely small size. It is true that the famous *Revenge* was of 500 tons burthen, and that Frobisher's ship at the Armada was 1,000 tons, but these were the fighting ships. The *Golden Hind* was only 100 tons. She drew 9 feet of water, was a mere 18 feet in the beam, and was 63 feet[1] in length, roughly three-quarters of the length of a lawn-tennis court. Somehow her full complement of 90 men or more, including carpenters, smiths, coopers, and not least musicians, were crowded aboard. This typical well-found ship of its day carried six cast-iron guns of 4½-inch bore on each broadside, two bronze bow-chasers, and four light guns which were breech-loaders and quickfirers. Contrary to prevailing ideas, breech-loaders came before muzzle-loaders. The former were forged guns, and had a rather clumsy system of spare charge chambers in the breech. In spite of their being quicker to load and fire (one shot every two minutes) they were only suitable as small weapons, and the larger heavy cast-iron cannon supplanted them as the main armament. The extreme range of her guns on the broadside was not more than 500 yards, throwing a 10 lb. shot. One lower gun deck was the rule; few ships, if any, had more. All ships at this period were square-rigged, with a square foresail, foretopsail, mainsail, and maintopsail, setting from yards which could be lowered to the deck. Sometimes there were light square topgallants above the topsails. There was also a square sail forward, called the spritsail, set on a yard beneath the bowsprit. There were no jibs or staysails to help in working to windward. The mizzen sail, set on the aftermost mast, was an exception to the rule of square sails, for it was triangular and very helpful in steering the ship.

[1] Perhaps 75 feet overall.

There were sometimes fighting tops on the foremast and mainmast.

The *Golden Hind*, small as she was for the amazing task she accomplished, must have seemed large and roomy beside many of the ships of these daring adventurers. Over and over again they sailed for weeks and months over stormy oceans in boats no bigger than a fishing smack. The *Squirrel*, in which Humphrey Gilbert was overwhelmed by a great wave and sent to the bottom of the North Atlantic, was only ten tons! On the other hand, the Queen's ships after 1577, when Hawkins was sent to the Navy Board, though dependent to a degree hard for this generation to realize upon the caprice of wind and wave and weather, were much larger, more seaworthy, faster and more powerful.

Hawkins set to work on a new plan. He increased the length of the ships in proportion to their beam. The result was that they completely outclassed all existing vessels in speed, sailing qualities, and in armament as well, for they carried more and heavier guns on the broadside. Up to this time ships had been used as floating castles to carry troops. A captain laid his ship aboard the enemy, and the soldiers armed with pike and sword poured on to his decks, and fought hand to hand. Guns were mounted in the fore and aft castles to shoot at the boarding parties. But now the power of the broadside began to be felt, and the guns were used to hull and sink the adversary. The English tactics against the Armada were not to board, but to dart in, fire a broadside, and swing away. The *Revenge*, Drake's flagship in the Armada fight, which was lost after Grenville's epic battle against fifty-three Spaniards, was the first of this new type, and was so successful that many more were built. A number of old ships also were rebuilt on these lines.

The "race-ship," the long, lean, low vessel of moderate tonnage, the *Revenge* class, came to take the place of the "galleon." The galleon was, however, a usual type during this era. Between the high poop and the forecastle was the "waist" of the ship, where stood the men working the sails, and where, when at sea, the pinnace and small boats were stowed away. The poop sloped up aft, and the whole structure at the stern overhung the sea for a considerable distance. Beneath the poop was the stateroom, where the captain dined, and entertained his guests. Here also were the cabins where he, the master, and the gentlemen slept, and here were the binnacle and steering gear. In the much smaller forecastle certain stores, like ropes, tackle, and blocks were kept, and some of the hands slept there. Most of the men slept and messed in the gun or lower deck, wrapped up in blankets or sleeping-bags on the bare boards. In some ships there was an orlop deck below the gun deck, and here were the petty officers' cabins. Below this again was the hold. In this were placed the powder magazines, store-rooms containing casks for salt meat and other provisions, beer-barrels and water-barrels, and under all, the ballast. The great danger of fire in these wooden ships made the position of the cook's galley an important and difficult problem. Usually it was placed on a brick floor over the ballast. This was fairly safe, but it had the disadvantage of tending to heat and spoil the provisions. In northern latitudes, the galley fires kept the ship warm, but in the tropics the heat must have been almost unbearable. As the overhang aft made the ship pitch in almost any sea, the bow was fitted with a wooden beak which broke the force of the waves and flung the water aside so that it was less likely to come aboard. The new ships, though their after superstructure was much smaller, still had this beak, though it was not so large. The lay-out of the vessel was much the same in the new ships as in the galleons, and in each there was much carving and gilding at the stern and a painted figurehead at the bows.

The galleon and the new ship were both rendering the galley and the galleasse obsolete. At Cadiz in 1587 it was shown that such ships in such hands could outfight the hitherto dreaded galleys. The beaked galley, with its ram, its slave-manned banks of oars, and its lateen sails, was in the first half of the sixteenth century without a rival as a ship of war in the Mediterranean Sea. The great advantage of the oared galley over other ships was its mobility, its independence of the winds. Its disadvantages were its unseaworthiness and its lack of sea endurance. Its necessary lightness, its fine lines, and its low freeboard all tended to make it a calm weather vessel. Its limited capacity for storage, and the number of mouths to be fed made it impossible to keep the sea for long periods. Moreover, the armament had to be confined to fore and aft guns. An improved vessel was evolved, the galleasse, which mounted a few guns on the broadside, but the difficulties were considerable. The English never took kindly to the galley, and those they had were not slave-oared. In the galleon, entirely propelled by sails, construction was on more seaworthy lines. It had less mobility, but there was vastly more storage space, and a much less numerous crew was needed for the actual handling of the vessel.

The armament of the war and merchant ship of the time was various. The guns already mentioned as being possessed by the *Golden Hind* were demi-culverins, but there was a much larger class, the muzzle-loading cannons proper. The Double Cannon, an 8½-inch 65-pounder, was rarely used, the Whole Cannon was an 8-inch 60-pounder, and the more usual Demi-Cannon a 7-inch 30-pounder. These were from ten to twelve feet long. The Culverins included the smaller muzzle-loading guns. The Whole Culverin was a 5-inch 17-pounder, a Demi-Culverin was a 4½-inch 9/10-pounder, the Saker was a 3½-inch 5-pounder, the Minion a 3-inch 4-pounder. These were also long guns, from 13 feet to 8 feet. Then same the smaller Falcon, Falconet, Robinet, and lastly the Base, a 1¼-inch breech-loader. Besides all these there were mortars for stone balls or for case shot, and a few more small types. The projectiles were mostly cast-iron cannon-balls kept in racks along the sides of the ship, but there was also case-shot, chain-shot (two shots linked by a short chain for cutting rigging), and bar-shot. The guns were mounted upon wooden carriages with small wheels. To load, the crew ran the gun back on the wheels by means of tackle and ropes, and the loader pushed a "cartridge" made of canvas or paper[1] down the muzzle. This was full of powder. Then came a wad of oakum[2] rammed well down, then the shot, and then another wad. The cartridge was punc-

---

[1] Hence the name "cartridge paper," now used by draughtsmen.

[2] Old ropes untwisted and teased into loose hemp. Also used for caulking seams of ships.

tured by means of a wire thrust down the touch-hole, which was filled with fine powder from the gunner's horn. Then the gun was run out and laid. To alter the elevation of the gun, the crew had to lift their piece with a crowbar or handspike so that a wedge could be manipulated beneath it. The gunner then took his burning match, which was twisted round a linstock or wooden fork, and with all standing clear for the recoil, applied it to the priming in the touch-hole. The recoil was checked to some extent by the breeching, a heavy piece of rope. In spite of all this labour, exact aim was impossible, as the shot was always much smaller than the bore of the gun. After firing a broadside a ship was out of action for five minutes at least. Further delay was caused as the guns quickly became hot, and had to be sponged through and allowed to cool. Nevertheless, with all their faults, the guns in use were not very much inferior to those of Nelson's day, two centuries later. As for the mortars, shells and bombs were used in them. Star shells were known, and shells containing "wild-fire," an inflammatory substance that water could not quench. Against the Armada the *Revenge* carried a thousand short arrows, of high penetrative power when fired from a musket. These arrows were a popular device among the English sailors, and could penetrate wooden baulks.

The officers of a ship were much the same as in modern days. The commanding officer was the captain, often in Elizabethan days a practical seaman. He might, however, be a merchant or a soldier. Under him was the master. He was always a seaman, and was in charge of the crew and all tackle. When there was no pilot on board, he acted as navigating officer, and if there was no lieutenant, he fulfilled his duties as well. The boatswain was in charge of the boats, sails, rigging, and anchors. There was sometimes a purser, and always a steward who looked after provisions and rations. There was a carpenter, a cooper, quarter-masters in charge of the watches, a coxswain, and a trumpeter. A very important member of the ship's company was the gunner, who was responsible for the guns and ammunition. He had to keep his pieces primed and matches lighted. He was also expected to have his guns well lashed in position, as in rough weather they might break loose and do very serious damage. A corporal was in charge of the muskets, bandoliers, pikes, cutlasses and bows. A well-found ship carried a chaplain and a surgeon. The pay of a naval captain was from 2s. 6d. to 6s. 8d. a day. The master drew £1 a month to two guineas, and a gunner 10s. with certain extras. The trumpeter, without which no ship was com-plete, was paid 15s. a month, which, surprisingly, was more than the gunner drew. Soldiers, if any, were under the orders of the sea officers. This was directly opposed to the practice in the Spanish navy, where soldiers were supreme, and the sailors had no more authority over them than had the slaves at the oars.

It is the fashion in some quarters to dismiss all the seamen of this era as pirates. The use of the opprobrious term "pirate" when applied to men like Drake cannot be too strongly condemned. To tar with the same brush Sir Francis Drake and a Barbary corsair is nonsense. It may not be easy to justify all the Elizabethan sea captains' exploits in terms of modern ethics, but in their own estimation and in the opinion of most of their English contemporaries they were no pirates. They thought they had the Bible behind them in spoiling the Egyptians (i.e. the Spaniards) or slaying the Amalekites (i.e. the Irish). It is true that they plundered to enrich themselves as well as their country, but it was their country's enemies they were attacking, and it must not be forgotten that very often they held a commission from the Queen. In fact, if they were pirates, she was the pirate queen. True pirates there were in plenty on the seas, men who looted indiscriminately, but it is not reasonable to class them all together, or to judge men of the sixteenth century by the European or American code of the twentieth. The nationalist passions and religious excitements of the age must be borne in mind. The seamen of Elizabeth were far from being saints, but even by the standards of to-day, which are supposed to be superior to those of Tudor times, their descendants at home or in the Newer Englands beyond the seas may be proud of their ancestry.

BOOKS CONSULTED

The English Voyages of the Sixteenth Century. Sir Walter Raleigh. Jackson Wylie & Co., Glasgow. 1928.

Drake and the Tudor Navy (2 vols.). Sir Julian Corbett. Longmans, Green & Co., London. 1898.

The Successors of Drake. Sir Julian Corbett. Longmans, Green & Co., London. 1900.

England under the Tudors. Arthur D. Innes. Methuen & Co., Ltd., London.

Voyages and Travels (2 vols.). C. Raymond Beazley, F.R.G.S. Archibald Constable & Co., Ltd., Westminster. 1903.

Queen Elizabeth and her Subjects. A. L. Rouse and G. H. Harrison. George Allen & Unwin Ltd., London. 1935.

Geographical Discovery and Exploration. J. N. L. Baker. Harrap, London. 1931.

Sir Martin Frobisher. William McFee. Golden Hind Series. Bodley Head, London. 1928.

Life of John Davis. Clements R. Markham, C.B., F.R.S. George Philip & Son, London. 1891.

Voyages and Works of John Davis the Navigator. Albert Hastings Markham, R.N., F.R.G.S. Hakluyt Society, London. 1880.

The Three Voyages of Martin Frobisher. Rear-Admiral Richard Collinson, C.B., Hakluyt Society, London, 1867.

Naval Miscellany. Vol. II. Navy Records Society.

England's Quest of Eastern Trade. Sir William Foster, C.I.E. A. & C. Black, Ltd., London. 1933.

The Voyages of Sir James Lancaster, Kt., to the East Indies. Hakluyt Society. 1877.

The Hawkins Voyages. Hakluyt Society. 1878.

The Great Armada. John Richard Hale. Thomas Nelson & Sons, London.

A History of Europe. Vol. II. Rt. Hon. H. A. L. Fisher. Eyre & Spottiswoode, London. 1935.

Transactions of the Devonshire Association. Vol. XV, 1883 ; Vol. XLIX, 1917.

The Principal Navigations Voyages Traffics and Discoveries of the English Nation. Richard Hakluyt. J. M. Dent & Sons, Ltd., London. (With an introduction by John Masefield.)

Sir Francis Drake Revived. Hakluyt Society.

New Light on Drake. Zelia Nuttall. Hakluyt Society, No. 34, London. 1914.

The World Encompassed. Hakluyt Society.

Cambridge Modern History. Vol. III. Cambridge University Press. 1904.

State Papers relating to the Defeat of the Spanish Armada, 1588. (2 vols.) Edited by J. N. Laughton, M.A., R.N. Navy Records Society. 1895.

The Great Tudors. Edited by Katherine Garvin. Ivor Nicholson & Watson Ltd., London. 1935.

Great Englishmen of the Sixteenth Century. Sir Sidney Lee. Thomas Nelson & Sons, London. 1907.

The Sailing Ship. Romola and R. C. Anderson. George G. Harrap & Co., Ltd., London. 1927.

INDEX

INDEX

PRINTED BY WESTERN PRINTING SERVICES LTD., BRISTOL